EXERCISES
in ENGLISH

Teacher Guide

LEVEL G

LOYOLAPRESS.

CHICAGO

The Workout That Brings Mastery in Grammar, Usage, and Mechanics

Exercises in English is the perfect teaching tool for educators who want their students to be educationally fit and READY—ready to communicate effectively when writing or speaking, ready for everyday language arts tasks, ready for accelerated English-language learning, and ready for assessment. Here are some ways that a workout with Exercises in English helps students become READY for any language arts task that they encounter:

R IGOROUS PRACTICE

Students are provided with a multitude of exercises on each page. With so many opportunities for learning, "practice makes perfect" is achievable!

E XAMPLES AND DEFINITIONS

Success comes with systematic instruction. Each new grammar, usage, or mechanics concept is clearly explained through examples and definitions.

A SSESSMENT

GUM scores increase as students are assessed and master their work with sentences, verbal agreement, and punctuation.

D IAGRAMMING FOR IN-DEPTH LANGUAGE STUDY

When students diagram sentences, they create visual representations of their learning—they can actually see how words work together to make correctly constructed sentences.

Y EARLONG REINFORCEMENT FOR LEARNERS AT EVERY LEVEL

With six books of varying levels and a multitude of lessons in each book, students are provided with learning opportunities that last a full school year and beyond.

Inside Exercises in English

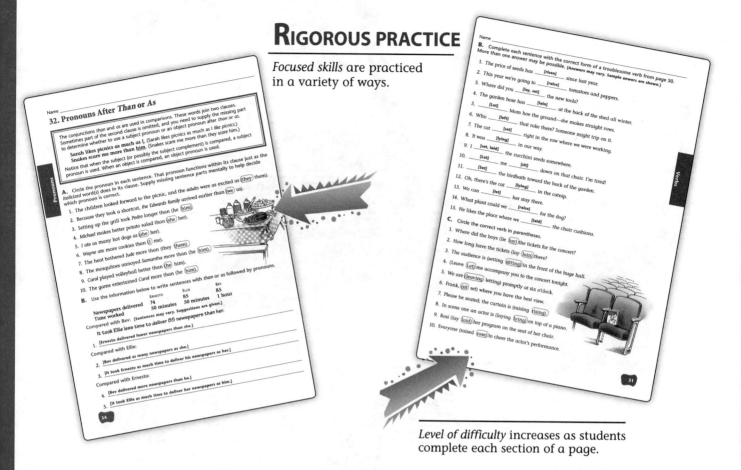

RIGOROUS PRACTICE

Focused skills are practiced in a variety of ways.

Level of difficulty increases as students complete each section of a page.

EXAMPLES AND DEFINITIONS

Clear definitions and numerous examples guide instruction.

Name _____

68. Participles

Verbals are words made from verbs. A **participle** is a verbal that is used as an adjective. It describes a noun or a pronoun.
- A present participle always ends in *-ing*, and the past participle of a regular verb ends in *-ed.*
- A **participial phrase** consists of the participle, its object or complement, and any modifiers.
- A participle can be active or passive, and it can show tense.
- A participial phrase that is essential to the meaning of a sentence is restrictive; a participial phrase that is not essential to the meaning is nonrestrictive and is set off by commas.

  <u>Donating money for social causes,</u> Peter Cooper set an example as a philanthropist.
  People <u>inspired by Cooper</u> give money to good causes.

A. Underline the participial phrase in each sentence.
Circle the noun or pronoun it describes.

1. Peter Cooper, known as an inventor and a philanthropist, lived from 1791 to 1883.
2. Completing only one year of formal education, Cooper started work at an early age.
3. Eventually, a craftsman making coaches hired Cooper as an apprentice.
4. Recognizing the young man's ability, the coach maker helped Cooper further his career.
5. Cooper, aided by his mentor, started a business that made machines for the cloth industry.
6. That business, being successful, permitted Cooper to enter other ventures and undertake new challenges.
7. Wanting to share his success, he founded Cooper Union.
8. The institution, dedicated to the education of the working poor, was set up in New York City.
9. Offering free courses in science, engineering, and art, the institution attracted many young students.
10. Any student meeting the requirements can still attend classes there.

B. Write the number of each sentence above that has a restrictive participial phrase.

[3, 10]

Peter Cooper founded a community institution to help the poor. Give an example of how you can help less fortunate people in your community.

73

ASSESSMENT

Comprehensive reviews allow for classroom assessment or preparation for standardized tests.

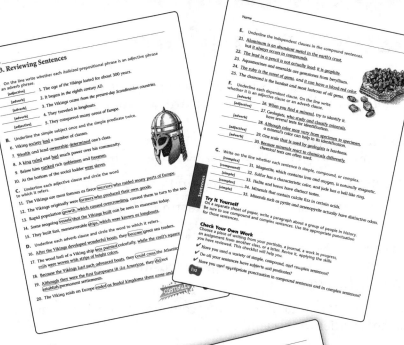

DIAGRAMMING FOR IN-DEPTH LANGUAGE STUDY

Sentence diagramming helps students better understand and remember concepts.

YEARLONG REINFORCEMENT FOR LEARNERS AT EVERY LEVEL

Leveled books allow for differentiated instruction. Determine which books to use based on individual student achievement rather than grade level.

Handbook of Terms invites all learners to refresh and expand their knowledge.

Mastery and More

When teachers and students use *Exercises in English,* they receive more than any other language arts workout offers.

Teachers receive MORE with
- easy-to-grade exercises that are always in multiples of five.
- perforated pages for easy grading and portfolio storage.
- embedded answers that make correcting a breeze.

Students receive MORE with
- grammar, mechanics, and usage lessons that support *Voyages in English.*
- cross-curricular content for reinforcement and enrichment in social studies and science.
- character-education lessons with positive role models as examples.
- practice in context for authentic writing opportunities and self-assessment.

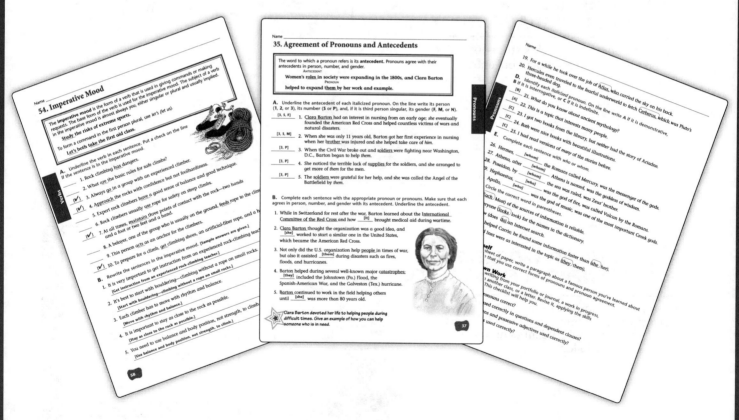

Comprehensive Scope and Sequence

Review the Scope and Sequence on pages T7–T11 to note how skill instruction is scaffolded across levels. Use the level or levels that best meet your students' needs.

Exercises in English—Scope and Sequence

SENTENCES	C	D	E	F	G	H
The Four Kinds of Sentences	✔	✔	✔	✔	✔	✔
Subjects and Predicates	✔	✔	✔	✔	✔	✔
Simple Subjects and Predicates		✔		✔	✔	✔
Compound Subjects and Predicates		✔	✔	✔	✔	✔
Direct Objects		✔	✔	✔	✔	✔
Complete Subjects and Predicates			✔	✔	✔	✔
Natural and Inverted Order in Sentences			✔	✔	✔	✔
Indirect Objects				✔	✔	✔
Compound Sentences				✔	✔	✔
Complex Sentences					✔	✔
Compound Complex Sentences						✔

NOUNS	C	D	E	F	G	H
Proper and Common Nouns	✔	✔	✔	✔	✔	
Singular and Plural Nouns	✔	✔	✔	✔	✔	✔
Possessive Nouns	✔	✔	✔	✔	✔	✔
Nouns Used as Subjects		✔	✔	✔		✔
Nouns Used as Objects		✔	✔	✔	✔	✔
Count and Noncount Nouns		✔	✔	✔		✔
Nouns Used as Subject Complements			✔	✔	✔	✔
Nouns Used in Direct Address			✔	✔		
Nouns Used as Objects of Prepositions			✔	✔	✔	✔
Appositives				✔	✔	✔
Collective Nouns				✔	✔	
Concrete and Abstract Nouns				✔	✔	
Words Used as Nouns and Verbs				✔		
Nouns Used as Object Complements						✔

VERBS	C	D	E	F	G	H
Regular and Irregular Verbs	✔	✔	✔	✔	✔	✔
Present Tense	✔	✔	✔	✔	✔	✔
Progressive Tenses	✔	✔	✔	✔	✔	✔
Past Tense	✔	✔	✔	✔	✔	✔
Future Tenses	✔	✔	✔	✔	✔	✔
Action Verbs	✔	✔	✔			
Verbs of Being	✔	✔	✔			
Helping Verbs	✔	✔				
Forms of *Bring*	✔					

	C	D	E	F	G	H
Forms of *Buy*	✔					
Forms of *Come*	✔					
Forms of *Eat*	✔					
Forms of *Go*	✔		✔			
Forms of *See*	✔		✔			
Forms of *Sit* and *Set*	✔		✔	✔		
Forms of *Take*	✔		✔			
Forms of *Write*	✔					
Forms of *To Be*	✔	✔	✔			
Forms of *Begin*		✔				
Forms of *Break*		✔	✔			
Forms of *Choose*		✔	✔			
Forms of *Do*		✔				
Verb Phrases		✔	✔	✔	✔	
Intransitive Verbs (Linking Verbs)		✔	✔	✔	✔	✔
There Is and *There Are*		✔		✔	✔	
Subject-Verb Agreement			✔	✔	✔	✔
Transitive Verbs			✔	✔	✔	✔
Doesn't and *Don't*			✔	✔	✔	✔
Let and *Leave*			✔	✔		
Teach and *Learn*			✔			
Lie and *Lay*			✔	✔		
Rise and *Raise*				✔		
Perfect Tenses				✔	✔	
Words Used as Nouns and Verbs					✔	
Active and Passive Voice					✔	✔
Modal Auxiliary Verbs					✔	✔
You Are and *You Were*					✔	
Compound Tenses						✔
Emphatic Verb Forms						✔
PRONOUNS	**C**	**D**	**E**	**F**	**G**	**H**
Singular and Plural Pronouns	✔	✔	✔			
Subject Pronouns	✔	✔	✔	✔	✔	✔
Possessive Pronouns	✔	✔	✔	✔	✔	✔
I and *Me*	✔	✔				
Pronouns Used as Subject Complements	✔		✔	✔	✔	✔
Pronouns Used as Direct Objects		✔	✔	✔	✔	✔
The Person of Pronouns		✔	✔	✔		
The Gender of Pronouns			✔			

	C	D	E	F	G	H
We and Us		✔				
Pronouns Used as Objects of Prepositions			✔	✔		
Pronouns Used in Contractions			✔	✔		
Reflexive Pronouns			✔	✔	✔	
Interrogative Pronouns				✔	✔	✔
Indefinite Pronouns				✔	✔	✔
Double Negatives				✔		
Pronouns Used as Indirect Objects					✔	✔
Who and Whom					✔	✔
Pronouns Used After Than and As					✔	✔
Relative Pronouns					✔	✔
Demonstrative Pronouns					✔	✔
Nothing and Anything					✔	
Pronouns Used as Objects of Prepositions						✔
Intensive Pronouns			✔			✔

ADJECTIVES	C	D	E	F	G	H
Descriptive Adjectives	✔			✔	✔	✔
Adjectives That Tell How Many	✔	✔	✔	✔		
Indefinite and Definite Articles	✔	✔	✔	✔	✔	
Demonstrative Adjectives	✔	✔	✔	✔	✔	✔
Comparative Forms of Adjectives	✔	✔	✔	✔	✔	✔
Possessive Adjectives		✔	✔	✔		
Common and Proper Adjectives		✔	✔			✔
Good and Bad		✔				
The Position of Adjectives			✔	✔	✔	✔
Superlative Forms of Adjectives			✔	✔	✔	✔
Adjectives Used as Subject Complements				✔		
Words Used as Adjectives or Nouns				✔	✔	✔
Those and Them				✔		
Interrogative Adjectives				✔		✔
Few and Little					✔	✔

ADVERBS	C	D	E	F	G	H
Adverbs of Time	✔	✔	✔	✔		
Adverbs of Place	✔	✔	✔	✔		
Good and Well	✔	✔	✔			
Comparative Adverbs		✔	✔	✔		✔
Adverbs of Manner		✔	✔	✔		
No, Not, and Never		✔	✔	✔		
Superlative Adverbs			✔	✔		
Real and Very			✔			

	C	D	E	F	G	H
Their and *There*			✔	✔		
To, Too, and *Two*			✔	✔		
Adverbs and Adjectives				✔	✔	✔
There, Their, and *They're*					✔	
Farther and *Further*					✔	✔
Interrogative Adverbs					✔	✔
Adverbial Nouns					✔	✔
As . . . As, So . . . As, and *Equally*						✔

PUNCTUATION, CAPITALIZATION, ABBREVIATIONS	C	D	E	F	G	H
End Punctuation	✔	✔	✔	✔	✔	✔
Periods After Abbreviations, Titles, and Initials	✔	✔				
Capital Letters	✔	✔	✔	✔	✔	
Titles of Books and Poems	✔		✔	✔	✔	
Commas Used in Direct Address	✔	✔	✔	✔		
Punctuation in Direct Quotations	✔	✔	✔	✔		
Apostrophes		✔	✔			
Commas After *Yes* and *No*		✔	✔	✔		
Commas Separating Words in a Series		✔	✔	✔		
Commas After Parts of a Letter			✔	✔		
Commas in Dates and Addresses			✔	✔		
Commas in Geographical Names			✔			
Commas Used with Appositives				✔		
Commas Used in Compound Sentences				✔		
Semicolons and Colons				✔	✔	✔
Apostrophes, Hyphens, and Dashes				✔	✔	✔
Commas and Semicolons						✔

PREPOSITIONS, CONJUNCTIONS, INTERJECTIONS	C	D	E	F	G	H
Prepositions and Prepositional Phrases			✔	✔	✔	✔
Interjections			✔	✔	✔	✔
Between and *Among*			✔	✔		
From and *Off*			✔			
Adjectival Phrases			✔			
Adverbial Phrases			✔			
Coordinate Conjunctions			✔			
Words Used as Prepositions and Adverbs				✔	✔	✔
At and *To*				✔		
Beside and *Besides, In* and *Into*				✔		
Coordinate and Correlative Conjunctions					✔	

Conjunctive Adverbs					✔	
Subordinate Conjunctions					✔	✔
Without and *Unless, Like, As,* and *As If*					✔	✔
PHRASES, CLAUSES	C	D	E	F	G	H
Adjectival Phrases				✔	✔	
Adverbial Phrases				✔	✔	
Adjectival Clauses					✔	✔
Adverbial Clauses					✔	✔
Restrictive and Nonrestrictive Clauses					✔	
Noun Clauses						✔
PARTICIPLES, GERUNDS, INFINITIVES	C	D	E	F	G	H
Participles						✔
Dangling Participles						✔
Gerunds						✔
Infinitives						✔
Hidden and Split Infinitives						✔
WORD STUDY SKILLS	C	D	E	F	G	H
Synonyms	✔	✔	✔	✔		
Antonyms	✔	✔				
Homophones	✔	✔	✔			
Contractions	✔	✔				
Compound Words		✔				

Correlation of Grade 7 *Voyages in English, 2006,* and Level G *Exercises in English, 2008*

CONJUNCTIONS AND INTERJECTIONS

PUNCTUATION AND CAPITALIZATION

Exercises in English, 2008

- Grammar is arranged in the same order as in *Voyages*, 2006, allowing students to work through the books simultaneously.

- Each grammar section in *Voyages* is supported by at least one lesson in *Exercises*.

- Some grammar sections in *Voyages* are supported by two or more lessons in *Exercises*. For example, Section 1.6 of *Voyages*, Grade 6, treats nouns used as objects. This section is supported by three lessons in *Exercises* that treat separately nouns used as direct objects, nouns used as indirect objects, and nouns used as objects of prepositions. This gives students extra practice in discrete grammar points.

- The grammar explanations in *Exercises* were rewritten to match those in *Voyages*, making it easy to move back and forth between books.

- An entire chapter of diagramming was added to *Exercises* to match that in *Voyages*. (This replaces the old Research Skills section. Research skills are taught in *Voyages* as part of the writing process, not as part of the grammar.)

- The Handbook of Terms for each level was rewritten to match that of *Voyages*.

- The TE front matter now contains a correlation of *Exercises* with the appropriate grade level of *Voyages*. (This replaces the old Sentence Analysis section.)

Features that were retained from the old *Exercises* include:

- Each exercise is based on grade-level science, social studies, or language arts content.
- The items in each exercise are divisible by 5 for easy grading.
- Character education lessons appear throughout each book.
- Section reviews provide regular assessment.
- Writing in context and self-assessment allow students to practice what they learn and to evaluate their own work.
- The TE contains overprinted answers.
- The TE front matter contains a scope and sequence chart of the entire program.

GRAMMAR WORKBOOK

EXERCISES
in ENGLISH

LEVEL
G

LOYOLAPRESS.

CHICAGO

Consultants

Therese Elizabeth Bauer
Martina Anne Erdlen
Anita Patrick Gallagher
Patricia Healey
Irene Kervick
Susan Platt

Linguistics Advisor

Timothy G. Collins
National-Louis University

Series Design: Loyola Press
Interior Art:
Jim Mitchell: 9, 15, 22, 37, 52, 73, 89, 121, 143.
Greg Phillips: 1, 75, 76, 78, 81, 82, 84, 86, 97, 106, 122, 124.
All interior illustrations not listed above are by Keith Ward.

ISBN-10: 0-8294-2345-1; ISBN-13: 978-0-8294-2345-7

ISBN-10: 0-8294-2339-7; ISBN-13: 978-0-8294-2339-6

Exercises in English® is a registered trademark of Loyola Press.

Manufactured in the United States of America.

06 07 08 09 10 11 12 VonH 10 9 8 7 6 5 4 3 2 1

06 07 08 09 10 11 12 VonH 10 9 8 7 6 5 4 3 2 1

Contents

Name _____

1. Singular Nouns and Plural Nouns

A **noun** is a name word. A **singular noun** names one person, place, thing, or idea. A **plural noun** names more than one. The plural of most nouns is formed by adding -*s* or -*es* to the singular form. For nouns ending in *y* preceded by a consonant, change the *y* to *i* and add -*es*. Some plural nouns are not formed by adding -*s* or -*es*. Check a dictionary for these forms.

A. Write the plural form for each noun.

1. highway   __[highways]__   6. goose   __[geese]__

2. cherry   __[cherries]__   7. gas   __[gases]__

3. college   __[colleges]__   8. box   __[boxes]__

4. fish   __[fish]__   9. path   __[paths]__

5. wish   __[wishes]__   10. species   __[species]__

B. Complete each sentence with the plural form of the noun.
Use a dictionary to check your answers.

enemy   1. In the Middle Ages, castles were built for defense against __[enemies]__ .

series   2. Castles had several __[series]__ of defenses, such as moats and walls.

ditch   3. Around some castles were moats, which were __[ditches]__ filled with water.

trench   4. Some of these __[trenches]__ were dry, however.

Sentry   5. __[Sentries]__ were soldiers who guarded the gates of the castle.

supply   6. Castles needed reserves of __[supplies]__ , including weapons and food.

siege   7. During __[sieges]__ opponents would surround a castle.

day   8. This kind of attack could last for __[days]__ or even months.

knight   9. Protecting a lord's castle was a duty of his __[knights]__ .

foot   10. The fighters often wore special metal armor that included protective covering for their __[feet]__ .

2. More Singular Nouns and Plural Nouns

Form the plural of nouns ending in *o* after a vowel by adding *-s* to the singular form. The plurals of some nouns that end in *o* after a consonant are formed by adding *-es* to the singular; others simply add *-s*. The plurals of some nouns ending in *f* or *fe* are formed by changing the *f* or *fe* to *ves*. For most compound words, form the plural by adding *-s*. For some compounds that consist of several words, make the principal word plural.

A. Write the plural form of each noun. Use a dictionary to check your answers.

1. shelf _____[shelves]_____   6. piano _____[pianos]_____

2. tomato _____[tomatoes]_____   7. half _____[halves]_____

3. mother-in-law _____[mothers-in-law]_____   8. spoonful _____[spoonfuls]_____

4. echo _____[echoes]_____   9. knife _____[knives]_____

5. break-in _____[break-ins]_____   10. cliff _____[cliffs]_____

B. Complete each sentence with the plural form of the noun.
Use a dictionary to check your answers.

Rodeo   1. _____[Rodeos]_____ are competitions in which cowboys demonstrate their skills in riding and roping.

bronco   2. Many people associate rodeos with cowboys and bucking _____[broncos]_____.

calf   3. Another rodeo image is that of the roping of _____[calves]_____.

cattle drive   4. Riding and roping were important skills during _____[cattle drives]_____ in the late 1800s.

ox   5. Cowboys had to be experts at herding _____[oxen]_____.

ranch   6. Cowboys date back to the _____[ranches]_____ of the Spanish in the Southwest.

hero   7. Movies often portray cowboys as _____[heroes]_____.

life   8. These movies generally romanticize cowboy culture, but hard work characterized the cowboys' _____[lives]_____.

hardship   9. Cowboys faced many _____[hardships]_____ and long hours in their saddles.

Cattle   10. _____[Cattle]_____ are fairly difficult animals to herd and control.

3. Nouns as Subjects and as Subject Complements

> A noun can be the subject or the subject complement of a sentence.
> A **subject** tells what the sentence is about. A **subject complement** is a
> noun that completes the meaning of a linking verb in a sentence.
> A subject complement renames or describes the subject.
>
> <u>Brazil</u> is in South America.
> <u>Brazil</u> is a <u>country</u> in South America.

A. Underline each subject. Circle each noun subject complement.

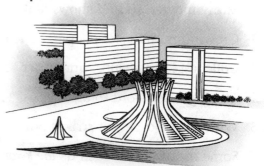

1. <u>Brazil</u> is a fast-growing (country).

2. The <u>capital</u> of the country is (Brasilia).

3. That <u>city</u> was built in the 1950s.

4. In Brazil, <u>Portuguese</u> is spoken.

5. <u>Brazil</u> is the economic (leader) of South America.

6. <u>Coffee</u> remains a major (export) of Brazil.

7. The <u>production</u> of automobiles has become an important (industry) for Brazil.

8. <u>Brazil</u> is the fifth largest (country) in the world in size and in population.

9. <u>Rio de Janeiro</u> and <u>São Paulo</u> are other important (cities) in Brazil.

10. The <u>beaches</u> of Rio de Janeiro are quite famous.

11. The <u>area</u> near the Amazon River is (home) to a large rain forest.

12. <u>Carnival</u> in Rio remains a popular (attraction) for Brazilians and tourists alike.

13. A <u>stew</u> with beans is a popular Brazilian (dish).

14. *Bossa nova* is a (type) of Brazilian music.

15. Will <u>Brazil</u> be a major (power) in the future?

B. Complete each sentence. On the line write **S** if you have added a subject or **SC** if you have added a subject complement. [Answers will vary.]

_[SC]_   1. The most important city in my area is _____.

_[S]_   2. _____ is a major attraction here.

_[S]_   3. _____ has become our most important product.

_[SC]_   4. A popular sport in the area is _____.

_[S]_   5. In this area _____ is a popular food.

Nouns

4. Nouns as Direct Objects

> A noun can be used as the direct object of an action verb.
> A **direct object** tells *whom* or *what* after the verb.
>
> **My mother practices <u>karate</u>.**

A. Underline the direct object in each sentence.

1. Over the past decades more and more people have shown an <u>interest</u> in karate.

2. Many movies and TV shows feature this <u>type</u> of martial art.

3. Growing numbers of people are learning <u>karate</u> as a means of defense.

4. Colleges, karate clubs, and other schools teach its <u>techniques</u>.

5. The Japanese word *karate* means "<u>empty hand</u>."

6. With karate a person strikes <u>parts</u> of another person's body.

7. Some martial arts, such as *tae kwon do*, emphasize <u>kicking</u>.

8. Others, such as *kung fu*, use a circular <u>motion</u> of the hands.

9. A karate blow can seriously injure a <u>person</u>.

10. In karate a person's hand may reach a <u>velocity</u> of 21 to 30 miles an hour.

11. Originally Buddhist monks used <u>karate</u> for protection against wild animals.

12. Today for many people in the United States, karate provides <u>fun</u> and <u>exercise</u>.

13. Groups sponsor karate <u>competitions</u>.

14. Karate competitors earn special <u>belts</u>.

15. The color of a belt indicates a person's <u>level</u> of expertise in the sport.

B. Complete each sentence with a noun used as a direct object. **[Answers will vary.]**

1. As far as sports go, I can play _____.

2. For exercise I often use _____.

3. When choosing sports on TV, I prefer _____.

4. Sports like tennis require _____.

5. To play a sport well, you need _____.

5. Nouns as Indirect Objects

> A noun can be used as an indirect object. An **indirect object** tells *to whom*, *for whom*, *to what*, or *for what* the action was done.
>
>
>
> INDIRECT OBJECT   DIRECT OBJECT
>
> Sally told her   **friend**   the   **story**   of her first job.
>
>

A. Underline the indirect object in each sentence. Circle the verb it goes with.

1. Mrs. Rivera ⟨offered⟩ <u>Sally</u> a job as a babysitter.

2. Mr. and Mrs. Rivera ⟨showed⟩ <u>Sally</u> their house.

3. They ⟨gave⟩ the <u>teenager</u> instructions.

4. Mrs. Rivera said, ⟨"Give⟩ the <u>baby</u> some juice when she wakes up."

5. She ⟨handed⟩ <u>Sally</u> a number to call in case of an emergency.

6. Sally ⟨read⟩ <u>Molly</u> a book about a dragon.

7. Sally ⟨tossed⟩ <u>Tommy</u> the bean bag.

8. Molly and Tommy ⟨drew⟩ <u>Sally</u> pictures.

9. Sally ⟨made⟩ the <u>children</u> sandwiches for supper.

10. Sally ⟨sang⟩ the <u>baby</u> lullabies in hopes that she would fall asleep.

11. The children ⟨told⟩ <u>Sally</u> stories about their favorite cartoon characters.

12. The children ⟨showed⟩ the <u>babysitter</u> their pet, a tiny hamster.

13. When Mrs. Rivera got home, she ⟨gave⟩ the <u>baby</u> a big kiss.

14. Mr. Rivera ⟨handed⟩ <u>Sally</u> money for her work.

15. Back home Sally ⟨wrote⟩ her <u>friend</u> a long e-mail about her first babysitting job.

B. Underline the indirect object in each sentence. Circle the direct object.

1. My grandfather told his <u>grandchildren</u> the ⟨story⟩ of his first job.

2. A family friend offered my <u>grandfather</u> ⟨work⟩ in an ice cream parlor.

3. At first my grandfather served <u>customers</u> ⟨sundaes.⟩

4. He usually gave <u>customers</u> extra-large ⟨scoops⟩ of ice cream.

5. My grandfather's boss soon gave my <u>grandfather</u> the ⟨job⟩ of washing dishes instead.

Nouns

6. Nouns as Objects of Prepositions

A noun can be the **object of a preposition**. A **preposition** shows place, time, direction, or relationship. Some common prepositions are *at, by, for, from, in, into, on, to, with,* and *without.*

	PREPOSITION		OBJECT			PREPOSITION	OBJECT
The centers	of	some	cities	are filled		with	skyscrapers.

A. Circle each preposition. Underline its object.

1. Skyscrapers are the pyramids and cathedrals (of) the modern age.

2. They show the age's amazing achievements (in) technology.

3. The Petronas Towers (in) Malaysia extend 1,483 feet (into) the sky.

4. The design (of) the towers is based (on) geometric characteristics (of) Muslim architecture.

5. (Without) the invention (of) the elevator, however, no skyscrapers would be practical.

6. Initially elevators were not considered safe (for) humans.

7. Then a special safety brake (for) elevators was invented (by) Elisha G. Otis.

8. Chicago is considered the birthplace (of) the skyscraper.

9. The first building (with) a frame (of) steel was built there (in) the late 19th century.

10. Early skyscrapers were covered (with) stone.

11. One example (of) this kind (of) skyscraper is the Empire State Building.

12. This building (in) New York was the tallest building (in) the world (for) many decades.

13. Buildings (in) several countries now exceed the Empire State Building (in) height.

14. Modern skyscrapers (throughout) the world usually feature construction (of) glass, steel, and concrete.

15. Streets (in) big cities (with) tall buildings are canyons made (by) humans.

B. Complete each sentence with an appropriate preposition. Underline the object of the preposition. **[Answers may vary.]**

1. Cesar Pelli was born and raised _____[in]_____ Argentina, but he lives _____[in]_____ the United States.

2. The Petronas Towers were designed _____[by]_____ Pelli.

3. Pelli wanted the buildings to offer good quality _____[to *or* for]_____ the people who used them.

4. The windows are shaded _____[with *or* by]_____ stainless steel bands to give protection _____[from]_____ the sun.

5. The Petronas Towers have been praised _____[for]_____ their design.

Name _____

7. Nouns as Object Complements

> A noun can be an object complement. A noun **object complement** renames the direct object. An object complement often occurs after one of the following verbs: *appoint, call, consider, elect, make, name,* or *select.*
>
> **The teacher made Kevin the <u>leader</u> of our group.**

A. On the line write **OC** if the italicized word(s) is an object complement. If it is not, leave the line blank.

_[OC]_ 1. The ancient Egyptians named their principal god *Ra.*

_____ 2. The Egyptians associated the *god* with the symbol of the sun.

_[OC]_ 3. They considered the rising sun a *symbol* of creation.

_____ 4. Other symbols for the god Ra were the *falcon* and the *bull.*

_[OC]_ 5. The Egyptians named the center of worship of this god *Iunu.*

_[OC]_ 6. The Greeks called this place *Heliopolis.*

_____ 7. The Egyptians made temples to the *god* but didn't put statues of him inside.

_____ 8. Over the centuries the Egyptians changed their stories and beliefs about *Ra.*

_[OC]_ 9. The Egyptians considered their ruler the *son* of Ra.

_[OC]_ 10. In fact, the ancient Egyptians considered the pharaoh a *god.*

B. Write sentences, combining each sentence part from Column 1 with an appropriate noun phrase that functions as an object complement from Column 2.

COLUMN 1	COLUMN 2
We made the gods of ancient Egypt	the presenter of the report.
We named our report	the topic of our report.
We designated Elizabeth	the best part of the report.
We considered the artwork by Omar	an excellent project.
The teacher may consider our work	"The Mysterious Gods of Ancient Egypt."

1. [We made the gods of ancient Egypt the topic of our report.]

2. [We named our report "The Mysterious Gods of Ancient Egypt."]

3. [We designated Elizabeth the presenter of the report.]

4. [We considered the artwork by Omar the best part of the report.]

5. [The teacher may consider our work an excellent project.]

8. Appositives

> An **appositive** is a word that follows a noun and helps identify it or adds more information about it. An appositive names the same person, place, thing, or idea as the noun it identifies. An **appositive phrase** consists of an appositive and its modifiers.
>
> **Biology, the <u>study</u> of plant and animal life, is a basic science.**

A. Underline the appositive in each sentence. Circle the noun it renames or describes.

1. The (cell,) the smallest <u>unit</u> of life, is a basic area of scientific research.

2. Every cell contains (DNA,) the <u>material</u> that determines the hereditary characteristics of all living things.

3. (Genes,) <u>sections</u> of DNA, govern all of life's processes.

4. Each (gene,) the structural <u>unit</u> of inheritance, is a segment of a DNA molecule with a specific purpose.

5. The (structure) of a DNA molecule, a twisting ladderlike <u>form</u>, is called a double helix.

6. Every human has unique DNA, except for identical (twins,) two <u>children</u> born from a single egg.

7. The (genome,) the <u>sequence</u> of genes within a type of organism, is being studied by scientists.

8. DNA's structure was discovered by (Francis Crick,) a British <u>scientist</u>, in the 1950s.

9. The (American) <u>James Watson</u> worked with Crick in making this discovery.

10. Along with a third (collaborator,) <u>Maurice Wilkins</u>, they were awarded the Nobel Prize.

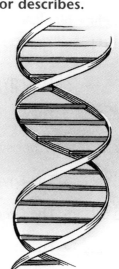

B. Use the phrase after each sentence as an appositive to explain the *italicized* noun. Add commas around the phrase.

1. Many advances are being made in *genetics*.   the scientific study of heredity
   [Many advances are being made in genetics, the scientific study of heredity.]

2. *Gregor Mendel* originated the study of genetics in the late 1800s.   an Austrian monk
   [Gregor Mendel, an Austrian monk, originated the study of genetics in the late 1800s.]

3. He is associated with *transmission genetics*.   a traditional branch of genetics
   [He is associated with transmission genetics, a traditional branch of genetics.]

4. This branch focuses on genes' *transmission*.   the passing of characteristics from parents to offspring

   [This branch focuses on genes' transmission, the passing of characteristics from parents

   to offspring.]

5. Mendel studied one *plant* through a number of generations.   a pea plant

   [Mendel studied of one plant, a pea plant, through a number of generations.]

9. More Appositives

> An appositive can be **restrictive** or **nonrestrictive**. A restrictive appositive is necessary to understand the meaning of the preceding noun. A restrictive appositive is not set off by commas. A nonrestrictive appositive gives extra information but is not essential to understand the sentence. A nonrestrictive appositive is set off by commas. Appositives of proper nouns are almost always nonrestrictive.

A. Underline the appositive in each sentence. Circle the noun or noun phrase that each explains. On the line write **R** if the appositive is restrictive and **N** if it is nonrestrictive.

__[N]__ 1. (Marian Anderson,) a famous singer, was born in Philadelphia in 1897.

__[N]__ 2. As a child, Anderson often sang (spirituals,) African American religious songs.

__[N]__ 3. Anderson soon discovered her (goal,) a career as an opera singer.

__[N]__ 4. To escape racism, prejudice based on her being an African American, (Marian) went to Europe and gained recognition there.

__[R]__ 5. The renowned (composer) Jan Sibelius heard her sing.

__[R]__ 6. He dedicated the (song) "Solitude" to her.

__[N]__ 7. She was the first African American to sing with the (Metropolitan Opera,) a prestigious opera company in New York City.

__[R]__ 8. She sang an important role in an opera by the Italian (composer) Giuseppe Verdi.

__[N]__ 9. In 1963 Anderson was awarded the (Presidential Medal of Freedom,) the nation's highest award for civilians.

__[N]__ 10. In 2005 she was honored with a stamp in the Black Heritage (series,) a collection of stamps in celebration of the achievements of African Americans.

B. Underline each appositive phrase. Add commas where necessary.

1. The world-famous singer Marian Anderson was the center of a famous episode in the fight against discrimination.

2. Discrimination, unequal treatment for African Americans, meant that Anderson was often denied access to hotels and restaurants.

3. In 1939 the impresario Sol Hurok tried to arrange a concert for Anderson at Constitution Hall, a large indoor hall in Washington, D.C.

4. The owners of the hall, a group called the Daughters of the American Revolution, refused the use of its hall.

5. With the encouragement of the president's wife, Eleanor Roosevelt, the U.S. government arranged for Anderson to give a concert at the Lincoln Memorial.

Marian Anderson had to fight against prejudice that resulted from racism.
Give an example of how you can fight prejudice in your everyday life.

10. Possessive Nouns

> A possessive noun expresses possession or ownership. To form the possessive of a singular noun, add -'s to the singular form of the noun. To form the possessive of a plural noun ending in s, add an apostrophe only. If the plural form of a noun does not end in s, add -'s.
>
> SINGULAR **The singer's voice was powerful and full.**
> PLURAL **Children's voices have qualities that differ from adults' voices.**

A. Write the singular possessive and the plural possessive of each noun.

	SINGULAR POSSESSIVE	PLURAL POSSESSIVE
1. neighbor	[neighbor's]	[neighbors']
2. enemy	[enemy's]	[enemies']
3. farmer	[farmer's]	[farmers']
4. uncle	[uncle's]	[uncles']
5. wife	[wife's]	[wives']
6. parent	[parent's]	[parents']
7. woman	[woman's]	[women's]
8. princess	[princess's]	[princesses']
9. camel	[camel's]	[camels']
10. sister-in-law	[sister-in-law's]	[sisters-in-law's]

B. Underline each possessive noun. Above the noun write **S** if it is singular, **P** if it is plural.

1. In ancient times the night air rang with the telling of <u>heroes'</u> [P] stories.

2. Storytelling was <u>humans'</u> [P] basic form of entertainment in the distant past.

3. <u>Homer's</u> [S] famous poems the *Iliad* and the *Odyssey* are classics from ancient Greece.

4. Some scholars say that the poems are not one <u>poet's</u> [S] work.

5. The poems arose from the ancient <u>Greeks'</u> [P] tradition of telling stories.

6. The *Iliad* tells about those who fought in the Trojan War and about the <u>warriors'</u> [P] bravery.

7. The *Odyssey* tells one <u>man's</u> [S] story—a Greek named Odysseus, who fought in the Trojan War.

8. The <u>hero's</u> [S] adventures were numerous during the 10-year return trip to his home.

9. The ancient Greeks believed in gods, and the <u>gods'</u> [P] roles in the poems are important.

10. The stories from the ancient <u>storytellers'</u> [P] creative imaginations still fascinate readers.

Name _____

11. More Possessive Nouns

> The possessive form of a noun expresses possession or ownership.

Complete each sentence with the possessive form of the noun at the left. Singular possessives are needed in some sentences and plural possessives in others.

Greek   1. The ancient _____[Greeks']_____ love of sports was expressed in the Olympics Games.

Frenchman   2. One _____[Frenchman's]_____ efforts resulted in the revival of the Olympic games in 1896.

Coubertin   3. _____[Coubertin's]_____ idea was to have an international gathering of athletes.

man   4. In the 1896 Olympics there were only _____[men's]_____ events.

woman   5. Since 1900 there have also been _____[women's]_____ events.

city   6. Cities bid to host the Olympics, and each _____[city's]_____ bid is analyzed by the Olympic committee.

committee   7. The _____[committee's]_____ decision is announced long before the start of the games.

winner   8. The _____[winners']_____ prizes in the original Olympics were crowns of laurel.

winner   9. A _____[winner's]_____ prize at the modern Olympics is a gold medal.

athlete   10. _____[Athletes']_____ names become instantly known today because TV broadcasts reach millions around the world.

minute   11. For many athletes years of training come down to a _____[minute's]_____ performance.

loser   12. Audiences see both a winner's joy and a _____[loser's]_____ disappointment.

crowd   13. One of the _____[crowd's]_____ favorites is the gymnastic events.

gymnast   14. A _____[gymnast's]_____ grace, strength, and skill are amazing.

individual   15. At the heart of the Olympics remain an _____[individual's]_____ effort and skill.

12. Separate Possession and Joint Possession

Nouns

If two or more people own something together, it is called **joint possession**. To show joint possession, add *-'s* after the last noun only. If two or more people own things independently, it is called **separate possession**. Add *-'s* after each noun.

JOINT POSSESSION   **Fred and Paul's band plays Latin music.** (one band)

SEPARATE POSSESSION   **Jason's and Peter's bands play rock music.** (two bands)

A. On the line write **J** if ownership is joint and **S** if ownership is separate.

___[S]___ 1. Mozart's and Haydn's symphonies are more than 200 years old but are still played.

___[J]___ 2. Leonard Bernstein and Stephen Sondheim's musical of 1957, *West Side Story*, was based on the story of Romeo and Juliet.

___[J]___ 3. Elton John and Tim Rice's musical *Aida*, set in ancient Egypt, was a popular Broadway show.

___[S]___ 4. Elvis Presley's and Chuck Berry's music was influential in the development of rock and roll in the 1950s.

___[S]___ 5. Ricky Martin's and Gloria Estefan's albums are representative of Latin pop music.

B. Combine the sentences into a single sentence that shows separate or joint possession, as appropriate.

1. Oscar and Ivan have a band. It plays jazz.

   [Oscar and Ivan's band plays jazz.]

2. Lillian has a band. Rita has a band. Their bands play country music.

   [Lillian's and Rita's bands play country music.]

3. Michael and Fiona have the same piano teacher. Her name is Ms. Suarez.

   [Michael and Fiona's piano teacher is Ms. Suarez.]

4. Ona and Petra sang together. Their song was judged the best in the recital.

   [Ona and Petra's song was judged the best in the recital.]

5. Wilson and Richard each have a new keyboard. The keyboards have great sound.

   [Wilson's and Richard's keyboards have great sound.]

Name _____

13. Reviewing Nouns

A. Complete each sentence with the plural form of the word at the left.

roof   1. The aerial photo showed the _____[roofs]_____ of several houses.

silo   2. Some of the buildings in the photos were _____[silos]_____ and barns.

Patch   3. _____[Patches]_____ of land made the earth look like a large quilt.

image   4. There were other interesting _____[images]_____ in the photo.

lens   5. Photographers use special _____[lenses]_____ to take photos of this type.

B. Above each *italicized* noun or noun phrase write how it is used. Write **S** if it is used as a subject, **SC** if it is used as a subject complement, **APP** if it is used as an appositive, and **OC** if it is used as an object complement.

         [S]
6. Does *Linda* know who developed Norse mythology?
         [S]   **[S]**   **[SC]**
7. In Norse mythology *gods* and *giants* are superhuman *creatures*.
   [S]   **[APP]**
8. *Asgard*, the *home* of the gods, is connected to the land of the humans by a bridge.
         [SC]   **[SC]**
9. Hel is the *goddess* of the dead, and Hel was also the *name* for the land of the dead.
   [S]   **[SC]**
10. *Valhalla* was the *home* of dead warriors, who fought during the day and feasted at night.
   [S]   **[SC]**
11. *Odin* is the supreme *ruler* in Norse mythology.
    [S]   **[APP]**   **[OC]**
12. The *Norse* considered Thor, Odin's oldest *son*, the *god* of thunder and lightning.
           [S]
13. In Norse myths a *tree* called Yggdrasil held up the world.
  [S]   **[APP]**
14. *Loki*, the evil *son* of a giant, causes the end of the world.
     [S]   **[DO]**   **[OC]**
15. Because *people* believed he was evil, they called *Loki* a *mischief maker*.

C. Underline the nouns in possessive form. Above each write **S** if it is singular or **P** if it is plural.

                         [P]
16. The development of the steam engine changed <u>humans'</u> lives.
                                [P]   **[S]**
17. Previously, people depended on their own power, <u>animals'</u> power, or <u>nature's</u> power.
   [P]
18. Many <u>inventors'</u> ideas went into the development of the steam engine.
                         [S]
19. Some books say that the engine was <u>James Watt's</u> invention.
                             [P]
20. His creation was an improvement on earlier <u>experimenters'</u> work, because it used less fuel.

CONTINUED

D. Write whether the *italicized* nouns show separate or joint possession.

_____[joint]_____ 21. The science-fair judges chose *Marco and Lillian's* project for first place.

_____[separate]_____ 22. *Roberto's and Guong's* entries tied for second place.

_____[separate]_____ 23. Everyone watched *Vic's and Sy's* faces as third place was announced.

_____[joint]_____ 24. They were disappointed; *Rose and Bob's* project came in third.

_____[separate]_____ 25. *Richard's and Robert's* projects were good, but they were both on photosynthesis.

E. Above each *italicized* noun or noun phrase, write **DO** if it is used as a direct object, **IO** if it is used as an indirect object, **OP** if it is used as an object of a preposition, or **APP** if it is used as an appositive.

26. France gave the *United States* [IO] the *Statue of Liberty,* [DO] a *symbol* [APP] of freedom.

27. It stands 46 meters high in the *harbor* [OP] of *New York.* [OP]

28. During each *year* [OP] countless tourists see the famous *sight.* [DO]

29. On the statue's *pedestal* [OP] visitors can read *"The New Colossus,"* [DO] a *poem* [APP] by *Emma Lazarus.* [OP]

30. The Statue of Liberty gives *people* [IO] the *promise* [DO] of *freedom* [OP] and *hope.* [OP]

Try It Yourself
Write a paragraph about a famous monument in the United States. Be sure that you spell plurals and possessives correctly.

_____

_____

_____

_____

_____

Check Your Own Work
Choose a piece of writing from your portfolio or journal, a work in progress, an assignment from another class, or a letter. Revise it, applying the skills you have reviewed. This checklist will help you.

✔ Have you used the correct forms of plural nouns?

✔ Have you used apostrophes in possessives correctly?

✔ Have you used nouns in a variety of ways?

Name _____

14. Descriptive Adjectives

> A **descriptive adjective** describes a noun or a pronoun by telling its number, color, size, type, or other quality.
>
> **The <u>large</u> <u>enthusiastic</u> audience began a <u>rhythmic</u> clapping to the music's beat.**
>
> Some adjectives come from proper nouns. Remember that a proper noun names a specific person, place, or thing.
>
> **The singer Nelly Furtado is of <u>Portuguese</u> descent.**

Underline each descriptive adjective. Circle each adjective that comes from a proper noun.

1. Gloria Estefan is a <u>popular</u> singer.
2. She sings (Latin) music.
3. As a child, Gloria had a <u>difficult</u> life.
4. Her family was of (Cuban) origin.
5. They had come to the United States because of <u>political</u> problems in Cuba.
6. As a <u>young</u> girl, Gloria became an <u>important</u> caregiver to her <u>ill</u> father.
7. Gloria, who spent much of her time at home, would listen to <u>popular</u> music and sing along with the <u>strong</u> beat of the music.
8. Gloria's mother encouraged her to sing with a <u>local</u> group.
9. Although Gloria was a <u>shy</u> performer at first, she became a <u>confident</u> entertainer.
10. Gloria's <u>smooth</u> voice made her a <u>huge</u> success with audiences.
11. (Latino) audiences appreciated the <u>original</u> sound of her group.
12. The group originally sang songs in the (Spanish) language only.
13. Her group then had a <u>big</u> hit with "Dr. Beat," a song in the (English) language.
14. Estefan now had the <u>successful</u> and <u>glamorous</u> life of a star.
15. Unfortunately, in 1990 Estefan was in a <u>serious</u> accident while riding in a bus.
16. She suffered a <u>severe</u> injury to her back that required <u>major</u> surgery.
17. Following her recovery, Estefan wanted to resume her <u>musical</u> career.
18. A <u>courageous</u> and <u>industrious</u> person, Gloria worked to reestablish herself.
19. Her efforts paid off, and she was able to rebuild her <u>successful</u> career.
20. Estefan performs in an <u>interesting</u>, <u>lively</u>, and <u>creative</u> way.

 Gloria Estefan is an example of a person who is determined to reach her goals. Give an example of how you can show determination to reach a goal.

15. Position of Adjectives

An adjective usually goes before the word it describes. An adjective, however, may directly follow the word it describes. An adjective that follows a linking verb is a subject complement. An adjective that follows an object and describes it is an object complement.

Corn and tomatoes were <u>Native American</u> crops. (before the noun)
Tomatoes, <u>rich</u> and <u>juicy</u>, can be eaten raw. (after the noun)
Popcorn is very <u>tasty</u>. (subject complement)
At first Europeans considered the tomato <u>exotic</u>. (object complement)

A. Underline each adjective. Identify its position by writing **BN** on the line if the adjective comes before the noun it describes, **AN** if it comes after the noun, **SC** if it is a subject complement, or **OC** if it is an object complement.

___[SC]___ 1. Popcorn isn't <u>new</u>.

___[BN]___ 2. At excavations in New Mexico, archaeologists have found <u>ancient</u> popcorn.

___[AN, AN]___ 3. The popcorn, still <u>fluffy</u> and <u>white</u>, had been in tombs for hundreds of years.

___[SC]___ 4. Native Americans were <u>creative</u> in their uses of popcorn.

___[BN]___ 5. They used popcorn in <u>decorative</u> headdresses and necklaces.

___[BN]___ 6. They even made an <u>unusual</u> soup from popcorn.

___[SC]___ 7. In the United States today popcorn is <u>popular</u>.

___[AN, AN]___ 8. People love to eat popcorn, <u>tasty</u> and <u>crunchy</u>.

___[BN, BN]___ 9. In a year the <u>average</u> American snacks on 73 quarts of popcorn.

___[BN]___ 10. Popcorn is a seed with a <u>tiny</u> embryo in it.

___[BN]___ 11. Around the embryo is a <u>starchy</u> substance.

___[SC]___ 12. This becomes <u>large</u> when the seed is heated.

___[BN]___ 13. The heating creates the <u>fluffy</u> material of the popcorn.

___[AN, AN]___ 14. Popcorn, <u>delicious</u> and <u>nutritious</u>, can be a snack almost anytime.

___[OC]___ 15. An excess of salt and butter, however, can make it <u>unhealthful</u> for a person.

B. Write the appropriate adjective(s) to complete each sentence. On the line identify the position of each. Use **BN**, **AN**, or **SC** as in Part A.

poisonous   decorative   popular   red, round   rich and thick

___[SC]___ 1. The tomato has become tremendously ___[popular]___ around the world.

___[BN]___ 2. The ___[red, round]___ tomato is actually a fruit and not a vegetable.

___[SC]___ 3. In times past Europeans thought that the tomato was ___[poisonous]___.

___[BN]___ 4. They used it only for ___[decorative]___ purposes.

___[AN]___ 5. Eventually the Italians made pasta sauces, ___[rich and thick]___, with tomatoes.

16. Demonstrative, Interrogative, and Indefinite Adjectives

> A **demonstrative adjective** points out a definite person, place, thing, or idea. The demonstrative adjectives are *this, that, these,* and *those.*
>
> An **interrogative adjective** is used in a question. The interrogative adjectives are *what, which,* and *whose. Which* is usually used to ask about one or more of a specific set of items. *What* is used for asking about people or things but is not limited to a particular group or set. *Whose* refers to possession.
>
> An **indefinite adjective** refers to any or all of a group. Indefinite adjectives include *all, another, any, both, each, either, few, many, more, most, much, neither, other, several,* and *some.*

A. Identify the type of the *italicized* adjective in each sentence. Write **A** for demonstrative, **B** for interrogative, or **C** for indefinite.

__[B]__   1. *Which* students have signed up to participate in the karaoke night?

__[A]__   2. *This* event is going to take place in the cafeteria.

__[C]__   3. *Every* participant has to choose the song he or she will sing.

__[C]__   4. Participants can choose *any* song from a list.

__[A]__   5. Students have to indicate their choices on *this* list.

__[C]__   6. *Many* students are choosing songs by their favorite groups.

__[B]__   7. *What* group is your favorite?

__[C]__   8. *Some* students want to sing with partners.

__[C]__   9. *Several* students have asked Michael to sing with them.

__[B]__   10. *Which* song do you think I should sing?

B. Complete each sentence with the type of adjective named. More than one answer may be correct. **[Answers may vary.]**

interrogative   1. __[Which, What]__ student do you think sang the best?

indefinite   2. Elena and Martina sang wonderfully; __[either, each]__ girl is worthy of the top prize.

indefinite   3. In fact, __[each, every]__ student received loud applause.

indefinite   4. __[Some, Several]__ student performers wore costumes for their song.

demonstrative   5. __[This, That]__ kind of event can be fun for everyone.

17. Demonstrative Adjectives

Adjectives

> *This* and *these* refer to objects that are near. *That* and *those* refer to objects that are farther away.
>
> **This** kind of backpack can hold all my books.
> **Those** tents are good for camping in the woods.

A. Circle the correct demonstrative pronoun in parentheses.

1. (this **these**) chairs
2. (this **these**) types of boots
3. (**that** those) camp stove
4. (**that** those) bag of apples
5. (this **these**) boxes of matches

6. (this **these**) compasses
7. (**that** those) sweater
8. (**that** those) pair of boots
9. (**that** those) bag of marshmallows
10. (**this** these) kind of sleeping bag

B. Complete each sentence with a demonstrative adjective.
Use the information at the left.

near   1. _____**[This]**_____ new type of tent isn't very bulky.

far   2. Don't forget _____**[those]**_____ tent stakes.

near   3. _____**[These]**_____ sleeping pads will be comfortable to sleep on.

far   4. We might take _____**[that]**_____ futon mattress instead.

far   5. _____**[Those]**_____ shirts will make good pillows for our heads.

near   6. _____**[This]**_____ recipe for campfire corn-on-the-cob sounds delicious.

far   7. Pack _____**[that]**_____ can of kidney beans for my easy chili.

far   8. We need to take _____**[that]**_____ can opener also.

near   9. I'll take _____**[these]**_____ bananas to grill for dessert.

near   10. _____**[This]**_____ type of camp stove burns propane gas.

near   11. _____**[These]**_____ boxes of plastic utensils will come in handy.

far   12. You should take _____**[those]**_____ warm socks.

near   13. Don't forget _____**[these]**_____ rain ponchos.

near   14. Put _____**[these]**_____ bottles of water into the cooler.

far   15. Can you carry all _____**[that]**_____ gear?

18. Comparative and Superlative Adjectives

Most adjectives have three degrees of comparison: **positive**, **comparative**, and **superlative**.

POSITIVE	COMPARATIVE	SUPERLATIVE
high	**higher**	**highest**

- For adjectives of one syllable and some adjectives of two syllables, the comparative degree is formed by adding *-er* to the positive form, and the superlative degree is formed by adding *-est* to the positive form: *old, older, oldest; funny, funnier, funniest.*

- For adjectives of three or more syllables and many adjectives of two syllables, the comparative degree is formed by using *more* or *less* with the positive form, and the superlative degree is formed by using *most* or *least* with the positive form: *careful, more (less) careful, most (least) careful.*

- Some adjectives have irregular comparisons: *good, better, best; bad, worse, worst.*

A. Write the comparative and superlative forms of each adjective.

1. short   [shorter]   [shortest]
2. efficient   [more/less efficient]   [most/least efficient]
3. charming   [more/less charming]   [most/least charming]
4. wide   [wider]   [widest]
5. long   [longer]   [longest]
6. popular   [more/less popular]   [most/least popular]
7. simple   [simpler]   [simplest]
8. colorful   [more/less colorful]   [most/least colorful]
9. cloudy   [cloudier]   [cloudiest]
10. graceful   [more/less graceful]   [most/least graceful]

B. Tell the degree of comparison of each *italicized* adjective.
Write **P** if it is positive, **C** if it is comparative, and **S** if it is superlative.

[S]   1. Some of the *most unusual* animals in the world are on the Galapagos Islands.

[S]   2. The flightless cormorant is one of the *oddest* creatures there.

[P]   3. It doesn't fly, but it is a *swift* swimmer.

[S]   4. The giant tortoises live the *longest* lives of all animals—more than 150 years.

[C]   5. The islands' giant tortoises live mostly at *higher* elevations.

Adjectives

19. More Comparative and Superlative Adjectives

Adjectives

The comparative degree is used when two things are compared. It is often used with *than*. The superlative degree is used when more than two things are compared.

COMPARATIVE   **Earth is much <u>smaller</u> than Jupiter.**
SUPERLATIVE   **Jupiter is the <u>largest</u> planet in the solar system.**

A. **Circle the correct form for the adjective used in each comparison.**

1. Of the planets Mercury is the one that is (closer (closest)) to the sun.

2. Temperatures on Mercury are the (more extreme (most extreme)) in the solar system.

3. Venus is the (brighter (brightest)) planet of all.

4. Venus looks ((brighter) brightest) than any other object in the sky except the Sun and the Moon.

5. Venus was considered the ((most beautiful) more beautiful) planet of all.

6. The (more enormous (most enormous)) volcano in the solar system is Olympus Mons, which is on Mars and reaches a height of about 16 miles.

7. Mars is much ((smaller) smallest) than Earth.

8. Earth is ((flatter) flattest) at the poles and ((wider) widest) in the middle than a true sphere would be.

9. The (more unusual (most unusual)) feature of Jupiter is its Red Spot, which is an intense storm of gases.

10. Jupiter is much ((larger) largest) than Earth—about 1,300 Earths would fit within it.

B. **For each sentence write the correct degree of comparison of the adjective given.**

cold   1. Pluto is the _____[coldest]_____ planet, with temperatures of −387°F.

long   2. Of all the planets, Pluto takes the _____[longest]_____ time to orbit the Sun.

remarkable 3. The __[most remarkable]__ feature of Saturn is the rings that circle its equator.

short   4. A year on Mercury is much _____[shorter]_____ than a year on Earth.

faint   5. The rings of Jupiter are _____[fainter]_____ than those of Saturn.

close   6. Venus comes _____[closer]_____ to Earth than any other planet does.

hot   7. Venus's clouds create a greenhouse effect that makes Venus the _____[hottest]_____ planet of all.

massive   8. Jupiter is ___[more massive]___ than the other planets.

important   9. Jupiter's name comes from the __[most important]__ Roman god.

interesting 10. What is the ___[most interesting]___ fact you've learned about the planets?

20. *Few* and *Little* with Count and Noncount Nouns

> **Count nouns** name things that can be counted: *days, watches, emotions.* **Noncount nouns**
> name things that cannot be counted: *time, jewelry, confidence.* Use the adjectives *few, fewer,*
> and *fewest* to compare count nouns. Use the adjectives *little, less,* and *least* to compare
> noncount nouns.
>
> COUNT   A basketball team has <u>fewer</u> players than an ice hockey team has.
> NONCOUNT A period in basketball takes <u>less</u> time than a period in ice hockey.

A. Circle the correct word in parentheses.

1. There were (fewer) less) students from our school at the basketball tournament this year than there were last year.

2. In fact, I think that our school had the ((fewest) least) fans of any school in the district.

3. (Fewer (Less)) applause than usual greeted the teams as they took the court.

4. Overall, there was ((less) fewer) enthusiasm for this tournament.

5. Our team scored ((fewer) less) points than its opponent did in the first half.

6. The other team made ((fewer) less) mistakes and deserved its lead.

7. Our team seemed to play with (fewer (less)) energy in the second half than it did at the beginning of the game.

8. There were ((few) little) cheers from the fans and the cheerleaders.

9. There was no longer the (fewest (least)) hope that our team would win.

10. Our best player scored the ((fewest) least) points of his career.

B. Complete each sentence with *fewer* or *fewest,* or *less* or *least.*

1. Basketball teams have __[fewer]__ players than baseball teams have.

2. A football quarter lasts __[less]__ time than a hockey period.

3. Of all the sports I know, polo has the __[fewest]__ minutes in a period—only seven and one half minutes.

4. Compared with residents of the other countries in the Western Hemisphere, the people in the United States seem to have the __[least]__ interest in professional soccer.

5. Of all major sports, hockey attracts the __[fewest]__ TV viewers for its championship games.

6. A football field covers __[less]__ area than a soccer field.

7. Soccer requires __[fewer]__ pieces of equipment than football does.

8. __[Fewer]__ points are scored in soccer than in many other sports.

9. Professional baseball players earned much __[less]__ money in the past than current players do.

10. Some people say that of the major sports, golf requires the __[least]__ pure athletic ability.

Name _____

21. Concrete Nouns and Abstract Nouns

> A **concrete noun** names something that can be seen or touched. An **abstract noun** names a quality, a condition, or a state of mind. It names something that cannot be seen or touched. Abstract nouns are often noncount nouns.
> CONCRETE **Teachers work in schools.**
> ABSTRACT **Teachers need energy and dedication.**

Circle the abstract nouns. Underline the concrete nouns.

1. Maria Montessori (1870–1952) was a pioneer in the (education) of children.

2. Through her (determination,) Maria was the first woman in Italy to become a doctor.

3. The young doctor began to work with children and study their (methods) of (learning.)

4. Montessori worked in a poor area of Rome.

5. Her (desire) to help children was strong.

6. Maria even had workers cut down chairs and desks for the (convenience) of small children.

7. Her basic (observation) was that children have a great (need) to work toward (goals.)

8. Educators need to establish the right (environment) so young learners can experiment independently.

9. The (philosophy) of Montessori was to present children with (challenges.)

10. There are many schools around the world that follow the (principles) of Montessori today.

11. In the classrooms you will see beads, blocks, and maps—all on low shelves.

12. In Montessori schools children work with materials that have specific (purposes.)

13. One such material is the pink tower, which is made of ten pink blocks.

14. For (success) with a tower, the child starts with the largest block first.

15. The tower helps children learn the (concept) of (size.)

Maria Montessori used her knowledge to help others.
Give an example of how you can use your talents to help others.

22

22. Adjective Phrases

> A **prepositional phrase** is made up of a preposition, the object of the preposition, and any modifiers of the object. A prepositional phrase can be used as an adjective. An **adjective phrase** describes a noun or a pronoun.
>
> **Christmas trees are a holiday tradition <u>in several countries</u>.**

A. Underline each adjective phrase.

1. The use <u>of decorated Christmas trees</u> started about 400 years ago.

2. Merchants <u>in Germany</u> held Christmas fairs.

3. Bakers carefully shaped decorations <u>from gingerbread</u> and sold them.

4. Families loved these souvenirs <u>from the fairs</u>.

5. Their placement <u>on Christmas trees</u> became common.

6. The tradition <u>of decorated Christmas trees</u> <u>in people's houses</u> grew.

7. Soon another decoration <u>for the tree</u> gained popularity—tinsel.

8. Tinsel <u>from real silver</u> was manufactured.

9. Some colonists <u>in the Americas</u> did not celebrate Christmas.

10. The Puritans did not like celebrations <u>with any showiness</u>.

11. The government <u>of Boston</u> outlawed the holiday.

12. About 150 years ago Prince Albert, originally the son <u>of a German duke</u>, gave his wife, Queen Victoria <u>of England</u>, the gift <u>of a Christmas tree</u>.

13. This event marked the Christmas tree's introduction <u>to the English-speaking world</u>.

14. The connection <u>between Christmas and Christmas trees</u> was established.

15. Trees <u>inside people's houses</u> meant Christmas was near.

B. Underline each adjective phrase. Circle the word each phrase describes.

1. (People) <u>in the United States</u> first used (ornaments) <u>from Germany</u>.

2. (Pioneers) <u>on the frontier</u> made their own (decorations) <u>for the Christmas trees</u>.

3. Their trees might have (lanterns) <u>with candles</u>.

4. The trees and Christmas provided (relief) <u>from the harsh</u> (life) <u>on the prairie</u>.

5. Some families made (garlands) <u>of popcorn</u>.

6. Later, (strings) <u>of blinking lights</u> became a popular (decoration) <u>for a tree</u>.

7. The ornaments themselves became a popular (gift) <u>for Christmas</u>.

8. (Danger) <u>from fire</u> and (concern) <u>for the environment</u> have spurred the (use) <u>of artificial trees</u>.

9. Decorated (trees) <u>on central</u> (plazas) <u>in large cities</u> are a yearly tradition.

10. Some people think that (Christmas) <u>without a tree</u> isn't really Christmas.

23. Adjective Clauses

> A **clause** is a group of words that has a subject and a predicate. A dependent clause does not express a complete thought. Some dependent clauses are **adjective clauses.** They describe nouns. Adjective clauses are introduced by *who, whom, whose, that, where,* or *when.*
>
> • A **restrictive adjective clause** is necessary to the meaning of a sentence.
>
> • A **nonrestrictive adjective clause** is not necessary to the meaning. Nonrestrictive clauses are set off with commas.
>
> RESTRICTIVE   **Europeans wanted the silk <u>that China produced.</u>**
> NONRESTRICTIVE   **China, <u>which was ruled by emperors</u>, remained mysterious to Europeans.**

A.   Underline the adjective clause in each sentence. Circle the noun or noun phrase it describes.

1. The (Silk Road) which was a 4,000-mile trading route, connected China to Europe.

2. According to legend, (General Zhang Qian,) who lived in the second century BC, was the first person to travel the route.

3. The (general,) to whom a Chinese emperor had given a special mission, spent 13 years on his journey to find trade partners in the west.

4. Silk was one of the (goods) that were carried to Europe along the route.

5. (Silk,) which only the Chinese knew how to make, was much prized in Europe.

6. (Goods) that went east along the route were wool, gold, and such foods as pomegranates.

7. A famous traveler along the Silk Road was (Marco Polo,) whose travel reports introduced the wonders of China to Europeans.

8. Part of the Great Wall of China was built to protect the route from (bandits) who attacked caravans.

9. One danger of the route was the (Takla Makan Desert,) whose name means "go in and you won't come out."

10. The Silk Road was actually the northernmost of three (routes) that were used for the transporting of goods from China to the west.

B.   Underline each adjective clause. Add commas where necessary.

1. One of the areas that the Silk Road crossed was Afghanistan.

2. The route went on to the Levant, which is a name for the countries on the eastern Mediterranean.

3. Ships that carried goods across the sea made the last leg of the journey.

4. Caravans, which included camels and horses, traveled at a slow pace.

5. The Silk Road, which was replaced by safer sea routes during the 1400s, was named by a German scholar in the 1800s.

24. Reviewing Adjectives

A. Identify the position of each *italicized* adjective by writing **BN** on the line if the adjective comes before the noun, **AN** if it comes after the noun, **SC** if it is a subject complement, or **OC** if it is an object complement.

__[BN]__ 1. People give meanings to *various* colors.

__[BN]__ 2. Here are some common meanings in *Western* culture.

__[AN]__ 3. Black, *stylish* and timeless, is a classic choice.

__[SC]__ 4. Black is *popular* even for casual clothes.

__[OC]__ 5. The color orange supposedly makes people *hungry*.

__[SC]__ 6. Red is *intense*.

__[BN]__ 7. Heads often turn when someone in a *red* outfit walks by.

__[BN]__ 8. Red cars are *chief* targets for thieves.

__[AN]__ 9. Blue, *peaceful* and calming, is the choice of many people.

__[SC]__ 10. Some scientists think that people are more *productive* in blue rooms.

__[BN]__ 11. Green is a *relaxing* color.

__[SC]__ 12. Green makes a good background color because it is *easy* on the eye.

__[AN]__ 13. This color, *cool* and refreshing, is used in many hospitals.

__[OC]__ 14. Yellow supposedly makes people *optimistic*.

__[BN]__ 15. Yellow is used for *legal* pads because it helps a person's concentration.

B. Identify the type of each *italicized* adjective.
Write **A** for demonstrative, **B** for interrogative,
or **C** for indefinite.

__[B]__ 16. *Which* color is your favorite?

__[A]__ 17. *Those* people chose the color blue.

__[C]__ 18. *Every* jacket in my closet is black.

__[A]__ 19. *That* jacket in red looks good on you.

__[C]__ 20. There are *few* purple jackets in the store.

CONTINUED

25

Adjectives

Adjectives

C. Underline the correct adjective for each sentence. Identify the degree of comparison by writing **P** if it is positive, **C** if it is comparative, or **S** if it is superlative.

21. The (shorter <u>shortest</u>) **[S]** day of the year in the Northern Hemisphere is usually on or about December 21.

22. On that day the North Hemisphere is actually tilted (closer <u>closest</u>) **[S]** to the sun.

23. In areas near the North Pole, the day is almost completely (<u>dark</u> darker). **[P]**

24. Days gradually become (<u>longer</u> longest) **[C]** after that date.

25. On the other hand, in the Southern Hemisphere, that very day is the (longer <u>longest</u>) **[S]** day of the year.

D. Circle the correct word for each sentence.

26. There are ((fewer) less) hours of daylight in the winter months.

27. (Fewer (Less)) sunlight makes me want to stay indoors.

28. Do owls catch ((fewer) less) mice in winter?

29. The zoo in our town has the (least (fewest)) snakes of any zoo in the state.

30. There is ((little) few) opportunity to acquire exotic animals, I'm told.

E. Circle the correct demonstrative adjective in each sentence.

31. ((This) These) planet has an axial tilt of almost 24 degrees.

32. ((That) Those) tilt causes solar rays to strike an area more or less intensely at different seasons of the year.

33. Where (this (these)) rays are most direct, the season is warmer.

34. Two days each year have nighttime hours equal to the daytime hours; (that (those)) days are called equinoxes.

35. ((This) These) word means "equal night."

Try It Yourself
On a separate sheet of paper, write a description of two places that you have visited. Tell how they are alike or different. Be sure to use comparisons correctly.

Check Your Own Work
Choose a piece of writing from your portfolio or journal, a work in progress, an assignment from another class, or a letter. Revise it, applying the skills you have reviewed. This checklist will help you.

✔ Have you chosen adjectives that create clear images of your subjects?

✔ Have you used the correct forms of adjectives in comparisons?

✔ Have you used commas correctly with adjective clauses?

Name _____

25. Personal Pronouns

> A **pronoun** is a word used in place of a noun. A **personal pronoun** changes form to indicate certain characteristics.
>
> - Personal pronouns reflect **person. First person** indicates the speaker: *I, me, mine, we, us, ours.* **Second person** indicates the person spoken to: *you, your, yours.* **Third person** indicates the person, place, or thing spoken about: *she, her, hers, he, him, his, it, its, they, them, theirs.*
>
> - Personal pronouns have **number:** singular or plural. The singular forms are *I, me, mine, you, yours, she, her, hers, he, him, his, it,* and *its.* The plural forms are *we, us, ours, you, yours, they, them,* and *theirs.*

A. Write **1** above each pronoun in the first person, **2** above each pronoun in the second person, and **3** above each pronoun in the third person.

             [2]
1. Where were you last night, Marcus?
            [1]
2. Sandy and I wanted to go to the movies.
   [3]   [3]
3. She heard some friends of hers talk about a scary movie playing at the theater.
   [3]   [1]
4. It was a film that none of us had seen.
   [1]
5. We met Sam and Ramona at the theater.
   [1]   [3]
6. We met them at the box office.
    [3]   [2]
7. They asked where you were.
           [1]   [3]   [3]
8. Sam treated us to popcorn; he already had his.
   [1]   [1]
9. I could hardly eat mine because the movie was so scary.
  [2]
10. You missed a great film!

B. Complete each sentence with the correct pronoun.

2nd, singular   1. Have ____[you]____ ever seen *Phantom of the Opera?*

1st, singular   2. ____[I]____ was really impressed by the musical.

3rd, singular   3. ____[It]____ was about a strange masked man who lived beneath the Paris Opera House.

3rd, singular   4. ____[He]____ falls in love with a beautiful singer.

3rd, plural   5. Lindy and John took me to the play, since ____[they]____ had an extra ticket.

26. More Personal Pronouns

In addition to changing form to reflect person (*first person, second person, third person*) and number (*singular* and *plural*), third person singular pronouns also change to indicate the **gender** of the person or thing spoken about. **Feminine gender** pronouns are *she, her,* and *hers.* **Masculine gender** pronouns are *he, him,* and *his.* **Neuter gender** pronouns are *it* and *its.*

A. Underline each personal pronoun. Use the columns to indicate its person, number, and gender. Use **1** for first person, **2** for second person, or **3** for third person; **S** for singular or **P** for plural; and for third person singular pronouns **M** for masculine, **F** for feminine, or **N** for neuter.

	PERSON	NUMBER	GENDER
1. Tony and <u>I</u> are building a model airplane.	[1]	[S]	
2. <u>It</u> should be good enough to enter into the science fair.	[3]	[S]	[N]
3. Naturally, <u>we</u> drew a design first.	[1]	[P]	
4. When Ilsa heard our plans, <u>she</u> quickly started her project.	[3]	[S]	[F]
5. Most of the students already had <u>theirs</u> partly finished.	[3]	[P]	
6. Are <u>you</u> going to do a science fair project, Al?	[2]	[S]	
7. <u>Ours</u> will be entered into the category titled "Flight."	[1]	[P]	
8. Tony has chosen which parts of the model <u>he</u> wants to build.	[3]	[S]	[M]
9. <u>I</u> want to do the wings.	[1]	[S]	
10. The judges said all applications must reach <u>them</u> by Friday.	[3]	[P]	

B. Complete each sentence with the correct pronoun. Use the same numbers and letters from Part A as a guide.

3, S, F 1. When Ms. Carter visits our school, I hope to meet __[her]__ personally.

3, P 2. I've seen her paintings at local art shows; __[they]__ always feature sports topics.

3, S, N 3. Sometimes a painting will have an amusing image in __[it]__, such as a pair of basketball sneakers with wings.

2, P 4. Don't __[you]__ all wish our basketball players had shoes like that?

1, P 5. Undoubtedly, __[we]__ would then have an undefeated team.

Name _____

27. Pronouns as Subjects

> A personal pronoun can be used as the subject of a sentence.
> The subject pronouns are *I, we, you, he, she, it,* and *they.*
>
> **I can play the guitar.**

A. **Circle the correct pronoun for each sentence.**

1. David and (him **he**) are philatelists, collectors of stamps.
2. Richard and (**they** them) sometimes go to shows for stamp collectors.
3. Alicia and (**I** me) know how to put up Web pages.
4. May (**we** us) help you design your Web page?
5. Pedro and (**she** her) can play the guitar and drums.
6. Are (**they** them) going to start a band?
7. Petra and (them **they**) take ballet lessons.
8. (**We** Us) have been invited to their dance recital.
9. Emilio and (him **he**) like to play soccer.
10. My friend and (**I** me) sometimes play with them.

B. **Replace the *italicized* word or words with the correct pronoun.**
Write it on the line.

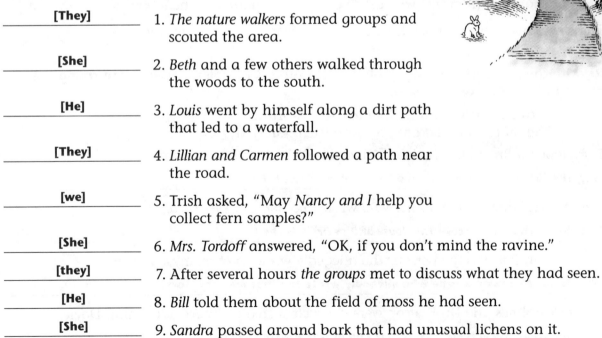

_____**[They]**_____ 1. *The nature walkers* formed groups and scouted the area.

_____**[She]**_____ 2. *Beth* and a few others walked through the woods to the south.

_____**[He]**_____ 3. *Louis* went by himself along a dirt path that led to a waterfall.

_____**[They]**_____ 4. *Lillian and Carmen* followed a path near the road.

_____**[we]**_____ 5. Trish asked, "May *Nancy and I* help you collect fern samples?"

_____**[She]**_____ 6. *Mrs. Tordoff* answered, "OK, if you don't mind the ravine."

_____**[they]**_____ 7. After several hours *the groups* met to discuss what they had seen.

_____**[He]**_____ 8. *Bill* told them about the field of moss he had seen.

_____**[She]**_____ 9. *Sandra* passed around bark that had unusual lichens on it.

_____**[They]**_____ 10. *Several students* showed drawings that they had made of plants.

28. Pronouns as Subject Complements

> A subject pronoun can replace a noun used as a subject complement. A subject complement follows a linking verb and refers to the same person, place, or thing as the subject.
>
> **The children who found the missing jewels were <u>they</u>.**

A. Circle the correct pronoun in each sentence.

1. The ones who wanted to watch the mystery on TV were (us **we**).

2. The man who asked us for directions to the library was (**he** him).

3. We learned later that the only person in the reference room was (him **he**).

4. Jennifer said the person who opened the library door was (**she** her).

5. Richard claimed the security guard was (**he** him) who turned off the lights.

6. Were the students who gathered in front of the library (them **they**)?

7. Is the gentleman in the gray suit (**he** him)?

8. Can the person who stole the jewels really be (her **she**)?

9. The librarian was (him **he**) who asked everyone to gather in the lobby.

10. The clever sleuth who named the guilty party was no other than (me **I**).

B. Rewrite the sentences, using a pronoun as a subject complement and confirming the information given. [Answers may vary.]

> EXAMPLE: **I think Sarah and Ed like mystery stories.**
> *Yes, Sarah and Ed are they who like mystery stories.*

1. Encyclopedia Brown is a fictional 10-year-old who helps solve crimes.

   [Yes, the fictional 10-year-old who helps solve crimes is he.]

2. Virginia Hamilton is the author who wrote *The House of Dies Drear*.

   [Yes, the author who wrote *The House of Dies Drear* is she.]

3. Edgar Allan Poe was the person who allegedly wrote the first mystery story.

   [Yes, Edgar Allan Poe was he who allegedly wrote the first mystery story.]

4. Sherlock Holmes and Dr. Watson were characters created by Arthur Conan Doyle.

   [Yes, the characters created by Arthur Conan Doyle were they.]

5. Agatha Christie has been called the queen of mystery.

   [Yes, Agatha Christie is she who has been called the queen of mystery.]

29. Pronouns as Direct Objects

> A personal pronoun can be used as the direct object of a verb.
> The object pronouns are *me, us, you, him, her, it,* and *them.*
>
> **My friends invited <u>us</u> to an international food fair.**

A. Circle the correct pronoun for each sentence.

1. My friends invited my sister and (I (me)) to the international food fair.

2. They called ((us) we) with the invitation, and we arranged to meet at noon.

3. We met Omar and (he (him)) near the entrance.

4. The workers directed my friends and (I (me)) to the ticket booth.

5. We saw Marietta and (she (her)) near the Mexican food booth.

6. The worker helped Peter and (they (them)) with directions to the Chinese booth.

7. Some people told Kathleen and (we (us)) about the tasty Thai spring rolls.

8. Some old friends of their family recognized Kent and (she (her)).

9. Unfortunately, I lost my sister and ((them) they) in the crowd.

10. Then I got an idea: I called (she (her)) on her cell phone.

B. For each sentence write the pronoun that correctly replaces the *italicized* word or words.

___[them]___ 1. Last week a distant cousin called *my mom and dad.*

___[us]___ 2. He was in town, and he wanted to see *my mom, my dad, my sister, and me.*

___[him]___ 3. We recognized *Paul* as he stepped off the plane.

___[her]___ 4. He surprised *my mom* with a gift—an album of family pictures.

___[him]___ 5. My mom thanked *Paul* for the gift.

___[her]___ 6. Paul told *my mom* about some of her family members.

___[them]___ 7. My mom hasn't seen *Paul's mother and father* for many years.

___[us]___ 8. Paul was seeing *my sister and me* for the first time.

___[him]___ 9. We liked *Paul* immediately.

___[them]___ 10. When he left, Paul thanked *my mom and dad* for their hospitality.

Name _____

30. Pronouns as Indirect Objects

> An object pronoun can be used as the indirect object of a verb.
> **George mailed <u>her</u> an invitation to the Halloween party.**

A. Circle the correct pronoun for each sentence.

1. George and David sent (I (me)) an invitation to their Halloween party.

2. Ann showed Juanita and ((me) I) her ghost outfit.

3. Her sister had lent (she (her)) the costume.

4. David's mother made his brother and (he (him)) skeleton costumes.

5. The hosts served (we (us)) apple juice and pretzels.

6. Lydia brought ((them) they) some pumpkin-shaped cookies.

7. I owed George and (he (him)) an apology for being late.

8. I told (they (them)) the problem: I couldn't get my Dracula teeth to stay in.

9. My sister gave (I (me)) some special adhesive for the teeth.

10. Dressing as salt-and-pepper shakers won Philippa and ((her) she) a prize for best costumes.

B. For each sentence write the object pronoun that correctly replaces the underlined word or words.

__[them]__ 1. In the *Aeneid* the ancient Greeks send <u>the Trojans</u> a huge horse.

__[them]__ 2. The horse affords <u>the Greek soldiers</u> a hiding place while they enter Troy.

__[him]__ 3. In a Roman myth the goddess Venus gives <u>Paris</u> some golden apples.

__[her]__ 4. Hippomenes wins a race against Atalanta when he throws <u>the young woman</u> the apples and distracts her.

__[him]__ 5. In the Bible Jacob gives <u>his son Joseph</u> a coat of many colors.

__[him]__ 6. The Magi bring <u>the baby Jesus</u> gold, frankincense, and myrrh.

__[them]__ 7. Tom Sawyer tells <u>his friends</u> a not-quite-true story about why he is painting a fence.

__[him]__ 8. The other children offer <u>Tom</u> things so that they too can paint the fence.

__[him]__ 9. In O. Henry's story "The Gift of the Magi," the wife gives <u>her husband</u> a chain for his watch.

__[her]__ 10. In the same story the husband buys <u>his wife</u> a set of combs for her hair.

Name _____

31. Pronouns as Objects of Prepositions

An object pronoun can be used as the object of a preposition.
The report was presented to <u>them</u> by Shirley and <u>me</u>.

A. Circle the correct pronoun for each sentence.

1. The work on the history project was divided among Jed, Jim, Valerie, Judy, and (I **me**).

2. Research on the Internet about the Incas was done by Jed and (she **her**).

3. The graphics were prepared by Judy and (**him** he).

4. All of (we **us**) decided on the organization of the project.

5. The section on the amazing road system of the Incas was prepared by Valerie and (she **her**).

6. The Mayas and the Incas were established civilizations, and we made comparisons between (**them** they).

7. The task of proofreading the report was divided between Valerie and (I **me**).

8. We asked Jed to make copies of our report for (**her** she).

9. Some excellent questions were asked by Richard and (he **him**).

10. We received some good feedback from Mr. Robertson and (they **them**).

B. For each sentence write the object pronoun that correctly replaces the *italicized* word or words.

___**[her]**___ 1. Tom and Sue presented a report on *Cleopatra*.

___**[them]**___ 2. She was a ruler of *the Egyptians* about 2,000 years ago.

___**[them]**___ 3. She was considered fascinating and alluring by *the people of her time*.

___**[them]**___ 4. For a while Cleopatra ruled Egypt with each of *her brothers*.

___**[him]**___ 5. Later Cleopatra was able to regain power with help from *Julius Caesar*.

___**[him]**___ 6. Eventually she was married to *Mark Antony, a Roman leader*.

___**[her]**___ 7. The aim of Antony and *Cleopatra* was to gain more power.

___**[them]**___ 8. They were defeated in several battles by *the Romans*.

___**[him]**___ 9. The story of Cleopatra and *Antony* ends unhappily.

___**[her]**___ 10. Many stories and plays have been written about *Cleopatra*.

32. Pronouns After *Than* or *As*

The conjunctions *than* and *as* are used in comparisons. These words join two clauses. Sometimes part of the second clause is omitted, and you need to supply the missing part to determine whether to use a subject pronoun or an object pronoun after *than* or *as*.

> **Sarah likes picnics as much as I.** (Sarah likes picnics as much as I *like picnics*.)
> **Snakes scare me more than him.** (Snakes scare me more than *they scare* him.)

Notice that when the subject (or possibly the subject complement) is compared, a subject pronoun is used. When an object is compared, an object pronoun is used.

A. Circle the pronoun in each sentence. That pronoun functions within its clause just as the *italicized* word(s) does in its clause. Supply missing sentence parts mentally to help decide which pronoun is correct.

1. The children looked forward to the picnic, and the *adults* were as excited as ((they) them).

2. Because they took a shortcut, *the Edwards family* arrived earlier than ((we) us).

3. Setting up the grill took *Pedro* longer than (he (him)).

4. *Michael* makes better potato salad than ((she) her).

5. *I* ate as many hot dogs as ((she) her).

6. *Wayne* ate more cookies than ((I) me).

7. The heat bothered *Jude* more than (they (them)).

8. The mosquitoes annoyed *Samantha* more than (he (him)).

9. *Carol* played volleyball better than ((he) him).

10. The game entertained *Carol* more than (he (him)).

B. Use the information below to write sentences with *than* or *as* followed by pronouns.

	ERNESTO	ELLIE	BEV
Newspapers delivered	74	85	85
Time worked	50 minutes	50 minutes	1 hour

Compared with Bev: [Sentences may vary. Suggestions are given.]

It took Ellie less time to deliver 85 newspapers than her.

1. [Ernesto delivered fewer newspapers than she.] _____

Compared with Ellie:

2. [Bev delivered as many newspapers as she.] _____

3. [It took Ernesto as much time to deliver his newspapers as her.] _____

Compared with Ernesto:

4. [Bev delivered more newspapers than he.] _____

5. [It took Ellie as much time to deliver her newspapers as him.] _____

Name _____

33. Possessive Pronouns and Possessive Adjectives

> A **possessive pronoun** shows possession or ownership. It takes the place of a possessive noun and stands by itself. The possessive pronouns are *mine, yours, hers, his, its, ours,* and *theirs.*
>
> **The yellow backpack is <u>hers</u>.** (The yellow backpack is *Mary's*.)
>
> A possessive adjective also shows possession or ownership, but it does not stand alone. A possessive adjective modifies a noun. The possessive adjectives are *my, your, her, his, its, our,* and *their.*
>
> **<u>Their</u> backpacks are navy blue.** (*The boys'* backpacks are navy blue.)

Pronouns

A. Underline each possessive pronoun. Circle each possessive adjective.

1. The things in the garage sale are <u>ours</u>.

2. (My) old Batman comic book sold for five dollars.

3. Deciding on prices is (her) job; <u>mine</u> is to give change.

4. (Their) offer for (his) bike was too low.

5. But that ugly painting is now <u>theirs</u>!

6. (My) coat is beside <u>hers</u> on the rack; those coats are not for sale.

7. You may use (my) pen if you have lost <u>yours</u>.

8. Someone bought (our) broken lamp for two dollars.

9. (His) old golf clubs got the highest price.

10. Come to (our) sale again next year.

B. On the first line at the left write a possessive that can replace the *italicized* words. On the second line write **A** if the word is a possessive adjective and **P** if it is a possessive pronoun.

[ours]	[P]	1. All the stuff in the attic was *my family's and mine.*
[mine]	[P]	2. Don't put those shabby stuffed animals on sale. They're *my stuffed animals.*
[her]	[A]	3. The table with the broken leg was in *Sally's* room. We can't sell it.
[his]	[P]	4. That obsolete phonograph was *my grandfather's.*
[his]	[A]	5. The guitar missing a string was once *Dad's* favorite possession.
[hers]	[P]	6. The box cameras were *Mom's.*
[theirs]	[P]	7. The nifty model planes were *my Dad's and his brother's.*
[mine]	[P]	8. These tiny baby shoes were once *my shoes.*
[her]	[A]	9. That was *my sister's* first tricycle.
[their]	[A]	10. The large wardrobe once was in *my grandparents'* house.

35

34. Intensive and Reflexive Pronouns

> Intensive and reflexive pronouns end in -self or -selves. An **intensive pronoun** emphasizes a preceding noun or pronoun. A **reflexive pronoun** is used as a direct object, an indirect object, or the object of a preposition.
>
> INTENSIVE   **Walt Disney himself did much of the work on his films.**
>   **Walt Disney did much of the work on his films himself.**
> REFLEXIVE   **Walt Disney had confidence in himself and gained success.**

A. Underline the reflexive or intensive pronoun in each sentence.
Circle the word(s) it refers to.

1. (Walt Disney) first established himself as an advertising cartoonist.

2. (He) then made a name for himself as a producer of cartoon features.

3. At first, (Disney) himself drew his cartoons.

4. Since (animals) lent themselves to animation, Disney's first character was a mouse.

5. (Disney) himself provided Mickey Mouse's voice.

6. (Mickey Mouse) would eventually earn himself a worldwide following.

7. Disney was not an overnight success; (he) slowly worked himself to the top.

8. (Snow White and the Seven Dwarfs) gained itself a place in movie history.

9. The cartoon's (characters) won permanent places for themselves in the hearts of audiences.

10. Even the (songs) from the films themselves are still sung today.

B. Complete each sentence with a reflexive or intensive pronoun. Circle the word(s) it refers to. On the line write **I** if the pronoun is intensive or **R** if it is reflexive.

__[I]__   1. (Rachel Carson) ___[herself]___ said that from an early age she loved nature.

__[R]__   2. (Carson) earned ___[herself]___ a degree in zoology in 1932.

__[R]__   3. Her (writings) about the ocean earned ___[themselves]___ a large audience.

__[R]__   4. (Carson) quit her job, and she devoted ___[herself]___ to scientific writing.

__[I]__   5. Carson studied the use of synthetic pesticides, and she decided that the (pesticides) ___[themselves]___ were a danger to the environment.

__[I]__   6. According to Carson, (we) ___[ourselves]___ are part of the ecosystem.

__[I]__   7. Pesticides might ultimately harm (humans) ___[themselves]___ .

__[R]__   8. Pesticide (manufacturers) aligned ___[themselves]___ against Carson's book about pesticides.

__[R]__   9. (Carson and her supporters) found ___[themselves]___ under attack.

__[I]__   10. (Carson) ___[herself]___ testified before Congress on behalf of the environment shortly before her death in 1964.

Pronouns

Name _____

35. Agreement of Pronouns and Antecedents

> The word to which a pronoun refers is its **antecedent**. Pronouns agree with their antecedents in person, number, and gender.
>
> ANTECEDENT
> **Women's <u>roles</u> in society were expanding in the 1800s, and Clara Barton**
> PRONOUN
> **helped to expand <u>them</u> by her work and example.**

A. Underline the antecedent of each italicized pronoun. On the line write its person (**1, 2,** or **3**), its number (**S** or **P**), and, if it is third person singular, its gender (**F, M,** or **N**).

__[3, S, F]__ 1. <u>Clara Barton</u> had an interest in nursing from an early age; *she* eventually founded the American Red Cross and helped countless victims of wars and natural disasters.

__[3, S, M]__ 2. When she was only 11 years old, Barton got her first experience in nursing when her <u>brother</u> was injured and she helped take care of *him*.

__[3, P]__ 3. When the Civil War broke out and <u>soldiers</u> were fighting near Washington, D.C., Barton began to help *them*.

__[3, P]__ 4. She noticed the terrible lack of <u>supplies</u> for the soldiers, and she arranged to get more of *them* for the men.

__[3, P]__ 5. The <u>soldiers</u> were grateful for her help, and she was called the Angel of the Battlefield by *them*.

B. Complete each sentence with the appropriate pronoun or pronouns. Make sure that each agrees in person, number, and gender with its antecedent. Underline the antecedent.

1. While in Switzerland for rest after the war, Barton learned about the <u>International Committee of the Red Cross</u> and how __[it]__ brought medical aid during wartime.

2. <u>Clara Barton</u> thought the organization was a good idea, and __[she]__ worked to start a similar one in the United States, which became the American Red Cross.

3. Not only did the U.S. organization help <u>people</u> in times of war, but also it assisted __[them]__ during disasters such as fires, floods, and hurricanes.

4. Barton helped during several well-known major <u>catastrophes</u>; __[they]__ included the Johnstown (Pa.) Flood, the Spanish-American War, and the Galveston (Tex.) hurricane.

5. <u>Barton</u> continued to work in the field helping others until __[she]__ was more than 80 years old.

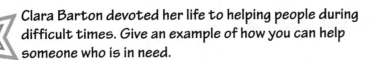

Clara Barton devoted her life to helping people during difficult times. Give an example of how you can help someone who is in need.

37

36. Interrogative Pronouns

> An **interrogative pronoun** is used to ask a question. The interrogative pronouns are *who, whom, whose, which,* and *what.*
>
> - *Who* refers to persons and is used as the subject of a question.
> - *Whom* refers to persons and is used as the object of a verb or a preposition.
> - *Whose* refers to possession.
> - *Which* refers to a group or class; it often pertains to a choice between two or more people or things.
> - *What* is used for asking about things, particularly when seeking information.

A. Circle the interrogative pronoun in each sentence.

1. By (whom) was *The Wizard of Oz* written?

2. (What) is a wizard?

3. (What) happens in the book?

4. (Which) of the characters lacks courage?

5. (What) did the scarecrow want?

6. (Who) were Dorothy's companions on the trip?

7. (Which) is Dorothy's home state—Kansas or Illinois?

8. (What) is a tornado?

9. (Who) starred in the movie version of *The Wizard of Oz?*

10. (Whose) book is this?

B. Complete each sentence with an interrogative pronoun.

1. ____[Who]____ wrote the Harry Potter books?

2. With ____[whom]____ did Harry Potter live at first?

3. ____[What]____ did Harry learn about himself when he was 11?

4. __[Who, What]__ were Harry's parents?

5. ____[What]____ is the name of Harry Potter's new school?

6. ____[Who]____ is Hermione?

7. ____[Which]____ of his classmates is Harry's main rival?

8. ____[Which]____ of the adventures in the books is the most exciting?

9. ____[What]____ makes the Harry Potter books special?

10. ____[Which]____ of the Harry Potter books have you read?

Pronouns

37. Demonstrative Pronouns

A **demonstrative pronoun** points out a specific person, place, or thing. The demonstrative pronouns are *this, that, these,* and *those. This* and *these* refer to what is near; *that* and *those* refer to what is distant.

> <u>This</u> is the best store in the area.
> <u>Those</u> over there are rotten apples.

A. Underline each demonstrative pronoun. On the line write **N** if it indicates an object that is near or **F** if it indicates an object that is farther away.

__[N]__ 1. <u>This</u> is the biggest supermarket in the area.

__[F]__ 2. Let's get one of <u>those</u> to hold our groceries.

__[N]__ 3. <u>This</u> is a large produce department.

__[N]__ 4. Do you think that <u>these</u> are the best-looking apples?

__[F]__ 5. Let's get some of <u>those</u>—they're on sale.

__[N, F]__ 6. <u>These</u> are more expensive than <u>those</u>.

__[F]__ 7. <u>That</u> is a good brand of cereal.

__[F]__ 8. Don't get near <u>that</u>—the whole stack might fall!

__[N]__ 9. <u>These</u> are the freshest loaves of bread.

__[F]__ 10. <u>That</u> is the shortest check-out line.

B. Complete each sentence with the correct demonstrative pronoun. Use the information at the left.

far   1. Is ___[that]___ the bag with the eggs? Be careful!

near   2. Are ___[these]___ all the bags we have?

far   3. ___[That]___ goes in the refrigerator.

near   4. Where does ___[this]___ belong?

far   5. ___[Those]___ go in the fruit bowl.

near   6. I can't carry ___[this]___—it's too heavy.

far   7. The bananas here look riper than ___[those]___.

near   8. ___[These]___ are great-looking grapes.

far   9. ___[That]___ is the largest can—put it on the bottom.

near   10. ___[This]___ is the last thing to put away. Hooray!

38. Relative Pronouns

A dependent clause contains a subject and a predicate but does not express a complete thought. When a dependent clause functions as an adjective, a **relative pronoun** is used to connect it to its antecedent in the main clause. The relative pronouns are *who, whom, which, that,* and *whose.*

- *Who, whom,* and *whose* usually refer to a person. *Who* is used as the subject of the dependent clause; *whom* is used as the object of a verb or a preposition.
- *Which* refers to an animal, a place, or a thing.
- *That* refers to a person, place, or thing.

Underline the relative pronoun in each sentence. Circle the noun or noun phrase that is its antecedent.

1. The present-day natural (wonder) that is called the Sacred Lake of Siberia lies near the border of Mongolia.

2. (Lake Baikal,) which is the deepest and oldest lake in the world, is a mile deep at its center and is estimated to be about 25 million years old.

3. Lake Baikal has an (area) that is slightly larger than the area of South Carolina, and to fill its basin would require all the rivers in the world to flow into it for one year.

4. Of the 2,635 plant and animal (species) that have been identified in the lake, more than 1,500 are not found anywhere else on earth.

5. Among the unusual species is a small fish called the (golomyanka,) or oil fish, about which there is a great deal of mystery.

6. This (fish,) whose body consists largely of oil rich in vitamin A, exists only in Lake Baikal and does not follow typical life patterns associated with fish.

7. Another (mystery) that fascinates scientists surrounds the nerpa, or Baikal seal.

8. (Scientists) who study Lake Baikal attempt to explain how other seals most similar to the nerpas exist only thousands of miles away.

9. Lake Baikal was first visited by (Russians) who were fur traders.

10. Later Benedykt Dybowski, a Polish scientist exiled to Siberia, discovered many rare species in the lake, (one) of which is named after him.

11. While in Siberia, Dybowski cofounded the field of science called (limnology,) which is the study of bodies of fresh water and their various properties.

12. The (lake,) which had been known for its great beauty and purity, became a victim of modern technology, with the construction of a paper mill on its shore in 1957.

13. Many Soviet (citizens) who heard about the project were alarmed, but their protests did not stop construction.

14. Meanwhile, the chemical (runoff) that threatens hundreds of unique species of the lake was blamed for the death of 78 nerpas found on the shore in 1999.

15. To decrease pollution, the United Nations is considering naming Lake Baikal a natural treasure of the world, a (move) that would give it international protection.

Pronouns

Name _____

39. Indefinite Pronouns

> An **indefinite pronoun** refers to any or all members of a group of persons, places, or things. Some common indefinite pronouns are *all, anybody, anyone, anything, both, each, either, everybody, everyone, everything, few, many, one, neither, nobody, no one, nothing, several, some, somebody, someone,* and *something.*
>
> **Many** enjoy the sport of ballooning.
> **Each** of the hot-air balloons was in bright colors.

A. Underline each indefinite pronoun.

1. My two brothers wanted to do <u>something</u> different during summer vacation.

2. <u>Both</u> of them are interested in sports and like a challenge.

3. A <u>few</u> of their friends had talked to them about hot-air ballooning.

4. My brothers went up in a balloon with <u>someone</u> who was an experienced pilot.

5. After <u>several</u> of the trips, they wanted to learn to pilot themselves.

6. They can take classes at <u>either</u> of the community colleges.

7. <u>Each</u> of the students would get 10 hours of flight experience with an instructor.

8. Passing a written examination was a requirement for <u>everyone</u> in the class.

9. <u>No one</u> who missed class would be able to get a license.

10. <u>Neither</u> of my brothers missed a class, and now they have their licenses.

B. Circle each indefinite pronoun. On the line write **S** if it is used as a subject, **DO** if it is a direct object, **IO** if it is an indirect object, or **OP** if it is the object of a preposition.

___[DO]___ 1. My brothers looked for ballooning sites on the Web, and they found (many.)

___[S]___ 2. (Neither) of them had known about the Balloon Fiesta in New Mexico.

___[OP]___ 3. The information they discovered really made an impression on (each) of them.

___[S]___ 4. (Somebody) told me that more than 1,000 balloonists participate in the fiesta.

___[S]___ 5. (Many) of the balloons are in odd shapes—such as a piggy bank or a motorcycle.

___[DO]___ 6. My brothers found (someone) who had been to the fiesta.

___[IO]___ 7. The person told (both) of them stories about the fiesta.

___[S]___ 8. (Either) of my brothers could participate in future fiestas.

___[OP]___ 9. The annual fiesta is open to (anyone) who qualifies.

___[OP]___ 10. I'll be rooting for (both) of them if they enter.

41

40. Agreement with Indefinite Pronouns

> Some indefinite pronouns are always singular; others are always plural.
> Depending on how they are used, some can be singular or plural.
>
> SINGULAR   another, anybody, anyone, anything, each, either, everybody, everyone, everything, much, neither, nobody, no one, nothing, one, other, somebody, someone, something
>
> PLURAL   both, few, many, others, several
>
> SINGULAR OR PLURAL   all, any, more, most, none, some

Circle the verb that agrees with the pronoun.

1. All of the cleanup volunteers (was (were)) supposed to bring their sign-up cards with them.

2. Everybody ((was mailed) were mailed) a sign-up card.

3. Each ((was) were) assigned to a work group for the day.

4. All of the work ((was) were) to be finished by dinnertime.

5. If anybody ((wants) want) gloves or shovels for the work, they are available.

6. A few of the volunteers ((have brought) has brought) their own gloves.

7. Nobody (have brought (has brought)) a shovel.

8. Several of the groups ((work) works) on the south end of the beach.

9. One of the groups (clean (cleans)) the parking areas.

10. Each of the volunteers ((fills) fill) his or her bag with garbage.

11. No one but the volunteers ((was allowed) were allowed) on the beach during the cleanup.

12. Many of the beach users (has left (have left)) garbage.

13. Most of the trash ((was put) were put) into bags.

14. Ed found a shoe. Someone ((has left) have left) the beach with only one shoe.

15. If anyone ((fills) fill) a bag, one of the two managers provides another bag.

16. After a couple of hours, neither of the beach managers ((has) have) any bags left.

17. Some of the bags (breaks (break)) when full.

18. Many of the groups (was finished (were finished)) early.

19. Others (works (work)) hard to complete their tasks.

20. Everyone ((was pleased) were pleased) with the results—a clean beach.

Name _____

41. Reviewing Pronouns

A. Circle the correct form of the pronoun for each sentence. On the line write
S if it is used as a subject, **SC** if it is a subject complement, **DO** if it is a direct object,
IO if it is an indirect object, or **OP** if it is the object of a preposition.

__[IO]__ 1. Ancient myths have given (we (us)) many famous characters.

__[OP]__ 2. Names such as Hercules are familiar to (we (us)) all.

__[SC]__ 3. Also well-known is the story of Daedalus. This Greek god
was ((he) him) who made wings of wax and feathers.

__[DO]__ 4. A king had imprisoned (he (him)) and his son Icarus.

__[S]__ 5. ((They) Them) wanted to escape.

__[S]__ 6. His son and ((he) him) were able to fly with the wings,
but the story ends unhappily for Icarus.

__[DO]__ 7. Daedalus had warned ((him) he) about the danger of the sun.

__[OP]__ 8. But the warning was forgotten by (he (him)) in the excitement of flying.

__[S]__ 9. The sun melted the wax on his wings, and ((they) them) came off.

__[S]__ 10. Both the wings and ((he) him) fell into the ocean.

B. Complete each sentence with a possessive pronoun, an intensive pronoun,
or a reflexive pronoun.

11. Zeus was the chief god, and the most important place on Mount Olympus was
_____**[his]**_____ .

12. He could turn _____**[himself]**_____ into an animal or a human.

13. The gods and goddesses often quarreled among _____**[themselves]**_____ .

14. They _____**[themselves]**_____ often behaved foolishly.

15. Despite this, the gods and goddesses were powerful, and the power over
humans was _____**[theirs]**_____ .

C. Underline each relative pronoun. Circle the noun or noun phrase
that is its antecedent.

16. (Hercules,) whose father was Zeus, was very powerful.

17. Hercules had to perform 12 difficult (tasks,) to which the name Labors of Hercules
was given.

18. Hercules wore the skin of a (lion,) which he had killed with his bare hands.

43

Pronouns

19. For a while he took over the job of (Atlas,) who carried the sky on his back.

20. Hercules even traveled to the fearful underworld to fetch (Cerberus,) which was Pluto's three-headed dog.

D. Identify each *italicized* pronoun. On the line write **A** if it is demonstrative, **B** if it is interrogative, or **C** if it is indefinite.

___[B]___ 21. *What* do you know about ancient mythology?

___[A]___ 22. *This* is a topic that interests many people.

___[C]___ 23. I got two books from the library, but *neither* had the story of Ariadne.

___[C]___ 24. *Both* were nice books with beautiful illustrations.

___[C]___ 25. I had read versions of *many* of the stories before.

E. Complete each sentence with *who* or *whom*.

26. Hermes, ___[whom]___ the Romans called Mercury, was the messenger of the gods.

27. Athena, after ___[whom]___ Athens is named, was the goddess of wisdom.

28. Poseidon, by ___[whom]___ the sea was ruled, was Zeus' brother.

29. Hephaestus, ___[who]___ was the god of fire, was called Vulcan by the Romans.

30. Apollo, ___[who]___ was the god of music, was one of the most important Greek gods.

F. Circle the correct word in parentheses.

31. ((Each) Most) of the sources of information is reliable.

32. Everyone ((looks) look) for the names in the dictionary.

33. A few (does (do)) an Internet search.

34. Mark helped Carrie; he found some information faster than ((she) her).

35. Lee and Inez were as interested in the topic as ((they) them).

Try It Yourself

On a separate sheet of paper, write a paragraph about a famous person you've learned about recently. Be sure that you use correct forms of pronouns and pronoun agreement.

Check Your Own Work

Choose a piece of writing from your portfolio or journal, a work in progress, an assignment from another class, or a letter. Revise it, applying the skills you have reviewed. This checklist will help you.

✔ Are the personal pronouns correct?

✔ Are *who* and *whom* used correctly in questions and dependent clauses?

✔ Are possessive pronouns and possessive adjectives used correctly?

✔ Are indefinite pronouns used correctly?

Pronouns

42. Principal Parts of Verbs

> A **verb** is a word that shows action or state of being. A verb has four principal parts: the **present** (or base), the **present participle**, the **past**, and the **past participle.**
>
> • The present participle is formed by adding -*ing* to the present part of the verb.
> • The past and the past participle of **regular verbs** are formed by adding -*d* or -*ed* to the present part.
> • The simple past and the past participle of **irregular verbs** are not formed by adding -*d* or -*ed* to the present part.
>
> | | PRESENT | PRESENT PARTICIPLE | PAST | PAST PARTICIPLE |
> |---|---|---|---|---|
> | REGULAR | live | living | lived | lived |
> | IRREGULAR | see | seeing | saw | seen |
>
> **Many nobles lived in castles. I have seen pictures of castles.**

A. Draw one line under the subject and two lines under the verb. On the line write whether the verb is regular or irregular.

__[regular]__ 1. During the Middle Ages most people lived in small villages.

__[regular]__ 2. The Middle Ages lasted from about AD 500 to AD 1400.

__[regular]__ 3. Society included three groups: nobles, peasants, and clergy.

__[irregular]__ 4. The nobles fought for the protection of the land and its people.

__[regular]__ 5. The nobles owned the land.

__[regular]__ 6. The nobles received their land from the king or queen.

__[regular]__ 7. The peasants farmed the land.

__[irregular]__ 8. The peasants gave part of their crops to the nobles.

__[irregular]__ 9. The clergy taught people about the Christian religion.

__[irregular]__ 10. The clergy held a great deal of power in medieval society.

B. Write the present participle, the past, and the past participle of each verb. If necessary, check your answers in a dictionary.

	PRESENT PARTICIPLE	PAST	PAST PARTICIPLE
1. fly	[flying]	[flew]	[flown]
2. decide	[deciding]	[decided]	[decided]
3. think	[thinking]	[thought]	[thought]
4. wear	[wearing]	[wore]	[worn]
5. eat	[eating]	[ate]	[eaten]
6. forget	[forgetting]	[forgot]	[forgotten]
7. fix	[fixing]	[fixed]	[fixed]
8. keep	[keeping]	[kept]	[kept]
9. sell	[selling]	[sold]	[sold]
10. hurt	[hurting]	[hurt]	[hurt]

43. Irregular Verbs

> The past and the past participle of irregular verbs are not formed by adding *-d* or *-ed.* If necessary, consult a dictionary.

A. Circle the correct form of the verb in parentheses.

1. The Hopi of Arizona have long (grew (grown)) corn and lived in pueblos.

2. They have also (hold (held)) ceremonies like the Snake Dance to call for rain.

3. Also, the Hopi have (tell (told)) a story about the origin of the sun and the moon.

4. The Hopi believed that they themselves had (risen) rose) to this world from the underworld.

5. The world they ((came) come) into was dark, and life was difficult for them.

6. One day they (seen (saw)) a light in the distance.

7. A messenger was (send (sent)) by the chiefs of the Hopi to find the source of the light.

8. In a field the messenger (find (found)) a great fire and a handsome man called Skeleton.

9. The Hopi were (gave (given)) corn for roasting by Skeleton.

10. With Skeleton's help, the Hopi (build (built)) fires and learned to grow crops.

B. Complete each sentence with the past or the past participle of the verb at the left.

make 1. The darkness of the world still __[made]__ life difficult for the Hopi.

have 2. The Hopi had __[had]__ a moon in the underworld, and so they decided to make one in this world.

cut 3. They __[cut]__ a huge circle from buffalo hide and painted it white.

put 4. The circle was __[put]__ on a huge wooden hoop.

throw 5. They __[threw]__ the circle into the sky.

sing 6. As they swung the circle, they __[sang]__ a magical song.

become 7. Suddenly there was a light in the sky that __[became]__ brighter and brighter—a moon for the earth.

do 8. There still wasn't enough light, so something else was __[done]__.

weave 9. The Hopi took a special piece of cloth that they had __[woven]__ in the underworld.

swing 10. They __[swung]__ the copper-colored cloth into the sky, and it became the sun.

Verbs

44. Verb Phrases

A **verb phrase** is two or more verbs that work together as a single verb. A verb phrase consists of the main verb and one or more **auxiliary,** or **helping,** verbs. The most common auxiliary verbs are forms of *be* and *have.*

Tropical rain forests <u>are found</u> near the equator.

<u>Can</u> you <u>describe</u> a rain forest?

Underline the verb or verb phrase in each sentence.

1. What <u>do</u> you <u>know</u> about tropical rain forests?

2. These rain forests <u>can</u> also <u>be called</u> jungles.

3. Their climate <u>is characterized</u> by high temperatures and abundant rain.

4. The rainfall <u>might reach</u> 400 inches a year!

5. Tropical rain forests <u>are located</u> in Asia, Africa, South America, and Central America.

6. A rain forest <u>is divided</u> into four levels.

7. Trees in the first, or emergent, level <u>grow</u> to 240 feet.

8. The next level, the canopy, <u>has</u> trees up to 200 feet tall.

9. The third level, with small trees and vines, <u>is called</u> the understory.

10. The fourth level <u>is</u> the forest floor.

11. The diversity of plant life in the rain forest <u>surpasses</u> that of any other habitat in the world.

12. Many medicinal plants <u>can be found</u> only in tropical rain forests.

13. An extraordinary variety of animal life <u>lives</u> there.

14. Scientists <u>discover</u> new species of insects and reptiles each year.

15. Unfortunately many species <u>are becoming</u> extinct.

16. Tropical rain forests <u>have existed</u> for about 300 million years.

17. <u>Will</u> they <u>survive</u> much longer?

18. Human activities severely <u>disrupt</u> the rain forests.

19. Millions of acres of rain forests <u>are destroyed</u> each year.

20. Farming, logging, and mining <u>may eliminate</u> them completely.

45. Transitive and Intransitive Verbs

A **transitive verb** expresses an action that passes from a doer to a receiver. The receiver of the action is the direct object.

	TRANSITIVE VERB	DIRECT OBJECT
The ancient Mayas	built	temples.

An **intransitive verb** does not have a receiver of its action. It does not have a direct object.

	INTRANSITIVE VERB	
The Mayas	lived	in Mexico and Central America. (no direct object)

Underline the verb in each sentence. On the line write **T** if the verb is transitive or **I** if it is intransitive. If the verb is transitive, circle the direct object.

[I] 1. In the rain forest of Central America stands a stone pyramid.

[T] 2. The pyramid honored the gods of the Mayas—the sun, the moon, and the rain.

[T] 3. The ancient Mayas built the pyramid about 1,000 years ago.

[I] 4. It rises to a height of almost 80 feet.

[T] 5. The pyramid has nine large stone terraces.

[I] 6. They lead to a temple at the top.

[I] 7. Only the priests went into the temple.

[T] 8. They sacrificed animals to the gods.

[T] 9. According to the Mayas, the gods needed blood for survival.

[T] 10. So the priests killed animals to satisfy their gods.

[I] 11. People from all classes of Mayas worshiped at the pyramid.

[I] 12. In 1952 Cuban archaeologist Alberto Ruiz Lhuiller explored deep within the pyramid.

[T] 13. He made an amazing discovery.

[T] 14. He found a secret crypt.

[I] 15. Inside the crypt lay the body of a king.

[T] 16. A shroud of cotton with sprinkles of red dye covered the body.

[I] 17. The Mayas believed that the king had fallen into the underworld at his death.

[T] 18. The king's followers put food into the tomb for his stay in the underworld.

[I] 19. A jade mask lay over the king's face.

[T] 20. The Mayas valued jade more than silver or gold.

46. Verbs That Can Be Transitive or Intransitive

Some verbs can be transitive or intransitive, depending on their use in a sentence.

	TRANSITIVE DIRECT OBJECT
TRANSITIVE	**The campers drove their new van.**
	INTRANSITIVE
INTRANSITIVE	**The campers drove to the lake.** (no direct object)

A. Underline the verb or verb phrase in each sentence. On the line write **T** if the verb is transitive or **I** if it is intransitive. If the verb is transitive, circle the direct object.

___[I]___ 1. I could see across the lake with my new binoculars.

___[T]___ 2. I saw a yellow-bellied (sapsucker) in a tree on my first day of camping.

___[T]___ 3. We roasted (corn) on the campfire.

___[I]___ 4. The corn cooked quickly in the open flames.

___[T]___ 5. Mari poured hot (cider) for us.

___[I]___ 6. The marshmallows burned quickly over the campfire.

___[T]___ 7. We burned (driftwood) for heating as well as for cooking.

___[I]___ 8. The rain poured down for the last two days of our trip.

___[I]___ 9. We could not play outside.

___[T]___ 10. Instead we played computer (games) inside our cabin.

B. Write two sentences for each verb at the left. Use the verb as transitive and as intransitive, in any form you choose. [Sample sentences are shown.]

sing

1. [We sang the national anthem at the baseball game.] _____

2. [The class sang together.] _____

hide

3. [Ann hid the cookies from the class.] _____

4. [George hides from his brothers.] _____

continue

5. [The group continued the tour of the art museum.] _____

6. [The game continued after the rain delay.] _____

burst

7. [Mary burst the water balloon.] _____

8. [The bicycle tires burst.] _____

play

9. [Jim and Bill played Monopoly.] _____

10. [Agnes and I played with the dog.] _____

Name _____

47. Troublesome Verbs

The verb *lie (lying, lay, lain)* means "to rest or recline." It doesn't take a direct object.

The bulbs have <u>lain</u> in the ground all winter.

The verb *lay (laying, laid, laid)* means "to put or place in position." It takes a direct object.

I've <u>laid</u> the gardening tools somewhere.

The verb *sit (sitting, sat, sat)* means "to have or keep a seat."

I <u>sat</u> on the wobbly lawn chair.

The verb *set (setting, set, set)* means "to put or place."

I <u>set</u> the rake against the wall.

The verb *rise (rising, rose, risen)* means "to ascend or move up." It doesn't take a direct object.

The first bulb sprouts <u>rose</u> from the ground in March.

The verb *raise (raising, raised, raised)* means "to lift up, put up, or elevate" or "to grow or breed." It takes a direct object.

We <u>raise</u> flowers in our front garden.

The verb *let (letting, let, let)* means "to permit or allow."

Mom <u>let</u> me plant the seeds.

The verb *leave (leaving, left, left)* means "to depart from" or "to allow to be."

I <u>left</u> my seed catalogs in the garden.

A. Circle the correct verb in parentheses.

1. My family (rises (raises)) vegetables for our use.

2. When the temperature ((rises) raises) in the spring, we get ready.

3. How long has that rake ((lain) laid) in the yard?

4. Don't ((sit) set) on that dirty chair; it's been outside all winter.

5. Don't ((lie) lay) down on the grass; it's wet and cold.

6. The key for the shed ((lay) laid) unnoticed in the grass all winter.

7. (Let (Leave)) the seed packages in the wagon.

8. ((Let) Leave) me do the raking.

9. I (lay (laid)) my gloves somewhere near the shed.

10. I'll (sit (set)) the seeds carefully in each hole.

11. Let's ((raise) rise) pumpkins this year.

12. Where can I ((set) sit) the tomato cages?

13. Just ((lay) lie) them in the corner.

14. We can (let (leave)) those chives where they are.

15. You should just ((lie) lay) down and rest.

Verbs

Name _____

B. Complete each sentence with the correct form of a troublesome verb from page 50. More than one answer may be possible. [Answers may vary. Sample anwers are shown.]

1. The price of seeds has __[risen]__ since last year.

2. This year we're going to __[raise]__ tomatoes and peppers.

3. Where did you __[lay, set]__ the new tools?

4. The garden hose has __[lain]__ at the back of the shed all winter.

5. __[Let]__ Mom hoe the ground—she makes straight rows.

6. Who __[left]__ that rake there? Someone might trip on it.

7. The cat __[sat]__ right in the row where we were working.

8. It was __[lying]__ in our way.

9. I __[set, laid]__ the zucchini seeds somewhere.

10. __[Let]__ me __[sit]__ down on that chair. I'm tired!

11. __[Set]__ the birdbath toward the back of the garden.

12. Oh, there's the cat __[lying]__ in the catnip.

13. We can __[let]__ her stay there.

14. What plant could we __[raise]__ for the dog?

15. He likes the place where we __[laid]__ the chair cushions.

C. Circle the correct verb in parentheses.

1. Where did the boys (lie (lay)) the tickets for the concert?

2. How long have the tickets (lay (lain)) there?

3. The audience is (setting (sitting)) in the front of the huge hall.

4. (Leave (Let)) me accompany you to the concert tonight.

5. We are ((leaving) letting) promptly at six o'clock.

6. Frank, ((sit) set) where you have the best view.

7. Please be seated; the curtain is (raising (rising)).

8. In scene one an actor is (laying (lying)) on top of a piano.

9. Rosi (lay (laid)) her program on the seat of her chair.

10. Everyone (raised (rose)) to cheer the actor's performance.

Verbs

51

48. Linking Verbs

A **linking verb** joins the subject of a sentence with a subject complement.
The subject complement renames or describes the subject. It can be a noun,
a pronoun, or an adjective. Verbs of being are the most common linking verbs.

> Helen Keller and Anne Sullivan <u>were</u> courageous, dedicated <u>people</u>.
> (*People,* a noun, is the subject complement; it renames *Helen Keller* and
> *Anne Sullivan.*)

> Helen Keller and Anne Sullivan <u>are</u> <u>famous</u> in American history.
> (*Famous,* an adjective, is the subject complement; it describes *Helen Keller*
> and *Anne Sullivan.*)

Circle each linking verb. Underline its complement. On the line write N if the subject complement is a noun, P if it is a pronoun, or A if it is an adjective.

__[A]__ 1. As a small child, Helen Keller (was) extremely <u>sick</u>.

__[N]__ 2. The effect of the illness (was) <u>loss</u> of sight and hearing.

__[N]__ 3. Helen's only means of contact with the world (was) the <u>sense</u> of touch.

__[A]__ 4. She (was) <u>eager</u> for communication with others.

__[N]__ 5. Anne Sullivan (was) Helen's <u>teacher</u>.

__[N]__ 6. The day of Anne's arrival (was) an important <u>day</u> in Helen's life.

__[P]__ 7. Anne (was) <u>someone</u> who would teach Helen to communicate.

__[N]__ 8. The method of communication (was) the <u>use</u> of finger movements for letters.

__[A]__ 9. Before this time Helen (had been) <u>lonely</u>, isolated in a world of her own.

__[A]__ 10. School attendance now (became) <u>possible</u> for Helen.

__[N]__ 11. By 1904 she (was) a college <u>graduate</u>.

__[N]__ 12. Later Helen (was) a <u>lecturer</u>.

__[N, N]__ 13. Her topics (were) often the <u>story</u> of her
life and <u>stories</u> of inspiration.

__[A]__ 14. Her lecture money (was) <u>helpful</u> in improving
conditions for those without sight.

__[A]__ 15. The story of Helen's life (is) <u>fascinating</u>
to readers of her autobiography.

Verbs (side tab)

**Helen Keller showed great courage to overcome her problems and help others.
Give an example of how you might show courage to overcome a problem.**

49. More Linking Verbs

> The verbs *appear, become, feel, grow, look, remain, seem, smell, sound, stay, taste,* and *turn* can be used as linking verbs. These verbs can be considered linking verbs if some form of the verb *be* can be substituted for them.
>
> **The Narnia chronicles <u>became</u> a well-loved <u>series</u> of books.**
> (*Series,* a noun, is the subject complement.)
>
> **The world of Narnia <u>seems</u> <u>green</u> and <u>fresh</u> at first.**
> (*Green* and *fresh,* adjectives, are the subject complements.)

A. Circle each linking verb. Underline its complement. On the line write **N** if the subject complement is a noun or **A** if it is an adjective.

__[N]__ 1. At the start of *The Chronicles of Narnia,* Digory and Polly (become) <u>friends</u>.

__[N]__ 2. They (become) <u>participants</u> in a magical world.

__[A]__ 3. There, an evil witch (appears) very <u>beautiful</u>.

__[A]__ 4. The lion's special song of creation (sounds) <u>sweet</u>.

__[A]__ 5. The lion's world of Narnia with its talking animals (seems) <u>wonderful</u>.

__[A]__ 6. Eventually the children (grow) <u>hungry</u>.

__[N]__ 7. In the magic land a piece of toffee candy (becomes) a toffee <u>tree</u>.

__[A, A]__ 8. Its fruit (tastes) <u>delicious</u> and <u>juicy</u>.

__[A]__ 9. Back at home the children (feel) <u>happy</u> about their adventures.

__[A]__ 10. Digory's mother (becomes) <u>well</u> through the magic of Narnia.

B. Underline the verb in each sentence. On the line write **T** if it is transitive, **I** if it is intransitive, or **L** if it is linking.

__[L]__ 1. C. S. Lewis <u>was</u> the author of the Narnia chronicles.

__[T]__ 2. Lewis <u>created</u> a world of talking animals and valiant battles.

__[T]__ 3. In the books the forces of evil <u>fight</u> the forces of good.

__[I]__ 4. Ordinary children, as well as mythical beings, <u>appear</u> as characters.

__[L]__ 5. The books <u>have become</u> popular around the world.

__[T]__ 6. This series of books <u>contains</u> seven volumes.

__[I]__ 7. According to Lewis, the idea for the stories <u>grew</u> from three images: a faun, a witch on a sled, and a magnificent lion.

__[T]__ 8. Lewis <u>wrote</u> *The Lion, the Witch and the Wardrobe* first, in 1950.

__[T]__ 9. As a professor, he <u>taught</u> literature at Oxford University.

__[L]__ 10. His children's books later <u>became</u> popular movies.

50. Active and Passive Voices

> When a transitive verb is in the **active voice**, the subject is the doer of the action.
>
> DOER
> **Renaissance artists painted religious and mythological subjects.**
>
> When a transitive verb is in the **passive voice**, the subject is the receiver of the action.
>
> RECEIVER
> **Religious and mythological subjects were painted by Renaissance artists.**
>
> Linking verbs are not action verbs; therefore, they do not have voice. Intransitive verbs are always active.

A. Underline the verb in each sentence. On the line write **A** if it is in the active voice, **P** if it is in the passive voice, or **L** if it is a linking verb.

___[P]___ 1. The period from about 1400 to about 1600 is called the Renaissance.

___[A]___ 2. *Renaissance* means "rebirth."

___[P]___ 3. The medieval focus on religion was rejected during the Renaissance.

___[P]___ 4. The works of ancient Greek and Roman authors were studied by Renaissance thinkers.

___[A]___ 5. Advances in science and technology occurred during this period.

___[A]___ 6. Botany and zoology developed from the study of ancient texts.

___[L]___ 7. Art became more realistic.

___[P]___ 8. Objects were drawn to scale and in proper perspective.

___[L]___ 9. The city of Florence in the central part of Italy was the center of the Renaissance.

___[P]___ 10. Many works of art were produced in Florence.

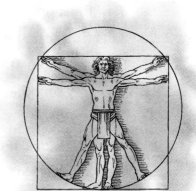

B. Rewrite the sentences, using the voice indicated.

1. Florence was ruled by rich, powerful families.

   active **[Rich, powerful families ruled Florence.]** _____

2. Wealthy families ordered many works of art.

   passive **[Many works of art were ordered by wealthy families.]** _____

3. The citizens of Florence appreciated art.

   passive **[Art was appreciated by the citizens of Florence.]** _____

4. Many churches and palaces were decorated by Florentine artists.

   active **[Florentine artists decorated many churches and palaces.]** _____

5. Thousands of tourists visit Florence each year.

   passive **[Florence is visited by thousands of tourists each year.]** _____

Verbs

Name _____

51. Simple Tenses

> The **simple present tense** tells about an action that is always true or that happens again and again.
>
> **Many people <u>like</u> ice hockey.**
>
> The **simple past tense** tells about an action that happened in past time.
>
> **Canadians <u>invented</u> the game of ice hockey.**
>
> The **future tense** tells about an action that will happen in future time.
>
> **The hockey season <u>will start</u> next October.**

A. Underline the verb in each sentence. Write its tense on the line: simple present, simple past, or future.

____[simple past]____ 1. The game of ice hockey <u>began</u> in Canada in the 1800s.

____[simple past]____ 2. The game <u>became</u> popular in other countries, including Russia and the United States.

____[simple present]____ 3. The fast-paced sport <u>is played</u> by two teams on an ice-covered rink.

____[simple present]____ 4. Five players plus a goalie <u>compose</u> a hockey team.

____[simple present]____ 5. A player <u>scores</u> by hitting the puck into the other team's net with a hockey stick.

____[future]____ 6. The team with more goals <u>will win</u> the game.

____[simple present]____ 7. Hockey <u>has</u> swifter action than many other sports.

____[future]____ 8. Aspiring hockey players <u>will require</u> excellent skating ability and balance.

____[simple present]____ 9. Spectators <u>need</u> quick reflexes to follow the fast-moving puck.

____[simple past]____ 10. Hockey <u>was established</u> as an Olympic sport in 1920.

B. Complete each sentence with the indicated tense and voice of the verb.

win—*future, active* 1. Who ____[will win]____ the Stanley Cup next year?

name—*present, passive* 2. The cup ____[is named]____ for Lord Frederick Stanley, a governor general of Canada.

give—*past, active* 3. He ____[gave]____ the cup annually as a prize for the best hockey team.

award—*past, passive* 4. The cup ____[was awarded]____ for the first time in 1893.

compete—*present, active* 5. National Hockey League teams ____[compete]____ for the cup.

Name _____

52. Progressive Tenses

> **Progressive tenses** express continuing action. The progressive tenses are formed with the present participle and a form of the auxiliary verb *be*.
>
> The **present progressive tense** tells about something that is happening right now.
>
>   Katherine <u>is paying</u> for summer camp.
>
> The **past progressive tense** tells about something that was happening in the past.
>
>   Jay <u>was paying</u> for summer school.
>
> The **future progressive tense** tells about something that will be happening in the future.
>
>   Elizabeth <u>will be paying</u> for all her music lessons next year.

A. Underline the verb in each sentence. Write its tense on the line: **A** for present progressive, **B** for past progressive, or **C** for future progressive.

[C] 1. Juan <u>will be kayaking</u> in Baja next summer.

[A] 2. His brother <u>is working</u> at a camp now.

[C] 3. His friend, Jorge, <u>will be counseling</u> for two more summers.

[A] 4. No one <u>is staying</u> home this summer.

[B] 5. I <u>was thinking</u> about going to school.

[A] 6. Dad and Uncle Pete <u>are planning</u> a fishing trip.

[C] 7. My music teacher <u>will be performing</u> in a musical.

[B] 8. Mom <u>was investigating</u> the schedule for swimming classes.

[A] 9. Am I the only one who <u>is</u> not <u>planning</u> something fun?

[B] 10. I <u>was looking</u> forward to a long rest.

B. Write a sentence for each verb listed. Use the verbs in the present progressive, past progressive, and future progressive tenses. **[Answers will vary. Sample answers are shown.]**

    get   act   grow   study   listen

1. **[Sarah is studying in her room.]**

2. **[She was acting very tired when she got home.]**

3. **[I'll be listening to my new CD in my room.]**

4. **[My CD collection is growing quite large.]**

5. **[I will probably be getting another CD for my birthday.]**

53. Perfect Tenses

> The **perfect tenses** are formed with a past participle and a form of the auxiliary verb *have*. The **present perfect tense** tells about an action that took place at an indefinite time in the past or that started in the past and continues into the present.
>
> **People <u>have used</u> computers in offices since the 1970s.**
>
> The **past perfect tense** tells about a past action that was completed before another past action started.
>
> **People <u>had used</u> typewriters before the invention of computers.**
>
> The **future perfect tense** tells about an action that will be completed before a specific time in the future.
>
> **People <u>will have developed</u> faster computers before the end of this decade.**

A. On the line write the tense of the *italicized* verb.

[present perfect] 1. The developments in technology *have occurred* quickly.

[present perfect] 2. The lives of people *have been changed* by these developments.

[past perfect] 3. Before the 20th century even started, some people *had foreseen* the world of the future.

[past perfect] 4. Before 1900 the French writer Jules Verne *had made* some accurate predictions.

[past perfect] 5. He *had predicted* skyscrapers of glass and steel and gas-powered cars.

[present perfect] 6. What *have* scientists *predicted* for the 21st century?

[future perfect] 7. Some predict that by 2025 self-driving cars *will have been developed*.

[future perfect] 8. By then tiny sensors *will have been placed* in highways to guide traffic.

[present perfect] 9. Already some car owners *have installed* a system for tracking the speed and position of the car ahead.

[future perfect] 10. *Will* people *have forgotten* the current rules of the road by 2030?

B. On the line write the tense and voice of the *italicized* verb.

[present perfect, active] 1. The term "digital electronics" *has existed* for only about the last 60 years.

[past perfect, active] 2. Before that time no one *had heard* the term.

[future perfect, active] 3. Some experts predict that electric plugs *will have disappeared* by the year 2025.

[future perfect, passive] 4. Appliances *will have been changed* to run on batteries or radio frequencies.

[present perfect, active] 5. Many inventions *have appeared* in homes over the last century.

54. Imperative Mood

> The **imperative mood** is the form of a verb that is used in giving commands or making requests. The base form of the verb is used for the imperative mood. The subject of a verb in the imperative mood is almost always *you*, either singular or plural and usually implied.
>
> **<u>Study</u> the risks of extreme sports.**
>
> To form a command in the first person plural, use *let's (let us).*
>
> **<u>Let's</u> both <u>take</u> the first aid class.**

A. Underline the verb in each sentence. Put a check on the line if the sentence is in the imperative mood.

_____ 1. Rock climbing <u>has</u> dangers.

_____ 2. What <u>are</u> the basic rules for safe climbs?

[✔] 3. Always <u>go</u> in a group with an experienced climber.

[✔] 4. <u>Approach</u> the rocks with confidence but not foolhardiness.

_____ 5. Expert rock climbers <u>have</u> a good sense of balance and good technique.

_____ 6. Rock climbers usually <u>use</u> rope for safety on steep climbs.

[✔] 7. At all times, <u>maintain</u> three points of contact with the rock—two hands and a foot or two feet and a hand.

_____ 8. A belayer, one of the group who is usually on the ground, <u>feeds</u> rope to the climbers.

_____ 9. This person <u>acts</u> as an anchor for the climbers.

[✔] 10. To prepare for a climb, <u>get</u> climbing shoes, an artificial-fiber rope, and a harness.

B. Rewrite the sentences in the imperative mood. [**Sample answers are given.**]

1. It is very important to get instruction from an experienced rock-climbing teacher.
   [Get instruction from an experienced rock-climbing teacher.]

2. It's best to start with bouldering—climbing without a rope on small rocks.
   [Start with bouldering—climbing without a rope on small rocks.]

3. Each climber has to move with rhythm and balance.
   [Move with rhythm and balance.]

4. It is important to stay as close to the rock as possible.
   [Stay as close to the rock as possible.]

5. You need to use balance and body position, not strength, to climb.
   [Use balance and body position, not strength, to climb.]

55. Indicative Mood

> The **indicative mood** is the form of the verb used in making statements and in asking questions.
>
> **What monument is being built to honor Crazy Horse?**
> **It is a massive sculpture in the Black Hills of South Dakota.**

A. Write the mood of each sentence: imperative or indicative.

[indicative]   1. A monument to the Sioux chief Crazy Horse has been under construction since 1948.

[indicative]   2. The sculptor Korczak Ziolkowski began work on the monument at the request of the Sioux chief Henry Standing Bear.

[indicative]   3. Would you believe the statue is carved right into the mountainside?

[imperative]   4. Let's see it when we visit the Black Hills.

[indicative]   5. Crazy Horse's face, completed in June 1998, is 88 feet high.

[indicative]   6. The statue, when finished, will be 563 feet high and 641 feet long.

[indicative]   7. Crazy Horse is considered a great leader by the Sioux.

[indicative]   8. How many people will visit the monument?

[imperative]   9. Read the story of the Sioux before you go.

[indicative]   10. The statue is an impressive sight.

B. Rewrite the sentences in the indicative mood. **[Sample answers are given.]**

1. Read the chapter on the Plains Indians tonight.
   [Our homework is to read the chapter on the Plains Indians tonight.]

2. Learn how they depended on the buffalo for food, clothing, and implements.
   [We will learn how they depended on the buffalo for food, clothing, and implements.]

3. Write the definitions of the vocabulary words.
   [Our assignment is to write the definitions of the vocabulary words.]

4. Let's do the map project together.
   [You and I can do the map project together.]

5. Don't forget to read the Internet article Mrs. Lauer assigned.
   [We need to read the Internet article Mrs. Lauer assigned.]

Verbs

56. Subjunctive Mood

> The **subjunctive mood** of a verb can express a wish or desire or a condition that is contrary to fact. The past and the past perfect verb forms are used when the subjunctive expresses these meanings. (*Were* is used with the subjects *I, he, she, it,* and singular nouns.)
>
> WISH   **I <u>wish</u> you <u>had seen</u> my cousin's ferret.**
>
> CONTRARY TO FACT   **If I <u>had</u> a pet, I would take good care of it.**
>
> The subjunctive is also used to express a demand or a recommendation after *that, if,* or *whether.* The base form of the verb is used when the subjunctive expresses one of these meanings.
>
> **My cousin <u>insisted</u> that my friend <u>pet</u> the ferret.**

A. Underline the verb or verb phrase in the subjunctive mood.
On the line write **W** if it expresses a wish, **C** if it expresses a condition contrary to fact, or **D** if it expresses a demand or a recommendation.

__[W]__   1. I wish I <u>had</u> an exotic pet like my cousin's, which is a ferret.

__[C]__   2. If I <u>had</u> the choice, I would buy a parrot.

__[C]__   3. If I <u>were</u> the owner of a parrot, I would teach it to talk.

__[C]__   4. If my parrot <u>were</u> smart, it might learn more than 100 words.

__[D]__   5. Experts insist, however, that any parrot owner <u>realize</u> that some parrots will never talk.

__[D]__   6. Experts recommend that a buyer <u>be</u> ready to give the care required by an exotic pet like a parrot.

__[C]__   7. One parrot owner I talked to said, "If I <u>were</u> you, I would get two parrots because they are happier with company."

__[D]__   8. My parents insist that I <u>care</u> for any pet myself.

__[D]__   9. They also insist that my pet <u>be</u> one that doesn't disturb the household.

__[W]__   10. I wish that my grandparents <u>had given</u> me a parrot for my birthday.

B. Circle the correct verb to complete the sentence in the subjunctive.

1. I wish I (have (had)) a job in a pet store, but I'm too young to get a real job.

2. This book recommends that anyone interested in animals ((volunteer) volunteers) in an animal shelter.

3. My friend said, "If I (was (were)) you, I'd volunteer at our local animal shelter."

4. If I (apply (had applied)) there last month, I could have become a volunteer, but now the shelter has a waiting list.

5. My mother recommends that I just (am (be)) patient; she says that eventually I will get a place.

Name _____

57. Modal Auxiliaries

An auxiliary verb that is not a form of the verb *be, have,* or *do* is called a **modal auxiliary.** Common modal auxiliaries are *may, might, can, could, must, should, will,* and *would.* They express possibility, permission, ability, necessity, obligation, and intention. Modal auxiliaries are used with main verbs in the base form.

POSSIBILITY	The students <u>might need</u> more items for the used-toy sale.
PERMISSION	Anyone <u>may participate</u>.
ABILITY	Jackson <u>can fix</u> old radios.
NECESSITY	The students <u>must put</u> all the clothes on racks.
OBLIGATION	We <u>should have paid</u> on time.
INTENTION	Martha <u>will sort</u> the used books.

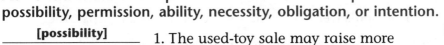

EVERYTHING $1.00

A. Underline the verb phrase. Write what each expresses: possibility, permission, ability, necessity, obligation, or intention.

[Answers may vary.]

__[possibility]__ 1. The used-toy sale <u>may raise</u> more money for charity this year than it did last year.

__[intention]__ 2. Amy <u>will collect</u> more sale items this year than she did last year.

__[ability]__ 3. Charlie <u>can assemble</u> tables faster than anyone else.

__[permission]__ 4. <u>May</u> I <u>help</u> you with that heavy box?

__[necessity]__ 5. You <u>must be careful</u> with the boxes of china.

__[ability]__ 6. Laura <u>could have helped</u> you unpack that box.

__[possibility]__ 7. Many people <u>may want</u> to look at the used clothes.

__[intention]__ 8. Barry <u>will get</u> another clothes rack.

__[obligation]__ 9. We <u>should have been</u> more careful with those old records.

__[possibility]__ 10. I <u>might like</u> to buy that red-and-white sweater.

__[necessity]__ 11. We <u>must clean</u> out the school basement completely.

__[possibility]__ 12. Most items <u>may be sold</u> before the sale ends.

__[ability]__ 13. We <u>can donate</u> any leftover items to another charity.

__[permission]__ 14. According to the principal, we <u>may have</u> another sale next year.

__[obligation]__ 15. We <u>should start</u> to collect right now.

B. Complete the sentences with a verb phrase containing a modal auxiliary verb. Use the verb and the meaning indicated at the left. **[Answers will vary.]**

plan—*necessity* 1. The students __[must plan, should plan]__ for the next sale.

make—*ability* 2. Elizabeth __[can make]__ signs on her computer.

make—*possibility* 3. She __[may make, might make]__ a flier for the sale.

collect—*necessity* 4. The students __[must collect]__ a variety of things.

store—*permission* 5. The students __[may store]__ items in lockers.

Name _____

58. Subject-Verb Agreement

> A verb agrees with its subject in person and number. The only variation in verb form occurs in the present tense with third person singular subjects. To make a verb agree with a third person singular subject, add -s or -es to the base form of a verb.
>
> **Our country <u>celebrates</u> special holidays.** (third person singular subject)
> **Mexicans <u>celebrate</u> the Day of the Dead.** (third person plural subject)

A. **Underline the subject in each sentence. Circle the correct verb form in parentheses.**

1. The <u>holiday</u> called Day of the Dead (**occurs** occur) on November 1 and 2.

2. <u>Mexican Americans</u> also (observes **observe**) this traditional holiday.

3. By remembering their dead, <u>Mexicans</u> (**honor** honors) the cycle of life and death.

4. The <u>holiday</u> (mark **marks**) a special time.

5. According to popular belief, dead <u>souls</u> (returns **return**) to their homes at this time.

6. <u>Families</u> (sets **set**) up special altars in their houses for their dead members.

7. The altar's <u>purpose</u> (**is** are) to welcome the souls of dead family members.

8. The <u>altar</u> (**honors** honor) the dead.

9. A special <u>bread</u> (**lies** lie) on the altar for the dead.

10. Sometimes candy <u>skulls</u> (is **are**) also placed there.

11. <u>Families</u> (goes **go**) to cemeteries to care for the graves of relatives.

12. A <u>picnic</u> (**is** are) sometimes held in the cemetery.

13. Traditional <u>music</u> played by a mariachi band (entertain **entertains**) the picnickers.

14. The <u>mood</u> (**is** are) joyful.

15. <u>People</u> (celebrates **celebrate**) the memory of dead relatives and friends.

B. **Complete each sentence with the present tense form of the verb at the left.**

have   1. The marigold _____[has]_____ a special role in the Day of the Dead.

drop   2. People _____[drop]_____ its petals along the route to the cemetery.

help   3. The flower's scent supposedly _____[helps]_____ the dead find their way home.

hold   4. Families _____[hold]_____ special ceremonies at the graveside.

place   5. A designated person _____[places]_____ a marigold in a special wreath for the dead.

Verbs

62

59. *Doesn't, Don't, You Are, You Were*

> Use *doesn't* if the subject of the sentence is the third person singular.
>
> **Doesn't mistletoe have poisonous berries?**
>
> Use *don't* if the subject of the sentence is the first or second person, or if it is the third person plural.
>
> **Don't farmers grow roses for perfumes?**
>
> Use *are* and *were* with *you*, whether it is singular or plural.
>
> **Are you going to use mistletoe in your holiday decorations?**

A. Complete each sentence with *doesn't* or *don't*.

1. Roses ___[don't]___ grow from bulbs.
2. ___[Doesn't]___ a Venus's-flytrap plant eat insects?
3. Venus's-flytraps ___[don't]___ trap insects in their flowers—they trap them in their leaves.
4. A cactus ___[doesn't]___ need a lot of water.
5. You ___[don't]___ know the name of your state flower!
6. ___[Don't]___ all states have a state flower?
7. Janet ___[doesn't]___ know the official state flower of Rhode Island.
8. ___[Don't]___ apples and pears belong to the family of rose plants?
9. ___[Doesn't]___ natural vanilla come from an orchid plant?
10. ___[Don't]___ sunflowers turn their heads to follow the sun?

B. Circle the correct verb form in parentheses.

1. You (is *are*) really an excellent gardener!
2. (Was *Were*) you the winner of the prize for best orchid at the floral show last year?
3. (*Was* Were) the garden wet this morning?
4. Someone said that you (is *are*) developing your own kind of orchid.
5. You (was *were*) on a gardening show on television last month, I heard.
6. (*Were* Was) you able to get a bulb for a purple tulip?
7. (*Is* Are) the flower show in June this year?
8. (Is *Are*) you going to show me your prize flowers?
9. You (is *are*) going to be a winner again this year for sure!
10. What (is *are*) you going to plant next spring?

Verbs

Name _____

60. *There Is* and *There Are*

> When *there* introduces a sentence, the sentence generally is inverted, so the subject follows the verb. *There is (was, has been)* should be used when the subject is singular. *There are (were, have been)* should be used when the subject is plural.
>
> PLURAL SUBJECT   **There <u>are</u> seven <u>continents</u> in the world.**
>
> SINGULAR SUBJECT   **There <u>is</u> one <u>country</u> that covers an entire continent.**

A. Circle the correct verb form in parentheses.

1. There (is (are)) more than 19 million people in Australia.

2. There ((have) has) been many new immigrants in the last 50 years.

3. There (is (are)) about 410,000 indigenous people in Australia.

4. How many stars (is (are)) there on the national flag of Australia?

5. In Australia there ((is) are) a prime minister who is the head of government.

6. There (is (are)) six states and two territories in the country.

7. There (is (are)) many farms and ranches in Australia.

8. (Is (Are)) there many natural resources?

9. There ((is) are) iron ore in Australia.

10. ((Was) Were) there a gold rush in Australia's past?

11. There (is (are)) large areas of empty dry land called the outback.

12. There ((is) are) a magnificent harbor in Sydney.

13. There (was (were)) many visitors to Sydney for the Olympic games in the year 2000.

14. There ((is) are) a huge rock formation in the middle of an area of flat land in Uluru National Park.

15. There ((is) are) an unusual Australian food, Vegemite spread, made from yeast extract, celery, and onions.

B. Complete each sentence with *is* or *are*.

1. There ____[is]____ a huge reef off the coast of Australia called the Great Barrier Reef.

2. There ____[are]____ approximately 1,500 species of fish in the reef's waters.

3. There ____[are]____ several animals found only in Australia, including kangaroos and koalas.

4. There ____[is]____ an unusual bird called the black swan.

5. ____[Are]____ there any questions about Australia?

Verbs

64

61. Agreement of Subjects and Verbs with Intervening Phrases

> Sometimes a phrase comes between a subject and a verb. The verb must agree with the subject, not with the noun or pronoun in the phrase.
>
> A <u>serving</u> of beans <u>is</u> one-half cup.
>
> <u>Milk</u>, together with yogurt and cheese, <u>forms</u> a basic food group.

A. Underline the subject of the sentence. Circle the correct verb form in parentheses.

1. <u>Fruit</u>, as well as vegetables, (**is** are) a basic food group.

2. <u>Meat</u>, along with fish, beans, eggs, and nuts, (**belongs** belong) to another group.

3. <u>Fats</u>, together with sweets and oils, (**are** is) to be eaten sparingly.

4. Vegetable <u>oil</u>, as well as butter and eggs, (**contains** contain) fat.

5. Two to four daily <u>servings</u> of fruit (is **are**) recommended per day.

6. Three to five <u>servings</u> of vegetables (is **are**) also recommended.

7. A <u>serving</u> of vegetables (**is** are) one cup of leafy vegetables.

8. A <u>serving</u> of fruit (**is** are) one piece of fruit.

9. <u>Carrots</u>, as well as spinach and cantaloupe, (supplies **supply**) vitamin A, which is important for good eyesight.

10. Citrus <u>fruit</u>, along with potatoes, (**has** have) vitamin C.

11. Grain <u>foods</u>, such as bread and rice, (**supply** supplies) carbohydrates, an excellent source of energy.

12. <u>Bread</u>, as well as broccoli and eggs, (**is** are) rich in vitamin B, which turns fat into energy.

13. <u>Milk</u>, together with cheese and sardines, (**contains** contain) calcium, which builds bones.

14. One <u>piece</u> of fudge (**has** have) as many calories as three slices of bread.

15. Thirty-five <u>stalks</u> of celery (has **have**) as many calories as one piece of fudge!

B. Complete each sentence with *is* or *are*.

1. A bowl of cabbage soup once a day _____**[is]**_____ recommended in one fad diet.

2. The opinion of nutritionists _____**[is]**_____ that fad diets don't work.

3. Recommendations for a balanced diet _____**[are]**_____ published by the government.

4. A diet low in fat and high in fruits and vegetables _____**[is]**_____ what almost everyone needs.

5. Moderate consumption of food, together with exercise, _____**[is]**_____ recommended.

62. Agreement with Compound Subjects

> Compound subjects connected by *and* usually are considered plural.
>
> **London and Edinburgh are the capitals of England and Scotland, respectively.**
>
> If the subjects connected by *and* refer to the same person, place, or thing or express a single idea, they are considered singular.
>
> **In Britain the prime minister and leader of the majority is the same person.**

A. Circle the correct verb form in parentheses.

1. England, Scotland, Wales, and part of Ireland (makes **make**) up the United Kingdom.
2. The nominal head of state and head of the church (**is** are) the monarch.
3. The prime minister and the cabinet (has **have**) the real executive power of government.
4. The prime minister and Parliament (shares **share**) the powers of government.
5. Rain and fog (characterizes **characterize**) London weather.
6. The stores and theaters (attracts **attract**) many tourists to London.
7. The Tower of London and Buckingham Palace (is **are**) important tourist sites.
8. A famous British writer and dictionary editor (**has** have) written, "When a man is tired of London, he is tired of life."
9. The monarch and the royal family (has **have**) a huge castle at Windsor, near London.
10. Fish and chips (**is** are) a popular English dish.
11. Scones and cream (is **are**) sometimes served at tea time.
12. Gardening and fishing (has **have**) long been popular pastimes in the countryside.
13. Soccer and cricket (is **are**) popular sports in England.
14. King Arthur and Robin Hood (was **were**) legendary figures in British history.
15. J. K. Rowling and Prince William (is **are**) famous current British citizens.

B. Complete the sentences with compound subjects and verbs that agree. **[Answers will vary.]**

1. _____ and _____ _____ important cities in my state.
2. _____ and _____ _____ important historical sites in the country.
3. _____ and _____ _____ important people in American history.
4. _____ and _____ _____ favorite pastimes in the area.
5. _____ and _____ _____ sometimes eaten for dessert.

Name _____

63. Agreement with Subjects Connected by *Or* or *Nor*

> When compound subjects are connected by *or* or *nor*, the verb agrees with the subject closer to the verb.
>
> **Either barbecued beef or hot dogs are served in the cafeteria every day.**
> **Hamburgers or chicken is served in many fast-food restaurants.**

A. Circle the correct verb form in parentheses.

1. Neither squash nor cucumbers (is **are**) really vegetables.
2. Also, neither pumpkins nor eggplant (**belongs** belong) to the vegetable family.
3. Either a cruller or a bismarck (**is** are) a good doughnut choice.
4. Sausage or mushrooms often (sits **sit**) on the top of a pizza.
5. Neither cheese nor tomatoes (tops **top**) all pizza in Italy.
6. Either potato pizza or vegetable pizza (**is** are) available.
7. Cucumber sandwiches or ham sandwiches (is **are**) often served at tea in England.
8. Neither apples nor wheat (**was** were) native to the Americas.
9. Neither lettuce nor carrots (was **were**) grown in the Americas before the arrival of Europeans.
10. Either a hoagie or a sub (**was** were) the large sandwich he ordered.
11. Soup or salad (**is** are) a common appetizer in the United States.
12. Bread, cheese, or olives (is **are**) sometimes eaten for breakfast in Turkey.
13. Rice porridge or dried pork (**is** are) sometimes eaten for breakfast in China.
14. Neither corn nor potatoes (was **were**) known in Europe until the 1500s.
15. Strawberries or grapes (is **are**) often made into jellies or jams.

B. Complete each sentence. Use verbs in the present tense.

1. Neither the firefighter nor the residents _____ [know how the fire started.]
2. Neither the boys nor the girls _____ [are at the fire scene.]
3. Either the smoke or the flames _____ [cause considerable damage.]
4. Neither the door nor the stairs _____ [are safe exits.]
5. Either the photos or the report _____ [is ready for review.]

[Answers will vary. Samples are given.]

Verbs

67

Name _____

64. Agreement with Indefinite Pronouns

An indefinite pronoun points out no particular person, place, or thing. The indefinite pronouns *another, anybody, anyone, anything, each, either, everyone, everybody, everything, much, neither, no one, nobody, nothing, one, other, someone, somebody,* and *something* are always singular.

Each of the newspaper issues <u>has</u> eight pages.
Somebody <u>has</u> the job of writing headlines.

A. Underline the subject in each sentence. Circle the correct form of the verb in parentheses.

1. <u>Everyone</u> in the school (gets) get) a copy of the school newspaper.

2. <u>Somebody</u> (places) place) copies of the newspaper in pickup boxes throughout the school.

3. <u>Everybody</u> in the school (waits) wait) eagerly for the next issue.

4. <u>Anyone</u> (is) are) eligible to work on the school newspaper.

5. Usually <u>one</u> of the issues (feature (features)) a teacher profile.

6. <u>Each</u> of the papers (contain (contains)) an interview with two students in school.

7. <u>Each</u> of the featured students (tells) tell) about his or her personal interests and goals.

8. <u>No one</u> (refuses) refuse) an invitation for an interview.

9. <u>Each</u> of the articles (is) are) illustrated with pictures.

10. <u>Neither</u> of the cartoons in the last issue (was) were) very funny.

B. Underline the subject in each sentence. Complete each sentence with the correct form of the present tense of the verb at the left.

have 1. <u>Each</u> of the articles in the newspaper __[has]__ a student as an author.

be 2. <u>Everyone</u> __[is]__ welcome to suggest topics for articles.

assign 3. In fact, <u>somebody</u> __[assigns]__ additional articles.

contain 4. <u>Each</u> of the issues __[contains]__ a fictional story.

want 5. <u>Everyone</u> who submits one __[wants]__ to see his or her story in the newspaper.

have 6. <u>Someone</u> __[has]__ a funny story about a magical horse in this issue.

put 7. For each issue <u>someone</u> __[puts]__ together a list of upcoming school events.

be 8. <u>Nothing</u> important __[is]__ missing.

appear 9. <u>Anything</u> especially interesting __[appears]__ on the front page.

work 10. <u>Everybody</u> __[works]__ to make the newspaper great.

65. Agreement with Collective Nouns

> A collective noun names a group of persons or things that are considered as a single unit, such as *audience* and *herd.* These nouns take a verb that agrees with the third person singular.
>
> **The school baseball team <u>uses</u> a field in the park.**
>
> When the meaning of a collective noun suggests that the members are being considered as individuals, the verb must agree with the third person plural subject.
>
> **The baseball team <u>use</u> their own equipment.**

A. Circle the correct verb form in parentheses.

1. The committee ((has) have) decided to improve park facilities.

2. The orchestra ((plays) play) in the band shell in the park.

3. The ensemble (needs (need)) separate backstage facilities for their instrument cases and personal items.

4. The audience ((needs) need) a roof in case of rain.

5. The local soccer team ((plays) play) its games in the park.

6. The marching band ((practices) practice) on the basketball court.

7. The band (wants (want)) individual lockers for their instruments.

8. A flock of swans ((swims) swim) in the pond.

9. The dance group (is (are)) looking for individual apartments.

10. The Irish dance group ((needs) need) a bigger outdoor stage for its performances.

11. The troop ((meets) meet) in the field house.

12. The city council ((are) is) arguing among themselves about new taxes.

13. The quilting club ((has) have) a meeting every week in the field house.

14. Our teachers union ((is) are) planning to lobby for more space.

15. The staff ((agrees) agree) that the field house needs to be remodeled.

B. Write sentences using the collective nouns as subjects.

[Sentences will vary. Sample answers are given.]

1. The orchestra [tunes up before the show begins.]

2. A herd of cattle [grazes on the prairie.]

3. The city council [meets once a month.]

4. A deck of flash cards [is what the teacher uses.]

5. A pod of whales [swims near the coastline.]

66. Agreement with Special Nouns

Some nouns are plural in form but singular in meaning; they require verbs that agree with the third person singular. These nouns include *aerobics, civics, economics, genetics, mathematics, measles, mumps, news,* and *physics.*

Other nouns are plural in form but refer to one thing; they require verbs that agree with the third person plural. These nouns include *clothes, goods, pliers, pants, proceeds, scissors, thanks, tongs, trousers,* and *tweezers.*

A. Circle the correct verb form in parentheses.

1. The clothes (is (are)) blowing off the clothesline.

2. My pants now (has (have)) a tear from the thorns on the rose bush.

3. The eaves of the house (is (are)) damaged and need to be repaired.

4. The ashes from the fireplace (is (are)) scattered over the carpet.

5. Mathematics ((is) are) a study of more than just numbers.

6. The news on television ((is) are) quite depressing.

7. Measles ((is) are) a disease that causes fever and red spots on the skin.

8. The scissors (is (are)) dull and should be sharpened.

9. The pliers I used yesterday (is (are)) missing.

10. Thanks (is (are)) in order for the person who returned the wallet.

B. Complete each sentence with the correct present tense form of the verb at the left.

be   1. Civics ____[is]____ the study of both the duties and the rights of a citizen.

be   2. Congratulations ____[are]____ due to all who passed the civics test.

present   3. The news ____[presents]____ a lot of information about civics and government.

be   4. Economics ____[is]____ the study of the production and distribution of goods.

be   5. Goods ____[are]____ important in the study of economics.

be   6. Aerobics ____[is]____ a good type of exercise with which to develop fitness.

promise   7. Genetics ____[promises]____ to aid in the cure of some diseases.

go   8. The proceeds of this fund-raising drive ____[go]____ to genetic research.

be   9. Thanks ____[are]____ due to researchers who devote their lives to its study.

interest 10. Physics ____[interests]____ me; I'm doing a physics project for the science fair.

Verbs

67. Reviewing Verbs

A. Write the past and the past participle of each verb. Write whether the verb is regular or irregular.

	PAST	PAST PARTICIPLE	REGULAR OR IRREGULAR
1. study	[studied]	[studied]	[regular]
2. lie	[lay]	[lain]	[irregular]
3. influence	[influenced]	[influenced]	[regular]
4. write	[wrote]	[written]	[irregular]
5. choose	[chose]	[chosen]	[irregular]

B. Underline each verb phrase.

6. <u>Have</u> you <u>read</u> any works by Charles Dickens?

7. You <u>should read</u> *A Christmas Carol*.

8. When <u>was</u> it <u>written</u>?

9. A made-for-TV version of the novel <u>will be aired</u> next week.

10. I <u>might watch</u> the original movie instead.

C. Underline the verb or verb phrase in each sentence. On the line write **T** if it is transitive, **I** if it is intransitive, or **L** if it is linking.

__[T]__ 11. Four ghosts <u>visit</u> Scrooge in *A Christmas Carol*.

__[L]__ 12. The ghosts <u>seem</u> very scary to Scrooge.

__[I]__ 13. Scrooge <u>goes</u> to past, present, and future time.

__[L]__ 14. <u>Will</u> Scrooge <u>be</u> different at the end of the book?

__[T]__ 15. <u>Read</u> the book for the answer.

D. Write the tense and voice of the *italicized* verbs.

	TENSE	VOICE
16. As a boy, Scrooge *had shown* generosity and friendliness.	[past perfect]	[active]
17. As a man, he *changed* into a miser.	[past]	[active]
18. Christmas *was* not *celebrated* by Scrooge.	[past]	[passive]
19. The story *is told* every Christmas.	[present]	[passive]
20. Film versions of the story *will be shown* again next Christmas.	[future]	[passive]

CONTINUED

Verbs

Verbs

E. Draw one line under the subject and two lines under the verb.
Write the tense on the line.

_____[simple past]_____ 21. Last month the science teacher announced
the date for the upcoming science fair.

_____[simple present]_____ 22. The topic of my project for the fair is solar energy.

_____[past perfect]_____ 23. I had already read many articles on the topic.

_____[future perfect]_____ 24. By next week I will have completed my solar-home model.

_____[future]_____ 25. According to Mom, my project will win a prize.

F. Underline the main verb or verb phrase. On the line write
whether it is in the indicative or the imperative mood.

_____[indicative]_____ 26. There are test tubes on the counter.

_____[imperative]_____ 27. Wear safety goggles and aprons at all times.

_____[imperative]_____ 28. Read all the directions carefully beforehand.

_____[indicative]_____ 29. You should not handle the equipment
without permission.

_____[imperative]_____ 30. Never leave a lighted burner unattended.

G. Write the correct form of the present tense of the verb at the left to
complete each sentence.

be 31. _____[Are]_____ you going to the mall, Teddy?

need 32. Lila and Serena _____[need]_____ a few things for their science project.

want 33. Each of them _____[wants]_____ a notebook to record results.

have 34. Every one of the projects _____[has]_____ a space at the science fair.

be 35. The best of all the projects _____[is]_____ the one that required most research.

Try It Yourself

On a separate sheet of paper, write a paragraph about a book that you have read
or a movie that you have seen recently. Tell about the plot and give your opinion.
Be sure to use the correct forms of verbs and correct verb agreement.

Check Your Own Work

Choose a piece of writing from your portfolio, a journal, a work in progress,
an assignment from another class, or a letter. Revise it, applying the skills
you have reviewed. This checklist will help you.

✔ Are all the verb forms correct?

✔ Are all the past tenses and past participle forms correct?

✔ Is the use of verb tenses consistent?

✔ Do all the subjects and verbs agree?

Name _____

68. Participles

> **Verbals** are words made from verbs. A **participle** is a verbal that is used as an adjective. It describes a noun or a pronoun.
>
> - A present participle always ends in *-ing,* and the past participle of a regular verb ends in *-ed.*
> - A **participial phrase** consists of the participle, its object or complement, and any modifiers.
> - A participle can be active or passive, and it can show tense.
> - A participial phrase that is essential to the meaning of a sentence is restrictive; a participial phrase that is not essential to the meaning is nonrestrictive and is set off by commas.
>
>   **Donating money for social causes, Peter Cooper set an example as a philanthropist.**
>   **People inspired by Cooper give money to good causes.**

A. Underline the participial phrase in each sentence.
Circle the noun or pronoun it describes.

1. (Peter Cooper,) known as an inventor and a philanthropist, lived from 1791 to 1883.

2. Completing only one year of formal education, (Cooper) started work at an early age.

3. Eventually, a (craftsman) making coaches hired Cooper as an apprentice.

4. Recognizing the young man's ability, the (coach maker) helped Cooper further his career.

5. (Cooper,) aided by his mentor, started a business that made machines for the cloth industry.

6. That (business,) being successful, permitted Cooper to enter other ventures and undertake new challenges.

7. Wanting to share his success, (he) founded Cooper Union.

8. The (institution,) dedicated to the education of the working poor, was set up in New York City.

9. Offering free courses in science, engineering, and art, the (institution) attracted many young students.

10. Any (student) meeting the requirements can still attend classes there.

B. Write the number of each sentence above that has a restrictive participial phrase.

[3, 10]

Peter Cooper founded a community institution to help the poor. Give an example of how you can help less fortunate people in your community.

69. Placement of Participles

A participle used as an adjective may precede or follow the noun it describes.

> **Near the poles, people can see lights <u>dancing</u> in the sky.**
> **<u>Watching</u> the lights, viewers are often treated to colorful exhibitions.**

A participle used as an adjective should not be confused with a participle that is part of a verb phrase.

> **The <u>respected</u> astronomer studied the northern lights.**
> (participle used as an adjective)
> **The astronomer's theories were <u>respected</u> by her colleagues.**
> (part of the verb phrase *were respected*)

A. Underline the participle used as an adjective in each sentence.
Circle the noun each describes.

1. The northern lights are <u>shimmering</u> (lights) in the sky.

2. Sometimes they are <u>waving</u> (streaks) of red, green, blue, or yellow.

3. The interaction between <u>charged</u> (particles) of the Sun and gases in Earth's atmosphere causes them.

4. According to Inuit tradition, the lights are <u>dancing</u> (spirits) in the sky.

5. According to another tradition, they are <u>flaming</u> (torches) of dead souls on their way to the afterlife.

B. Underline each participle. On the line write **A** if it is an adjective or **V** if it is part of a verb phrase.

___[V]___ 1. The northern lights are also <u>called</u> the aurora borealis.

___[V]___ 2. They were <u>named</u> for the Roman goddess of dawn.

___[V]___ 3. They can be <u>viewed</u> near the North and South poles.

___[A]___ 4. The best <u>viewing</u> times for the northern lights are during the winter when the sky is relatively dark.

___[A]___ 5. Many people take trips to Alaska at that time despite the <u>freezing</u> temperatures.

___[A]___ 6. People go to unusual lengths to see a display of the <u>dazzling</u> lights.

___[A]___ 7. <u>Dedicated</u> Alaskans will put on their parkas and lie in the snow for a good view.

___[V]___ 8. Few people are <u>disappointed</u> by the sight of the lights.

___[V]___ 9. People today are still <u>talking</u> about one of the rarest sights, a red aurora that occurred on February 11, 1958.

___[A]___ 10. The <u>astonishing</u> phenomenon of the northern lights is a natural wonder.

70. Dangling Participles

> A participle or a participial phrase that does not describe a noun or a pronoun in a sentence is called a **dangling participle**. A dangling participle is incorrect and should be corrected.
>
> INCORRECT   **Liking fables, my bookshelves contain many of them.**
>   (no word for *liking* to describe)
> CORRECT   **Liking fables, I have many books of them on my bookshelves.**

A. Underline each participial phrase. On the line write **D** for any that are dangling participles. If the participial phrase is used correctly, leave the line blank.

__[D]__   1. Reading a book of Aesop's fables, one fable stood out.

_____   2. It was the story of a very ill farmer worried about the future of his sons.

__[D]__   3. Thinking of his sons' futures, a plan developed.

__[D]__   4. Knowing about his sons' laziness, a spur to make them work was needed.

_____   5. Calling his sons around his deathbed, the father told them a secret.

__[D]__   6. Buried in the vineyard, something was hidden.

_____   7. Soon after, the man died, leaving his sons his property.

__[D]__   8. Thinking about the buried treasure, the vineyard was dug up.

__[D]__   9. Not finding anything, disappointment followed.

_____   10. The field, having been well plowed, however, yielded an abundance of grapes and taught that the fruits of one's toil are a person's most valuable treasure.

B. Rewrite the sentences, correcting the dangling participles. Add a noun or a pronoun for the participle to describe. **[Answers may vary.]**

   1. Leaving the book on the sink, its cover got wet.

     [Leaving the book on the sink, I caused its cover to get wet.]

   2. Returning the book to the library, a fine was probable.

     [Returning the book to the library, I knew that a fine was probable.]

   3. Examining the damage, a price was set to cover the book's replacement.

     [Examining the damage, the librarian set a price to cover the book's replacement.]

   4. Being a paperback, the price wasn't much.

     [Being a paperback, the book's replacement wasn't much.]

   5. Vowing to be more careful, several more library books are in my room.

     Vowing to be more careful, I plan to return the library books in my room.]

71. Gerunds as Subjects

> A **gerund** is a verb form ending in *-ing* that is used as a noun.
> A gerund phrase consists of the verb, its object or complements, and any modifiers. It can be used as the subject of a sentence.
>
> **<u>Traveling to other countries</u> is an educational experience.**

A. Underline each gerund phrase. Circle the gerund.

1. (Touring) <u>Japan</u> was my family's first choice for a vacation.
2. (Shopping) <u>at the Ginza Market in Tokyo</u> is an activity popular with tourists.
3. (Seeing) <u>all the electronic stores at Akihabara</u> is a fun thing to do.
4. (Playing) <u>computer games in an arcade</u> was a highlight of my trip.
5. (Trying) <u>a special kind of pinball game</u> was a new experience for me.
6. (Meeting) <u>Japanese kids in the arcade</u> contributed to my good time.
7. (Speaking) <u>English</u> seemed fun for them too.
8. (Eating) <u>sushi wrapped in nori</u> became my regular routine.
9. (Slurping) <u>noodles from your bowl</u> is not bad manners in Japan.
10. (Putting) <u>plastic food as samples in restaurant windows</u> is a common practice.
11. (Understanding) <u>only a few words of Japanese</u> made it difficult for me to communicate.
12. (Reading) <u>Japanese characters</u> is not an easy task—even for Japanese children.
13. (Taking) <u>exams</u> is a regular part of school life for Japanese children.
14. (Reading) <u>illustrated comic books called *manga*</u> is common for both adults and children.
15. (Wearing) <u>kimonos</u> is usually limited to special occasions such as weddings.
16. (Climbing) <u>Mount Fuji</u> is an experience for Japanese and tourists alike.
17. (Ascending) <u>the mountain</u> has religious significance for many Japanese.
18. (Attending) <u>a tea ceremony</u> made me appreciate the beauty of their native rituals.
19. (Buying) <u>souvenirs for my friends and family</u> required much time and thought.
20. (Packing) <u>my suitcase for the return trip</u> is going to be difficult!

B. Complete the sentences. Use the words in parentheses in gerund phrases. Try to use your own experiences. **[Answers will vary. Sample answers are given.]**

1. _____**[Visiting New York City]**_____ was a great vacation. (visit)
2. _____**[Seeing all the skyscrapers]**_____ was fascinating. (see)
3. _____**[Walking in Central Park]**_____ should be relaxing. (walk)
4. _____**[Talking to people from different countries]**_____ can be wonderful. (talk)
5. _____**[Waiting for my next vacation trip]**_____ will be difficult. (wait)

Verbals

72. Gerunds as Subject Complements

> A gerund can be used as a subject complement. It follows the verb *be* or other linking verbs.
>
> **One step in the learning process is <u>improving your study skills</u>.**

A. Underline each gerund phrase used as a subject complement. Circle the gerund.

1. A necessity for success in school is (having) good study skills.
2. An important step is (establishing) a set place to study.
3. A bad habit is (studying) late in the evening.
4. One key to success is (concentrating) on the material without distractions.
5. Another key to success is (setting) manageable goals.
6. The result will be (avoiding) discouragement when you can't complete everything.
7. Another tip for a productive study session is (doing) the most difficult task first.
8. When that is completed, the result should be the (gaining) of a sense of accomplishment.
9. Another advantage is (approaching) the most difficult task with a fresh mind.
10. An effective way to keep track of your assignments is (using) an agenda book.
11. A good plan to make sure you study is (working) with a friend at a set time.
12. One way to do this is (chatting) online.
13. For difficult homework assignments, one approach is (asking) your parents or older siblings for help.
14. A good starting point for an assignment is (choosing) a topic that interests you.
15. Something to work toward is (finding) the best methods for you as an individual.

B. Complete each sentence, using the words in parentheses as a gerund phrase. Write **S** if the gerund is used as a subject or **SC** if it is used as a subject complement. **[Answers will vary. Sample answers are given.]**

__[SC]__ 1. For homework assignments, one help is _____**[writing down the assignment]**_____ . (write down the assignment)

__[S]__ 2. _____**[Understanding the assignment]**_____ is important. (understand the assignment)

__[SC]__ 3. One suggestion is _____**[asking the teacher any questions you have]**_____ . (ask the teacher any questions you have)

__[S]__ 4. _____**[Doing your homework the first thing]**_____ means that you can use the rest of the evening for other things. (do your homework the first thing)

__[S]__ 5. _____**[Budgeting your time]**_____ will allow you to finish all your other chores. (budget your time)

Verbals

73. Gerunds as Objects

> A gerund can be used as a direct object or the object of a preposition.
>
> **Would you consider <u>owning a macaw</u>?** (gerund as direct object)
> **Macaws are famous for <u>learning words</u>.** (gerund as object of a preposition)

A. Underline each gerund phrase. On the line write **DO** if it is a direct object of a verb or **OP** if it is the object of a preposition.

[DO] 1. Because of macaws' beauty and intelligence, people enjoy <u>having them as pets</u>.

[DO] 2. Macaw owners love <u>teaching their birds new words</u>.

[OP] 3. Macaws possess a good capability for <u>remembering locations</u>.

[OP] 4. This ability is necessary for <u>recalling the location of trees with fruit</u>.

[OP] 5. At any one time, only a relatively small number of trees in the rain-forest home of the macaws are actually producing fruit suitable for <u>eating</u>.

[OP] 6. A good memory for location is useful in <u>finding those trees</u>.

[OP] 7. The macaw's claws are handy for <u>grasping nuts and fruits</u>.

[OP] 8. Its beak is designed for <u>cracking hard nuts</u>.

[OP] 9. All in all, macaws benefit from <u>finding food relatively easily</u>.

[DO] 10. This means <u>having more "free time."</u>

[DO] 11. Free-time activities for macaws include <u>playing, preening, and resting</u>.

[DO] 12. Some macaws seem to prefer <u>hanging from branches of trees</u>.

[OP] 13. Their population unfortunately is being reduced by <u>trapping</u>.

[OP] 14. The purpose of <u>trapping macaws</u> is often to capture live birds to sell as pets.

[DO] 15. For this reason, many people prefer <u>buying macaws from local breeders</u>.

B. Complete each sentence, using a phrase from the list to create a gerund that functions as a direct object.

work there last fall   help to feed the animals   clean the cages

have birds or fish as pets   volunteer at the animal shelter

1. Do you prefer [having birds or fish as pets]?

2. My free-time activity for the community is [volunteering at the animal shelter].

3. I began [working there last fall].

4. At the shelter I don't like [cleaning the cages].

5. Whenever possible, however, I enjoy [helping to feed the animals].

Verbals

Name _____

74. Gerunds as Appositives

> A gerund can be used as an appositive. An appositive is a word or group of words immediately after a noun that identifies the noun or gives more information about it.
>
> **A current trend, <u>traveling to remote places in support of their natural environments</u>, can help natural and wildlife conservation.**

A. In each sentence underline the gerund phrase used as an appositive.

1. The role of the rain forest, <u>serving as a mass producer of oxygen</u>, is essential to the earth's survival.

2. Deforestation, <u>cutting down of trees</u>, continues at an alarming rate in rain forests.

3. Some people point out that the reason for the removal of trees, <u>using the wood for industrial purposes</u>, is important to business.

4. A new approach to preservation, <u>using ecotourism to provide income for local residents</u>, is gaining ground.

5. Ecotourism, <u>traveling for enjoyment of the natural environment</u>, appeals to many environmentalists.

B. Underline the gerund phrase in each sentence. Rewrite any sentence with a gerund used as an appositive, adding commas as appropriate.

1. One way to help preserve the rain forest <u>writing letters to companies engaged in deforestation</u> is supported by many people.

   [One way to help preserve the rain forest, writing letters to companies engaged in deforestation, is supported by many people.]

2. These companies destroy the rain forest by <u>logging the trees</u> and thus reduce the amount of oxygen for earth's inhabitants.

   _____

   _____

3. One letter-writing campaign <u>getting a bank to suspend loans for a project harmful to the rain forest</u> shows the positive effect of letters.

   [One letter-writing campaign, getting a bank to suspend loans for a project harmful to the rain forest, shows the positive effect of letters.]

4. We can encourage all people to help in <u>preserving the environment</u>, including the rain forest.

   _____

   _____

5. Individually, we can stop <u>wasting such things as paper, gasoline, and plastic</u>.

   _____

   _____

75. Possessives with Gerunds, Using *-ing* Verb Forms

A gerund may be preceded by a possessive form—either a possessive noun or a possessive adjective. This possessive describes the doer of the action expressed by the gerund.

<u>My</u> deciding to join the marching band surprised my family.

It is possible for an *-ing* form to be a gerund, a participle used as an adjective, or a participle in a progressive verb phrase.

The bands were practicing for <u>entertaining</u> the crowd at halftime. (gerund)

<u>Entertaining</u> the crowds at halftime, the band received a lot of applause. (participle used as an adjective)

An <u>entertaining</u> program of songs was played. (participle used as an adjective)

The band was <u>entertaining</u> the crowd at halftime. (participle used as part of a progressive verb)

Verbals

A. Underline the correct form.

1. The selection (committee <u>committee's</u>) choosing our marching band to participate in the state tournament was a surprise.

2. (Everyone <u>Everyone's</u>) being excited by the news was no surprise.

3. Our (band <u>band's</u>) deciding to apply to the tournament was a last-minute action.

4. As the band director silently read the committee's response to our application, we watched (<u>him</u> his), waiting in eager anticipation.

5. Our (principal <u>principal's</u>) allowing us to hold a fund raiser to raise money for the trip was a big help.

6. (She <u>Her</u>) promoting the event was much appreciated.

7. (<u>Kevin</u> Kevin's) kept suggesting a garage sale as a way to motivate us.

8. (Us <u>Our</u>) organizing the sale required weeks of planning.

9. (<u>Our</u> Us) earning several hundred dollars helped pay for the cost of the bus to the tournament.

10. (People <u>People's</u>) donating so generously to us also made the trip possible.

B. On the line write **A** for each *italicized -ing* word that is used as a gerund, **B** for each participle that is used as an adjective, or **C** for each participle that is used as part of a progressive verb.

__[B]__ 1. Our band was one of several in the *marching* band competition.

__[B]__ 2. *Marching* around the field, our band played its best.

__[C]__ 3. We were *marching* along with bands from several other schools.

__[A]__ 4. *Marching* down the field in formation was one part of the competition.

__[A]__ 5. Our supporters cheered loudly as we started *marching* before the judges.

76. Infinitives as Subjects and Complements

An **infinitive** is a verb form, usually preceded by *to*, that is used as a noun, an adjective, or an adverb. Infinitives may have objects and complements and be modified by adverbs and adverb phrases. When used as a noun, an infinitive can function as a subject or a subject complement.

To see the Iditarod race is my brother's dream. (subject)
My brother's dream is to see the Iditarod race. (subject complement)

Underline each infinitive phrase. Write **S** if it is used as a subject or **SC** if it is used as a subject complement.

__[S]__ 1. To defeat the elements is one of the challenges of the Iditarod Great Sled Race in Alaska.

__[S]__ 2. To drive a dogsled 1,150 miles from Anchorage to Nome is the task for the drivers in the race.

__[SC]__ 3. One reason for the race is to preserve the tradition of transportation by dogsled.

__[S]__ 4. To commemorate an important dogsled trip in the 1920s is another reason for the modern race.

__[SC]__ 5. The purpose of that trip was to bring medicine to sick children in Nome; at that time the only method of transport was the dogsled.

__[S]__ 6. To use dogs was common in the far north in the past.

__[SC]__ 7. The dogs' specialty was to travel over rough terrain.

__[S]__ 8. To carry supplies to gold-mining camps in the interior was the reason for establishing the Iditarod Trail.

__[SC]__ 9. The motivation for the first Iditarod race in 1967 was to celebrate the centennial of the purchase of Alaska from Russia.

__[SC]__ 10. The goal of many people from all walks of life is to drive in the race.

__[S]__ 11. To be a good driver is not enough for success.

__[SC]__ 12. A requirement for a driver is to show perseverance.

__[S]__ 13. To decide on tactics for the race is each driver's responsibility.

__[S]__ 14. To drive by day or by night is the decision of each racer.

__[S]__ 15. To pull the sled is the work of powerful draft dogs.

__[S]__ 16. To reach the finish line takes 9 to 12 days.

__[SC]__ 17. A requirement for victory is to travel up to 12 hours a day.

__[S]__ 18. To run fast is a basic requirement for competent sled dogs.

__[SC]__ 19. Another quality is to have the desire and willingness for racing.

__[S]__ 20. To understand and even communicate with one's dogs is necessary for a dogsled driver, who is called a musher.

Verbals

81

77. Infinitives as Objects

> When an infinitive functions as a noun, it can be used as a direct object in a sentence.
>
> **In the early 1900s many people tried <u>to reach the North and South poles</u>.**
>
> An infinitive used as a direct object may be preceded by a noun or a pronoun.
> This word tells the doer of the infinitive. The infinitive and its subject form an **infinitive clause**. The object form of a pronoun is used as the subject of an infinitive.
>
> **Ernest Shackleton persuaded <u>them to finance his expeditions</u>.**
> (*Them* is the subject of the infinitive, *to finance*.)

Underline each infinitive or infinitive phrase used as a direct object.
Circle the verb of which it is the direct object.

1. As a boy, Ernest Shackleton (wanted) <u>to go to sea</u>.

2. A the age of 16, he (began) <u>to pursue a career as a sailor</u>.

3. Within eight years he (managed) <u>to obtain certification as a ship's commander</u>.

4. With a taste for new adventures, he (asked) <u>to accompany Robert Scott and Dr. Edward Wilson on an expedition to Antarctica</u> in 1902.

5. At the time, many people (sought) <u>to be the first at the South Pole</u>.

6. Scott's expedition (failed) <u>to reach the pole</u>.

7. Shackleton, however, (vowed) <u>to return on his own expedition</u>, but that too failed in 1909.

8. After Roald Amundsen reached the pole in 1911, Shackleton (decided) <u>to change his focus</u>.

9. He (planned) <u>to cross Antarctica on foot</u>, and he began by sailing there on the ship *Endurance*.

10. A thick ice pack in the Antarctic (did) not (allow) <u>the ship to move</u>, and the ice eventually crushed the ship.

11. Stranded with his crew in a hostile environment, Shackleton (tried) <u>to maintain his crew's morale</u>.

12. For example, Shackleton (encouraged) <u>them to play sports</u>.

13. The crew (needed) <u>to keep up their spirits</u>.

14. Floating in small boats, after 16 months on the ice, the crew (managed) <u>to reach a small uninhabited island</u>.

15. With a few crew members, Shackleton then (hoped) <u>to reach an inhabited island to the north</u>.

16. He (promised) <u>to return with help</u>, and he did.

17. To everyone it seemed miraculous that all of the crew (managed) <u>to survive such an ordeal</u>.

18. Still lured by the challenge of Antarctica, Shackleton next (undertook) <u>to circumnavigate the continent</u>.

19. He (refused) <u>to turn back</u> despite a heart attack; he died shortly thereafter, in 1922.

20. During his lifetime Shackleton (dared) <u>to face many difficult challenges</u>.

Verbals

78. Infinitives as Appositives

> An infinitive functioning as a noun can be used as an appositive. An appositive is a word or a group of words used after a noun that identifies the noun or gives more information about it.
>
> **Bridget's chief goal during summer vacation, to read a good novel each week, seems an attainable one.**

A. Underline each infinitive phrase used as an appositive. Circle the word that the appositive explains.

1. Dorothy's (wish,) to return to Kansas, forms the main plot of *The Wizard of Oz*.

2. Harry Potter's (challenge,) to face the evil Lord Voldemort, is a recurring theme in J. K. Rowling's series.

3. The (goal) of the children in *From The Mixed-up Files of Mrs. Basil E. Frankweiler,* to teach their parents a lesson, soon turns into something quite different.

4. In *Chasing Vermeer*, two children undertake a special (mission,) to find a stolen painting by the famous Dutch artist Jan Vermeer.

5. Meg and Charles's (quest) in *A Wrinkle in Time,* to find their father, leads them into space.

B. Underline each infinitive phrase. Rewrite any sentence with an infinitive used as an appositive, adding commas as necessary.

1. In Lois Lowry's *The Giver* people freely choose to give up their humanity in return for a more stable society.

   _____

   _____

2. The main character's important decision to reject this stable society provides the force behind his actions.

   [The main character's important decision, to reject this stable society, provides the force behind his actions.]

3. In *A Single Shard* by Linda Sue Park, Tree-Ear's overriding goal to become a potter seems impossible for the homeless orphan in 12th-century Korea.

   [In *A Single Shard* by Linda Sue Park, Tree-Ear's overriding goal, to become a potter, seems impossible for the homeless orphan in 12th-century Korea.]

4. After he breaks one of the potter's vases, Tree-Ear works for the potter to make amends.

   _____

   _____

5. Ultimately the potter entrusts him with an important job to take two pots to the emperor in hopes of a royal commission.

   [Ultimately the potter entrusts him with an important job, to take two pots to the emperor in hopes of a royal commission.]

Verbals

79. Infinitives as Adjectives

> An infinitive can be used as an adjective to describe a noun or a pronoun. An infinitive used as an adjective follows the word it describes.
>
> **There are many simple inventions <u>to improve everyday life</u>.**
> (The infinitive phrase describes the noun *inventions*.)

Underline each infinitive phrase used as an adjective.
Circle the noun or the pronoun it describes.

1. Women have successfully shown their (capacity) <u>to create new things and processes</u>.

2. In 1809 Mary Dixon Kies received a U.S. patent for a (process) <u>to weave straw with silk and thread</u>.

3. This patent was the (first) <u>to be issued to a woman</u>.

4. Her process resulted in a more efficient (way) <u>to produce hats</u>.

5. Martha Coston's husband had the idea for nighttime (flares) <u>to communicate at sea</u>.

6. After his death Martha completed his (work) <u>to produce a system of workable flares</u>.

7. The (system) <u>to communicate at night at sea</u> was tested by the U.S. Navy.

8. The Navy thenbought the (right) <u>to use Martha's invention</u>.

9. Margaret Knight, born in 1838, was always thinking of (ways) <u>to improve things</u>.

10. Her (machine) <u>to make flat-bottomed paper bags</u> is still in use.

11. More important, Knight also invented a stop-motion (device) <u>to halt the operation of textile machines</u>.

12. Its (ability) <u>to shut down a machine quickly</u> helped in preventing accidents and thus saved lives in textile mills.

13. A primitive (machine) <u>to wash dishes</u> was first patented in 1850.

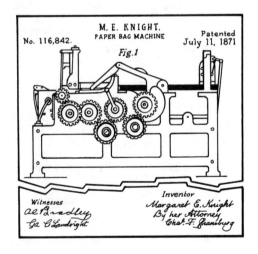

M. E. KNIGHT.
PAPER BAG MACHINE
No. 116,842.
Fig.1
Patented
July 11, 1871

Witnesses
Al Bradley
Ga C Landright

Inventor
Margaret E. Knight
By her Attorney
Chas. F. Fransburg

14. This first dishwasher was little more than a (wheel) <u>to splash water on dishes</u>.

15. Josephine Cochran felt that all the existing (devices) <u>to wash dishes</u> were inadequate.

16. Therefore, in the 1890s she made an (effort) <u>to invent a practical appliance</u>.

17. Cochran founded a (company) <u>to manufacture her dishwashers</u>.

18. Her (attempts) <u>to sell her dishwashing machine to the public</u>, however, failed at first.

19. The only (people) <u>to buy the machines</u> were those who ran hotels and restaurants.

20. Eventually, however, (products) <u>to ease household labor</u> became increasingly attractive and led to greater sales in the mid-20th century.

Name _____

80. Infinitives as Adverbs

An infinitive can be used as an adverb to describe a verb, an adjective, or another adverb.

The students looked on the Internet to get information on places for a field trip. (describes the verb *looked*)

They were pleased to find an interesting place. (describes the adjective *pleased*)

It was close enough to be a choice for the trip. (describes the adverb *enough*)

Underline each infinitive phrase used as an adverb. Circle the word it describes. On the line write the part of speech of each circled word: **V** for verb, **Adj** for adjective, or **Adv** for adverb.

[V] 1. The seventh-grade class (went) to participate in a special program at a space camp.

[V] 2. They (attended) to learn about space and space travel.

[V] 3. The camp (is designed) to simulate an astronaut-training program.

[Adj] 4. The students were (happy) to attend the program.

[V] 5. They first (were trained) to be "astronauts."

[V] 6. They (used) a special jet pack to travel through the air, off the ground.

[V] 7. To experience the gravitational pull of a walk on the Moon, they (tried) a microgravity chair.

[V] 8. The students also (took) rides in a multi-axis chair to feel the sensation of reentry into Earth's atmosphere in a space capsule.

[V] 9. They next (visited) a special area to participate in a simulated trip in a space shuttle.

[V] 10. They (were divided) into three teams to learn different tasks.

[V] 11. Students on the mission control team (were assigned) to track the shuttle.

[Adj] 12. After training, they were (ready) to handle emergencies!

[V] 13. Some students (practiced) to become proficient in space walks.

[V] 14. Others (were prepared) to operate the shuttle controls.

[V] 15. Those "on board" the shuttle (worked) to perform experiments on crystal and plant growth in space.

[V] 16. Later, the students (went) to a museum to see the rockets that launch spaceships.

[V] 17. As part of the training program, student groups (worked) together to build a model rocket.

[Adj] 18. All the groups were (proud) to launch the rocket successfully.

[Adj] 19. The students were (excited) to get hands-on experience in space tasks.

[Adv] 20. Two days was not (enough) to do all they would have liked.

81. Hidden and Split Infinitives

> The word *to* is called the sign of the infinitive, but sometimes an infinitive appears in a sentence without the *to*. Such an infinitive is called a **hidden infinitive.**
>
> **We heard friends <u>talk</u> about a dinosaur-dig center in Colorado.**
>
> An adverb placed between *to* and the verb results in a **split infinitive.** Good writers try to avoid split infinitives.
>
> SPLIT INFINITIVE   **We hope <u>to</u> soon <u>visit</u> the camp.**
>
> IMPROVED   **We hope <u>to visit</u> the camp soon.**

A.   Underline the hidden infinitive in each sentence.

1. My parents let me <u>go</u> with my friend Emily's family to a real dinosaur dig.

2. On the first day we heard people <u>explain</u> how the dig operated.

3. They helped us <u>find</u> a digging site.

4. They also helped us <u>learn</u> the best methods for digging.

5. I watched Emily's father <u>brush</u> dirt from a dull object in the ground.

6. Emily's father let me <u>help</u> him.

7. He made me <u>work</u> slowly and carefully.

8. We saw a dinosaur fossil slowly <u>appear</u>!

9. We dared not <u>hope</u> for such a exciting find on our first dig!

10. I felt my heart <u>race</u> at the thought of possibly finding more fossils.

B.   Rewrite the sentences so that they do not contain split infinitives. **[Answers will vary.]**

1. I learned to carefully work on the dig site.

   [I learned to work carefully on the dig site.]

2. I managed to effectively use the brushes and other tools.

   [I managed to use the brushes and other tools effectively.]

3. I hope to eventually find a fossil myself.

   [Eventually I hope to find a fossil myself.]

4. I don't expect to quickly find one.

   [I don't expect to find one quickly.]

5. I need to patiently keep digging.

   [I need to keep digging patiently.]

Verbals

82. Reviewing Verbals

A. Underline each participle or participial phrase. Circle the word it describes.

1. <u>Advancing from Scandinavia,</u> the (Vikings) invaded parts of eastern and western Europe from 793 to 1066.

2. <u>Being fierce warriors and able sailors,</u> (they) dominated sea travel.

3. Vikings built powerful <u>sailing</u> (vessels.)

4. The (Vikings,) <u>establishing settlements as far away as Greenland and Iceland,</u> became the first European settlers in the New World.

5. The remains of a Viking (settlement,) <u>hidden for centuries,</u> were found by archaeologists in Newfoundland, Canada, during the 1960s.

6. <u>Confirming the old stories of a Viking colony on the North American continent,</u> the (discovery) was an important find.

B. Rewrite each sentence with a dangling participle to improve the sentence.
[Answers will vary. Sample sentence are given.]

7. Preparing a social studies project, the story of the Vikings was focused on.

   [Preparing a social studies project, I focused on the story of the Vikings.]

8. Watching a TV program on Vinland, much new information was obtained.

   [Watching a TV program on Vinland, I obtained much new information.]

9. Being interested in the topic, I read a few books about the Vikings.

_____

C. Underline each gerund or gerund phrase. On the line describe how it functions:
S for subject, **SC** for subject complement, **DO** for direct object, **OP** for object of a preposition, or **AP** for appositive.

__[S]__ 10. <u>Establishing colonies</u> was a common practice of the Vikings.

__[OP]__ 11. The Vikings abandoned their colonies in North America apparently after <u>facing opposition from Native Americans.</u>

__[S]__ 12. <u>Finding mention in Norse stories of a place in North America called Vinland</u> has led to speculation among historians about the location of this colony.

__[A]__ 13. One issue, <u>establishing whether Viking settlements reached as far south as modern-day Massachusetts,</u> has created controversy among historians.

__[S]__ 14. <u>Interpreting the name *Vinland* as "a place of grapevines,"</u> as some people do, suggests an area with a climate suitable for these plants.

__[OP]__ 15. Other historians counter by <u>interpreting the meaning of *Vinland* as "a meadow."</u>

__[DO]__ 16. Many historians prefer <u>identifying Vinland with the Viking colony in Newfoundland.</u>

__[OP]__ 17. Archaeologists can prove the existence of a colony along the east coast of the United States only by <u>finding remains of such a colony.</u>

CONTINUED

__[SC]__ 18. The difficulty is <u>determining a specific place to look</u>.

__[S]__ 19. <u>Conclusively identifying the exact location of Vinland</u> may be impossible.

D. Underline each infinitive phrase. On the line describe how it functions: **S** for subject, **SC** for subject complement, **DO** for direct object, **AP** for appositive, **ADJ** for adjective, or **ADV** for adverb.

__[S]__ 20. <u>To learn more about Leif Ericson</u> is my plan.

__[DO]__ 21. Leif Ericson may have tried <u>to establish a colony on mainland North America</u>.

__[SC]__ 22. The hope of many archaeologists is <u>to find this colony</u>.

__[DO]__ 23. Some archaeologists believe <u>the colony to be at L'Anse aux Meadows, Newfoundland</u>.

__[DO]__ 24. They managed <u>to find Viking-type houses and hearths and some metal objects there</u>.

__[ADV]__ 25. They were excited <u>to discover the remains of a colony</u>.

__[AP]__ 26. The colony's fate, <u>to be forgotten for centuries</u>, added intrigue.

__[ADJ]__ 27. The mystery <u>to be solved</u>, the history of Vinland, may never have a definitive solution.

E. Rewrite each of the sentences to correct the split infinitive. **[Answers may vary.]**

28. I managed to quickly find information on Vinland on the Internet.
   [I managed to find information on Vinland quickly on the Internet.]

29. I wanted to thoroughly research the topic, however.
   [I wanted to research the topic thoroughly, however.]

30. I needed to slowly analyze the information.
   [I needed to analyze the information slowly.]

Try It Yourself

On a separate sheet of paper, write about something that you have recently studied in school or something that you have recently learned about that interests you. Be sure to use verbals correctly.

Check Your Own Work

Choose a selection from your writing portfolio, a journal, a work in progress, an assignment from another class, or a letter. Revise it, applying the skills you have learned. This checklist will help you.

✔ Have you used participles, gerunds, and infinitives correctly?

✔ Have you used possessives correctly with gerunds?

✔ Have you used avoided dangling particples and split infinitives?

Name _____

83. Types of Adverbs

An **adverb** is a word that describes a verb, an adjective, or another adverb. An adverb generally describes the time, place, manner, or degree of the word it modifies. It may also indicate affirmation (telling whether a statement is positive or giving consent or approval) or negation (expressing a negative condition or refusal).

TIME	We should leave <u>now</u>.	DEGREE	The park was <u>rather</u> far.
PLACE	I've never been <u>there</u>.	AFFIRMATION	It <u>certainly</u> was a great trip.
MANNER	We left <u>quickly</u>.	NEGATION	We could <u>not</u> try all the rides.

Underline each adverb. On the line tell what type of adverb it is: **T** for time, **P** for place, **D** for degree, **M** for manner, **A** for affirmation, or **N** for negation.

[A] 1. The Wright brothers did <u>indeed</u> invent the first successful airplane.

[T] 2. They had experimented <u>previously</u> with a five-foot biplane kite.

[T] 3. <u>Then</u> they had worked with a glider that could carry a person.

[D] 4. The lifting power of their glider was <u>rather</u> disappointing.

[N] 5. Despite many setbacks they did <u>not</u> give up their dream of flying.

[M] 6. They <u>cleverly</u> developed a better wing design.

[M] 7. They <u>carefully</u> studied books about flight and about birds.

[T] 8. They <u>usually</u> went to North Carolina to test their planes.

[P] 9. The winds <u>there</u> were good for flying.

[D] 10. The first airplane flight on December 17, 1903, was <u>quite</u> short.

[D] 11. The airplane <u>barely</u> got off the ground.

[M] 12. Its body seemed to move <u>uncontrollably</u>.

[P] 13. The plane moved <u>forward</u> in the air 120 feet in 12 seconds.

[M] 14. Within two years the Wright brothers' airplane could <u>easily</u> fly 20 miles.

[M] 15. The Wright brothers had <u>actively</u> tested flying machines for four years before their success.

ORVILLE   WILBUR

Orville and Wilbur Wright worked cooperatively to achieve their goals. Give an example of how you work cooperatively with others to achieve goals.

84. Interrogative Adverbs

An **interrogative adverb** is used to ask a question. The interrogative adverbs are *how, when, where,* and *why.* They are used to ask about reason, place, time, or method.

METHOD **How did King Arthur become king?**

TIME **When did the stories take place?**

PLACE **Where did you find these stories?**

REASON **Why has King Arthur been so popular?**

A. Underline each interrogative adverb once. Underline other adverbs twice.

1. <u>When</u> did the story of King Arthur begin?

2. It appeared <u>originally</u> during the early Middle Ages.

3. According to old writings, a king named Arthur <u>bravely</u> fought the invaders of England.

4. The stories about the king and his knights of the Round Table became <u>extremely</u> popular.

5. People <u>gradually</u> invented more and more stories about the king.

6. <u>Then</u> the stories were gathered into a poem called *Le Morte d'Arthur.*

7. <u>Why</u> has the popularity of the stories lasted <u>so</u> long?

8. In the stories Arthur <u>highly</u> values the virtues of peace, duty, and friendship.

9. <u>Where</u> is Arthur's legendary home?

10. <u>Annually</u> many tourists visit Cadbury Castle, one of several supposed sites of Camelot.

B. Complete each sentence with one of the following adverbs.
Use the clues at the left for the class of adverb. [**Suggested answers are given.**]

easily	foolishly	how	not	soon
speedily	suddenly	unsuccessfully	truly	why

interrogative 1. _____[How]_____ did King Arthur become king?

negation 2. Arthur did _____[not]_____ know he was a king's son.

manner 3. One day Sir Kay, his companion, _____[foolishly]_____ forgot to bring his sword to a tournament.

manner 4. Arthur rode _____[speedily]_____ back to town for the sword.

time 5. Along the way he _____[suddenly]_____ noticed a sword in a stone.

manner 6. He _____[easily]_____ pulled it from the stone and returned with it.

interrogative 7. _____[Why]_____ did the knights at the tournament look in amazement at Arthur and the sword?

degree 8. According to legend, whoever pulled the sword from the stone would be a _____[truly]_____ great king.

manner 9. Many knights had tried _____[unsuccessfully]_____ to remove the sword.

time 10. _____[Soon]_____ Arthur was declared king.

Adverbs

85. Adverbial Nouns

> An **adverbial noun** is a noun that functions as an adverb. It generally modifies a verb and expresses time, measure, value, or direction.
> **Lewis and Clark spent several years on an expedition to the Northwest.**

A. Underline each adverbial noun. On the line tell what it expresses. Write **T** for time, **M** for measure, **V** for value, or **D** for direction. [**Some answers may vary.**]

[V] 1. The United States paid France 15 million <u>dollars</u> for the Louisiana Territory.

[M] 2. The territory covered more than 800,000 square <u>miles</u>.

[V] 3. The United States spent only three <u>cents</u> for each acre!

[V] 4. Thomas Jefferson requested $2,500 <u>dollars</u> for exploration of the territory.

[T] 5. The <u>day</u> after the announcement of the purchase, Meriwether Lewis began to organize an expedition.

[T] 6. It took ten <u>months</u> to organize the expedition, which began on May 14, 1804.

[M] 7. Lewis and William Clark traveled some 7,200 <u>miles</u> to the Pacific coast and back.

[T] 8. The expedition took two and one-half <u>years</u>.

[M] 9. They traveled the Missouri River on a keelboat that measured 55 <u>feet</u>.

[M] 10. On a good day they could travel 14 <u>miles</u> by boat.

[T] 11. Did Sacagawea know the journey to the Northwest would take <u>years</u>?

[D] 12. She did not guide the expedition <u>west</u>, but she helped communicate with the Shoshone people.

[D] 13. The expedition pushed <u>west</u> to the Continental Divide and then to the Pacific Ocean.

[D] 14. The group returned <u>east</u> to St. Louis on September 23, 1806.

[T] 15. The journals of Lewis and Clark make interesting reading <u>today</u>.

B. Complete each sentence with one of the following adverbial nouns.

days   east   hours   miles   today

1. In 1889 a fictional book told of a trip around the world that lasted 80 __[days]__ .

2. Nellie Bly traveled __[east]__ , through England, Egypt, Japan, and back to New York.

3. She traveled some 23,000 __[miles]__ by boat, train, rickshaw, and donkey.

4. It took her 72 days and 6 __[hours]__ for the trip.

5. __[Today]__ most people don't know of this woman's outstanding feat.

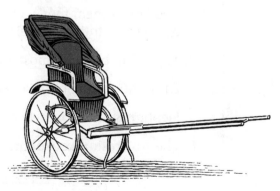

86. Comparative and Superlative Adverbs

The comparative and superlative degrees of most adverbs that end in -ly are formed by adding *more* or *most* (or *less* or *least*) before the positive form of the adverb.
slowly, more slowly, most slowly

The comparative and superlative degrees of most adverbs that do not end in -ly are formed by adding -er and -est.
fast, faster, fastest

Some adverbs, such as *well* and *much,* have irregular comparative and superlative forms.
well, better, best   **much, more, most**

A. Complete the chart with degrees of comparison.

POSITIVE	COMPARATIVE	SUPERLATIVE
1. confidently	[more/less confidently]	[most/least confidently]
2. [thoughtfully]	more thoughtfully	[most thoughtfully]
3. early	[earlier]	[earliest]
4. [hurriedly]	[less hurriedly]	least hurriedly
5. easily	[more/less easily]	[most/least easily]
6. [enthusiastically]	less enthusiastically	[least enthusiastically]
7. [late]	later	[latest]
8. [carefully]	[less carefully]	least carefully
9. graciously	[more/less graciously]	[most/least graciously]
10. [soon]	[sooner]	soonest

B. Underline the adverb in each sentence. On the line write the degree of comparison— **P** for positive, **C** for comparative, or **S** for superlative.

__[P]__ 1. Arctic ground squirrels sleep almost <u>continuously</u> for nine months.

__[C]__ 2. Mayflies die <u>sooner</u> after birth than most animals do; they live only a few hours.

__[S]__ 3. Desert locusts may well be the world's <u>most destructive</u> insects.

__[P]__ 4. Swarms of them move across vast areas, <u>quickly</u> devouring all the vegetation in their paths.

__[S]__ 5. Migrating birds fly <u>most efficiently</u> in a V formation.

__[S]__ 6. Of all migrating birds, the arctic tern travels <u>farthest</u> in its migrations.

__[P]__ 7. Elephants <u>affectionately</u> entwine their trunks as a way to communicate.

__[C]__ 8. The Australian kookaburra sings <u>more noisily</u> than most other birds.

__[S]__ 9. Cheetahs run <u>most rapidly</u> of all animals.

__[C]__ 10. Hares can run <u>faster</u> than horses.

Adverbs

Name _____

87. *Farther* and *Further*

> *Farther* refers to distance. *Further* means "in addition to."
> Both words are used as adjectives and as adverbs.
>
> **Spacecraft allow humans to see <u>farther</u> into space.**
>
> **Scientists continue to encourage <u>further</u> space research.**

A. Circle the correct word in parentheses.

1. Mathematicians predicted the existence of the planet Neptune in the 1840s, and (farther (further)) events proved them right.

2. Because of changes in Uranus's orbit, they concluded that there was a planet ((farther) further) out in space than Uranus.

3. After the time of Galileo, (farther (further)) scientific studies produced better telescopes.

4. The telescopes of the 1800s could see ((farther) further) than earlier ones.

5. In the 1840s (farther (further)) efforts by astronomers confirmed Neptune's existence through direct observation.

6. Usually Pluto is ((farther) further) from the Sun than any other planet.

7. Sometimes Neptune's orbit takes it ((farther) further) than Pluto from the Sun.

8. Some scientists think that Pluto should not be called a planet, but (farther (further)) discussion will be needed to decide the issue.

9. Scientists have found many small bodies ((farther) further) out in space than Neptune in what is known as the Kuiper Belt.

10. They will undoubtedly study the topic (farther (further)).

B. Complete each sentence with *farther* or *further*.

1. Since people landed on the Moon, there has been _____**[further]**_____ space exploration.

2. Space probes have gone _____**[farther]**_____ and _____**[farther]**_____ into space.

3. They have discovered _____**[further]**_____ details about nearly all the planets.

4. New information has spurred _____**[further]**_____ discoveries by scientists.

5. *Voyager 1* and *Voyager 2* explored planets at _____**[farther]**_____ distances than the Sun is from Earth.

6. *Voyager 1* traveled _____**[farther]**_____ into space than any other spacecraft.

7. Scientists _____**[further]**_____ expect to get information about the solar system.

8. *Pioneer 10* once traveled _____**[farther]**_____ into space than any other object from Earth.

9. _____**[Further]**_____ missions are planned—including one to Jupiter's moon Europa.

10. A spacecraft will go _____**[farther]**_____ than Jupiter to explore the nature of Pluto.

Adverbs

93

88. *There, Their,* and *They're*

> *There* is an adverb of place.
> > **The heart is a major organ of the human body; blood is pumped <u>there</u>.**
>
> *There* is sometimes an introductory word, usually before the verb *be* and its forms.
> > **<u>There</u> are two main types of blood vessels—veins and arteries.**
>
> *They're* is a contraction for *they are*. *Their* is a possessive adjective.
> > **Veins are blood vessels. <u>They're</u> filled with dark red blood.**
> > **<u>Their</u> role is to carry blood toward the heart.**

A. Write **A** if *there* is used as an adverb or **I** if it is used as an introductory word.

___[I]___ 1. There are 206 bones in the human body.

___[A]___ 2. Bones support the human body, and blood cells are produced there.

___[I]___ 3. Within the human body there are 12 pairs of ribs.

___[I]___ 4. There is a small worm-shaped pouch called the appendix
at the beginning of the large intestine.

___[A]___ 5. There, according to scientists, very little that is useful happens.

___[I]___ 6. Within the cerebrum there are gray cells.

___[A]___ 7. There in the cerebrum is where thinking takes place.

___[I]___ 8. There is white nerve fiber in the brain that carries signals.

___[A]___ 9. The forebrain includes the diencephalon and the cerebrum;
heartbeat and body temperature are regulated there.

___[A]___ 10. The cerebellum is an important part of the brain because balance
and movement are controlled there.

B. Complete each sentence with *there, their,* or *they're*.

1. ___[There]___ are four chambers in the human heart.

2. ___[Their]___ function is to pump blood throughout the body.

3. Deoxygenated blood is pumped from the right atrium and the right ventricle to the
lungs; when the blood reaches the lungs, it obtains fresh oxygen ___[there]___.

4. Oxygenated blood goes to the left atrium and the left ventricle: ___[they're]___
partners in the next step of the process.

5. Blood cells carry food and oxygen to the body; without ___[their]___
services all other body cells would die.

89. *Well* and *Good*

> *Good* is an adjective. It is used to describe a noun or a pronoun but never a verb. The word *well* is an adverb that generally describes a verb.
>   **I am a good painter in acrylics. Do you do well in art class?**
>
> *Well* may be used as an adjective but only when it refers to health.
>   **Armand was not in art class; he has not been well since Monday.**

Underline the correct word to complete each sentence.

1. There were many (good well) exhibits at the school hobby show.

2. Ariane showed some extraordinarily (good well) portraits done in pencil.

3. She really draws (good well).

4. She designed a (good well), colorful poster for the show itself.

5. Many of us did not know that Louis could take photographs so (good well).

6. He finds (good well) subjects in ordinary places—even in the school halls!

7. Had he felt (good well), he would have prepared a larger display of his work.

8. Jason does origami (good well); he had some intricately folded pieces in the show.

9. He says that the local community center is a (good well) place to learn origami.

10. Learning to do origami (good well) doesn't take long, he says.

11. Eli likes models of aircraft, and he makes them (good well).

12. He gave us some (good well) tips for learning how model planes are constructed.

13. Many (good well) collections are on display in the show.

14. Ashley did (good well) in presenting her collection of snow globes.

15. She arranged the globes (well good), according to size and color.

16. Brian has a (good well) collection of baseball cards.

17. He explained (good well) how to start a collection of this type.

18. The show registered a (good well) attendance, much better than last year's.

19. The organizers thought that everything had gone (good well).

20. Everyone spoke (good well) of the show.

Adverbs

90. *Bad* and *Badly*

> *Bad* is an adjective, and *badly* is an adverb. When the predicate of a sentence is a linking verb, it must be followed by *bad,* not *badly.* Remember that some verbs can function as linking verbs or as action verbs.
> **Some animals hear <u>badly</u>.**
> **The songs of a whale may sound <u>bad</u> to us, but they probably do not sound that way to whales.**

Underline the correct word to complete each sentence.

1. Sharks see (bad <u>badly</u>), but their sense of smell is superior.

2. Some animals smell (<u>bad</u> badly)—their terrible scent acting as a defense to ward off enemies.

3. Bright colors can warn predators that an animal tastes (<u>bad</u> badly).

4. Penguins walk (bad <u>badly</u>), but they are expert swimmers.

5. A crow sings (bad <u>badly</u>).

6. The cry of the peacock also sounds (<u>bad</u> badly) to humans' ears.

7. Bats do not have (<u>bad</u> badly) eyesight; it is almost as good as that of humans.

8. Electric eels can shock other animals (bad <u>badly</u>); their shock can actually knock over an adult person wading nearby.

9. Some jellyfish sting (bad <u>badly</u>), and their poison can kill a human in 30 seconds.

10. In their fangs vipers and cobra produce a (<u>bad</u> badly) venom that can kill humans.

11. The venom of some snakes is not deadly, but it can hurt other animals (bad <u>badly</u>).

12. An insect sting can cause (<u>bad</u> badly) swelling in a human.

13. For 1 percent of the people stung by insects, the results are not just (<u>bad</u> badly), they are fatal.

14. Beaver habitats are being (bad <u>badly</u>) damaged by humans.

15. Male lions may be considered (<u>bad</u> badly) providers for their families; lionesses do most of the hunting.

16. When a member of an elephant herd dies, the other elephants take it so (bad <u>badly</u>) that they seem to cry.

17. Most birds migrate to the tropics in winter to escape the (<u>bad</u> badly) effects of cold weather.

18. A frightened grasshopper releases an oozy substance that smells (<u>bad</u> badly).

19. Termites can harm wood (bad <u>badly</u>).

20. An infestation of crown-of-thorns sea stars can affect a coral reef (bad <u>badly</u>), destroying much of the coral.

91. Adverb Phrases

Prepositional phrases can be used as adverbs to describe verbs, adjectives, and other adverbs. Prepositional phrases used in this way are called **adverb phrases**.

   Some lichens grow in extremely hot or cold environments.

Underline the adverb phrase in each sentence. Circle the word it describes.

1. In a lichen two totally different parts (complement) each other.

2. An alga and a fungus (live) together in this unusual plant.

3. With sunlight the alga (can make) food.

4. The fungus, however, (can)not (make) food by itself.

5. The alga (passes) a form of sugar to the fungus.

6. The fungus (uses) the sugar for the plant's growth.

7. It (contributes) to the plant in other ways.

8. The fungus (helps) the plant through its water-absorption ability.

9. Some lichens (grow) in soil.

10. Most (live) on rocks or on tree bark.

11. Some lichens (can survive) in hostile environments.

12. They (can be found) in the Arctic and in deserts.

13. Animals and humans (benefit) from lichens.

14. Lichens (provide) reindeer and caribou with food.

15. During the winter lichens (represent) an important food supply.

16. Lichens (are used) in manufacturing.

17. Manufacturers (use) them in perfumes, after-shave lotions, and soap.

18. They (act) as fixatives, substances that prevent rapid evaporation.

19. Certain skin disorders (may be treated) with lichens.

20. Can you believe that people also (make) Christmas decorations from lichens?

Adverbs

92. Adverb Clauses

A clause is a group of words that has a subject and a predicate. A dependent clause does not express a complete thought. A dependent clause that acts as an adverb is called an **adverb clause.** Some subordinate conjunctions used to introduce adverb clauses are *after, although, as, because, if, since, so that, unless, until, when, whenever, wherever, whether,* and *while.*

Tornadoes occur <u>when certain atmospheric conditions are present</u>.

A. Underline the adverb clause. Circle the word(s) it modifies.

1. Tornadoes (frighten) us <u>because they can cause sudden, violent destruction.</u>

2. <u>Although there are tornadoes all over the world,</u> they (occur) most often in North America.

3. <u>Unless there is a thunderstorm,</u> a tornado (does) not (occur.)

4. Thunderstorms (are produced) <u>when warm, moist air meets cold, dry air.</u>

5. A tornado (forms) <u>as warm, moist air gets trapped below a layer of stable cold, dry air.</u>

6. <u>If conditions are right,</u> the warm, moist air (spins) its way through the stable air.

7. The warm air (spirals) upward <u>as its heat is released.</u>

8. The rotating air (gains) speed <u>when it moves up.</u>

9. <u>If tornadoes hit the ground,</u> they (can travel) huge distances.

10. Some tornadoes (darken) <u>after they pick up dust and debris.</u>

11. <u>If this happens,</u> you (can see) the twisting spiral of the tornado.

12. <u>Because there are so many tornadoes in Texas, Oklahoma, and Kansas,</u> this area (is called) Tornado Alley.

13. <u>Although tornadoes can strike any time of the day,</u> they (happen) most frequently in the afternoon.

14. <u>While tornadoes whirl counterclockwise in the Northern Hemisphere,</u> they (turn) clockwise in the Southern Hemisphere.

15. <u>Before tornadoes hit,</u> scientists (can predict) dangerous weather conditions.

B. Complete each sentence with an independent clause. **[Answers will vary. Sample answers are given.]**

1. Before you leave the house, _____ [check the weather report] _____ .

2. After the storm ended, _____ [a beautiful rainbow appeared in the sky] _____ .

3. While I was swimming, _____ [I suffered a cramp in my right leg] _____ .

4. _____ [Our team has not lost a game] _____ since Julie became the goalie on our team.

5. _____ [I usually go to sleep at 10 o'clock] _____ unless the next day is a school holiday.

Adverbs

Name _____

93. Reviewing Adverbs

A. Underline each adverb. On the line write whether it is an adverb of manner, degree, time, or affirmation.

_____[degree]_____ 1. Annie Oakley was an <u>extremely</u> talented sharpshooter of the Old West.

_____[manner]_____ 2. At 15 she <u>confidently</u> took part in a shooting match and defeated Frank Butler.

_____[time]_____ 3. <u>Later</u>, Annie joined Buffalo Bill's Wild West Show.

_____[manner]_____ 4. During the show Frank <u>courageously</u> held a dime in his hand for Annie to shoot.

_____[affirmation]_____ 5. Annie did <u>indeed</u> have an adventurous life.

B. Complete each sentence with an appropriate interrogative adverb. **[Answers may vary.]**

6. _____[When]_____ was the era of the cowboy?

7. _____[Why]_____ was the age of the cowboy so short?

8. _____[Where]_____ did cowboys come from?

9. _____[Where]_____ was the Chisholm Trail located?

10. _____[How]_____ did cowboys prevent stampedes?

C. Underline each adverbial noun. Tell what each expresses. On the line write **T** for time, **M** for measure, **V** for value, or **D** for direction. **[Some answers may vary.]**

__[T]__ 11. The era of the cattle drive lasted only 20 <u>years</u>.

__[M]__ 12. The drive could cover only 10 to 20 <u>miles</u> in a day.

__[T]__ 13. A drive took several <u>months</u> to complete.

__[D]__ 14. The Chisholm Trail went <u>north</u>, from Texas to Abilene, Kansas, which was a rail center.

__[V]__ 15. Ranchers earned more <u>dollars</u> by selling their cattle to markets in the East.

D. Complete the chart with the missing adverbs.

Positive	Comparative	Superlative
16. energetically	[more/less energetically]	[most/least energetically]
17. [cautiously]	[more cautiously]	most cautiously
18. [badly]	[worse]	worst
19. [far]	farther	[farthest]
20. late	[later]	[latest]

Adverbs

E. Complete each sentence with *farther* or *further*.

21. In the 1800s people wanted ships that traveled _____[farther]_____ and faster.

22. The first steamships traveled _____[farther]_____ in a day than sailing sloops.

23. Early steamships had paddle wheels, however, and _____[further]_____ development was needed before they were suitable for ocean travel.

24. _____[Further]_____ improvements made the first solely steam-powered crossing of the Atlantic possible in 1838.

25. Eventually there was no _____[further]_____ need for vessels with sails.

F. Complete each sentence with *there, their,* or *they're*.

26. We went to the museum mainly to see the replica of a clipper ship _____[there]_____.

27. Although other exhibits _____[there]_____ were interesting, the clipper replica was my favorite.

28. When discussing the clippers, the tour guide said _____[their]_____ speeds were up to 20 knots per hour.

29. _____[Their]_____ days of glory ended quickly.

30. _____[They're]_____ still remembered as beautiful vessels.

G. Underline the adverb phrase or the adverb clause in each sentence. Circle the word it modifies.

31. Clipper ships (moved) smoothly across ocean waters.

32. If they were required to do so, these ships (could move) speedily also.

33. As a matter of fact, they (were designed) for just one thing—speed.

34. With their clouds of canvas and graceful lines, clipper ships (have fascinated) the American public for more than 150 years.

35. Because many people still love the romance of the beautiful clipper ships, vacation cruise lines (feature) trips on modern-day clippers.

Try It Yourself
On a separate sheet of paper, write a paragraph related to a means of transportation such as a train or an airplane. Be sure to use the correct forms of adverbs.

Check Your Own Work
Choose a selection from your portfolio or journal, a work in progress, an assignment from another class, or a letter. Revise it, applying the skills you have reviewed. This checklist will help you.

✔ Have you included appropriate adverbs of time, place, degree, and manner?

✔ Have you used the correct adverb forms for comparisons?

✔ Have you used *there, their,* and *they're* correctly?

Adverbs

94. Single and Multiword Prepositions

A **preposition** is a word that shows the relationship between a noun or a pronoun and another word in a sentence. A **prepositional phrase** contains a preposition, the object of the preposition, and any words that describe the object. Most prepositions are one word; however, some have more than one word. Common **multiword prepositions** include *according to, because of, in spite of, instead of,* and *on account of.*

The samurai were members <u>of</u> the warrior caste <u>in</u> Japan.
<u>According to</u> this Japanese history book, the samurai prized personal honor.

Underline each preposition and circle the object of the preposition.

1. Samurai were knights <u>in</u> feudal (Japan).

2. They defended the estates <u>of</u> (aristocrats) <u>in</u> the (provinces).

3. The samurai fought <u>with</u> long, curved (swords).

4. They were equipped <u>with</u> special (armor) made <u>of</u> (pieces) <u>of</u> (iron).

5. The armor was effective protection <u>against</u> (cuts) <u>from</u> (swords).

6. <u>In</u> damp (climates) iron would rust, so the armor was lacquered <u>with</u> a black (coating).

7. <u>During</u> the 11th and 12th (centuries) the samurai developed a code <u>of</u> (values).

8. They showed an unfailing loyalty <u>to</u> their (overlords) and an indifference <u>to</u> (pain).

9. The code <u>of</u> (honor) was called bushido <u>by</u> the (samurai).

10. <u>In</u> (defeat) some samurai would kill themselves <u>for</u> the (preservation) <u>of</u> their (honor).

11. The samurai were the dominant group <u>in</u> (Japan) <u>for</u> (centuries) <u>because of</u> their fighting (skills).

12. <u>In spite of</u> their warlike (nature) the samurai and their culture were responsible <u>for</u> many (customs) <u>of</u> (Japan).

13. <u>Among</u> (these) was the tea ceremony.

14. Ronin, who were samurai <u>without</u> (masters), eventually became a social problem <u>in</u> (Japan).

15. Although they were needed <u>in</u> (times) <u>of</u> (war), the ronin were a burden <u>on</u> (society) <u>in</u> (times) <u>of</u> (peace).

16. <u>In</u> the 17th (century) direct control <u>of</u> the (villages) was taken <u>from</u> the (samurai).

17. <u>Prior to</u> that (time) they lived <u>in</u> (villages), but they eventually were moved <u>into</u> (towns).

18. <u>After</u> the (move) they assumed jobs <u>as</u> (bureaucrats).

19. <u>Because of</u> this (change) <u>in</u> their (lifestyle), the samurai lost their fighting ability <u>over</u> (time).

20. <u>By</u> the (end) <u>of</u> the 19th (century), the central powers <u>in</u> (Japan) had changed, and samurai, <u>as</u> a (class) <u>of</u> (society), were abolished.

Name _____

95. More Single and Multiword Prepositions

> A preposition shows the relationship between a noun or a pronoun and another word in a sentence. A preposition may be one word or more than one word.

Complete each sentence with a preposition from the list of prepositions shown with each set of sentences. Use each preposition in a set once.

according to   among   at   during   from   of

1. __[According to]__ legend, William Tell was a hero _____[of]_____ the Swiss _____[during]_____ the 14th century.

2. _____[At]_____ that time the Swiss were trying to gain their independence _____[from]_____ the Austrians.

3. _____[Among]_____ the Swiss leaders was William Tell.

into   on top of   over   through   with

4. A tyrant named Gessler ruled _____[over]_____ Tell's territory.

5. Gessler placed a cap _____[on top of]_____ a pole.

6. Gessler threatened to put _____[into]_____ jail anyone who did not salute the cap.

7. One day William Tell was walking _____[through]_____ the town _____[with]_____ his son.

about   as   in front of   off   without

8. Tell passed the pole _____[without]_____ a glance, and so soldiers captured Tell and brought him __[in front of]__ Gessler.

9. Gessler knew _____[about]_____ Tell's skills _____[as]_____ an archer.

10. He said, "I'll let you go free if you shoot this apple _____[off]_____ your son's head."

at   from   in   of   with

11. Tell looked _____[at]_____ Gessler _____[with]_____ an expression _____[of]_____ contempt.

12. Tell took two arrows _____[from]_____ his quiver.

13. The crowd watched _____[in]_____ horror as Tell shot an arrow.

on account of   from   in   to   with

14. The apple split _____[in]_____ half and fell _____[to]_____ the ground; Tell's son was safe.

15. Tell later shot the tyrant _____[with]_____ the second arrow, and __[on account of]__ Tell's heroic actions the Swiss regained their independence _____[from]_____ a foreign country.

Prepositions

102

96. Troublesome Prepositions

Beside refers to position; it means "next to." *Besides* means "in addition to."
> **My CD collection is beside my desk.**
> **Besides CDs I have some old vinyls.**

Use *between* to speak of two persons, places, or things. Use *among* to speak of more than two.
> **My father split his record collection between my brother and me.**
> **I divided my old CDs among my three best friends.**

You *differ with* someone when you disagree. You *differ on* things. *Differ from* describes the differences between persons and things.
> **I differ with my brother about the best kind of music.**
> **My brother and I differ on the topic of music.**
> **Current rock differs from classic rock in many ways.**

A. Underline the correct preposition in parentheses.

1. Kathy differs (with on) her sister Betty in many ways.

2. They differ (from with) each other in personality: Kathy is serious, and Betty is easygoing.

3. For example, they differ (with on) the issue of borrowing.

4. There is little agreement (among between) the two sisters on this topic.

5. Betty and Kathy differ (on with) the question of whether it is okay to borrow things without asking in advance.

6. Betty often just borrows clothes; (beside besides) that, Betty also uses her sister's CDs and CD player without asking.

7. There was a big row (between among) Betty and Kathy after Betty took some of her sister's CDs without asking.

8. Kathy wants an agreement (among between) all the family members about not borrowing without asking in advance.

9. (Beside Besides), Kathy wants Betty to return all the things she has borrowed.

10. (Among Between) themselves, however, the family members differ (on with) how to enforce the agreement.

B. Complete each sentence with the correct preposition from the list of troublesome prepositions.

1. I usually differ ____[from]____ my brother on choice of music.

2. We differ ____[on]____ the subject of classical music: he likes it and I don't.

3. My musical choices are usually ____[among]____ rap, heavy metal, and punk rock.

4. __[Between]__ my brother and me, we have hundreds of CDs.

5. He asked to borrow some of my CDs and was surprised to find ____[among]____ the songs an updated version of a Bach motet!

Prepositions

97. More Troublesome Prepositions

> *Like* is a preposition and is used in prepositional phrases. *As* and *as if* are conjunctions; they introduce dependent clauses.
>
> **Plants <u>like</u> weeds seem to thrive in any climate.**
> **Mom grew tired, <u>as</u> she had worked in the garden all afternoon.**
> **Dad looks <u>as if</u> he also has been working hard in the garden.**
>
> One is *angry with* a person but *angry at* a thing.
>
> **Mom was <u>angry with</u> me for pulling out some plants that were not weeds.**
> **We were <u>angry at</u> the decision to close the herb garden in the park.**
>
> *From* can indicate removal or separation. *Off* means "away from." Use *off*, not *off of*, to indicate movement from.
>
> **I borrowed a rake <u>from</u> my neighbors.**
> **We took the old leaves <u>off</u> (*not* off of) the rose trellis.**

A. Underline the correct word or words in parentheses.

1. The backyard looked (like <u>as if</u>) no one had tended it for a while.

2. The gigantic sunflower, (<u>like</u> as) a tall scarecrow, stood above all the other plants.

3. The surrounding fence looked (like <u>as if</u>) it hadn't been painted in years.

4. The creaky old gate swung back and forth (like <u>as</u>) the wind blew.

5. The scent of roses was (<u>like</u> as) a sweet but subtle perfume.

B. Complete each sentence with *angry with* or *angry at*.

1. The neighbors were very ____[angry at]____ the poor state of our backyard.

2. My mother was ____[angry with]____ my father and me for not giving it better care.

3. My father was ____[angry with]____ me for not cutting the grass regularly.

4. I was ____[angry at]____ the entire situation.

5. I think that everyone in our house is ____[angry at]____ something or ____[angry with]____ someone.

C. Underline the correct word(s) in parentheses.

1. We had to remove the weeds (off of <u>from</u>) the backyard.

2. We borrowed a special grass cutter (off <u>from</u>) a friend.

3. We also took the vines (off of <u>from</u>) the walls.

4. I got an old straw hat (off <u>from</u>) my mom.

5. Because of the sun, I didn't take it (off of <u>off</u>) my head until evening.

Name _____

98. Words Used as Adverbs and Prepositions

> An adverb tells how, when, or where. A preposition shows the relationship between its object and another word in the sentence. Some words can be used as adverbs or as prepositions.
>
> PREPOSITION   We looked <u>under</u> the cabinet.
> ADVERB   The puppy frequently crawls <u>under</u> to escape the cat.

A. On the line write **A** if the *italicized* word is an adverb or **P** if it is a preposition.

___[A]___ 1. Have you made a terrarium *before?*

___[P]___ 2. A terrarium basically consists of plants grown *inside* a container.

___[A]___ 3. The water cycle occurs on a small scale *inside*.

___[A]___ 4. Here are the steps to go *through*.

___[P]___ 5. *Before* starting, get what you need: a plastic or glass container with a cover, charcoal, soil, and plants.

___[A]___ 6. Look *around* in garden stores for potting soil and plants.

___[A]___ 7. Choose plants of different heights and colors in order to achieve a balanced visual effect *throughout*.

___[A]___ 8. Place the charcoal mentioned *above* inside the container.

___[P]___ 9. *Over* the charcoal place a layer of the potting soil.

___[A]___ 10. Center the tallest plant and push its roots *down* into the soil.

___[P]___ 11. Put the smaller plants *around* the edges and then cover the container.

___[P]___ 12. After a few days check that no water is coming *down* the sides.

___[P]___ 13. If there is water, remove the cover *from* the terrarium.

___[A]___ 14. Then let the terrarium dry *out* for a short time.

___[P]___ 15. Enjoy looking *through* the clear sides at your plants.

B. Complete each sentence with one of the following words. On the line write **A** if it is used as an adverb or **P** if it is used as a preposition.

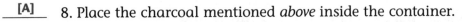

inside   into   off   on   up

___[A]___ 1. You can set ____[up]____ a terrarium inside a two-liter plastic soda bottle.

___[P]___ 2. Cut the sloping top ____[off]____ the bottle.

___[A]___ 3. Place a layer of charcoal and then a layer of soil ____[inside]____.

___[P]___ 4. Press the plants' roots ____[into]____ the soil carefully.

___[A]___ 5. Put the top back ____[on]____.

Name _____

99. Prepositional Phrases as Adjectives

Prepositional phrases can be used as adjectives; such phrases describe nouns or pronouns. Prepositional phrases used in this way are **adjective phrases**.
Amy Tan is a well-known writer <u>of Chinese American origin</u>.

Underline each adjective phrase. Circle the word it describes.

1. The (homeland) <u>of Amy Tan's family</u> is China.

2. When Tan was young, she rejected (things) <u>from Chinese culture</u>.

3. She felt (embarrassment) <u>about her family's Chinese customs</u>.

4. There was (conflict) <u>between Tan and her mother</u>.

5. Her mother thought the best career (choice) <u>for her daughter</u> was to be a doctor.

6. Tan's (rejection) <u>of her mother's plan</u> led to a bad (split) <u>between them</u>.

7. Later Tan helped her mother fulfill a (wish) <u>for a</u> (trip) <u>to China</u>.

8. The (trip) <u>with her mother</u> was a (revelation) <u>to Tan</u>.

9. The trip gave her a new (perspective) <u>on China and her mother's difficult life there</u>.

10. Tan's (interest) <u>in China</u> grew.

11. She began to write (stories) <u>about China and Chinese Americans</u>.

12. The (success) <u>of her first novel</u> made Tan famous.

13. The (title) <u>of the book</u> was *The Joy Luck Club*.

14. It describes the (relationship) <u>between Chinese-born mothers and their American-born daughters</u>.

15. The book tells the (stories) <u>of four mothers and four daughters</u>.

16. (Events) <u>in the book</u> reflect (jumps) <u>in time</u>.

17. It includes dramatic (tales) <u>of the Chinese mothers' early lives</u>.

18. Tan has also written several (books) <u>for young readers</u>.

19. (One) <u>of these</u> is *The Moon Lady*.

20. It retells (some) <u>of the</u> (stories) <u>from *The Joy Luck Club*</u>.

 Amy Tan's trip to China helped her to understand and respect her mother. Give an example of how you show respect to your parents.

Name _____

100. Prepositional Phrases as Adverbs

> Prepositional phrases can be used as adverbs; such phrases describe verbs, adjectives, or other adverbs. Prepositional phrases used in this way are **adverb phrases**.
> **Mosquitoes feed on blood and other liquids.**

A. Circle the word(s) that each *italicized* adverb phrase describes. On the line write **V** if the word described is a verb, **Adj** if the word is an adjective, or **Adv** if it is an adverb.

___[V]___ 1. People (view) mosquitoes *as pests.*

___[V]___ 2. Malaria and yellow fever (are spread) *by mosquitoes.*

___[Adj]___ 3. Not all kinds of mosquitoes, however, are actually (responsible) *for the spread* of disease.

___[Adj]___ 4. Most people are (allergic) *to mosquitoes' saliva.*

___[Adv]___ 5. The reaction to the saliva from a bite is usually strong (enough) *for the production* of a welt.

B. Underline each adverb phrase. Circle the word it describes.

1. Mosquitoes (develop) through four stages.

2. They (begin) life as eggs.

3. They (go) from a larva stage to a pupa stage.

4. After those stages they (become) adults.

5. Many mosquitoes (lay) eggs on stagnant water.

6. A mosquito egg (hatches) quickly into a larva.

7. A mosquito larva (is shaped) like a comma.

8. Larvae (grow) rapidly during hot summer months and become pupae.

9. Adult mosquitoes (emerge) from the pupae within seven days.

10. At this stage, adult mosquitoes (mate.)

11. The female mosquito (needs) blood for her eggs.

12. She (can produce) eggs after each bite.

13. Male mosquitoes (die) within a short time.

14. Because of stagnant water, mosquitoes often (breed) in huge numbers.

15. Mosquitoes can be (dangerous) to humans, but they are (important) in the planet's food chain.

101. Prepositional Phrases as Nouns

A prepositional phrase can be used as a noun. It can be used in any position where a noun is used—as a subject, a subject complement, or an object of a preposition. **On the Web is a good place to find information on many topics.**

A. Underline the prepositional phrase used as a noun in each sentence. On the line write **S** if the phrase is used as the subject, **SC** if it is used as the subject complement, or **OP** if it is used as the object of a preposition.

[S] 1. For protection was the main reason that a medieval castle needed thick walls.

[S] 2. Around the castle's outer wall was the best location for a protective moat.

[SC] 3. The usual way to enter a castle was through a guarded gateway.

[S] 4. During a siege was the time when the portcullis, an iron or wooden grating suspended over the gateway, was lowered to block the entrance.

[OP] 5. Soldiers in the castle fired arrows from behind narrow, slanted wall slits.

[S] 6. Inside the keep—a tower inside the castle—was the safest place of refuge for the defenders of the castle.

[SC] 7. The main area for eating in a medieval castle was in the great hall.

[S] 8. On the floor was an acceptable place to throw scraps of food.

[OP] 9. Dogs ate the scraps from under the tables.

[S] 10. On bread was an accepted way to eat soft and mushy foods.

[S] 11. With a knife was a way to eat such foods as meat because the fork hadn't yet come into use in Europe.

[S] 12. At curfew was the time the gates of a medieval town were shut.

[SC] 13. The time for townspeople to buy candles, shoes, and other goods was on market day.

[S] 14. Around his neck was where a knight wore a collarlike piece of armor called a bevor.

[S] 15. On his feet was where a knight wore sabatons, or metal shoes.

B. Complete each sentence with a prepositional phrase used as a noun.
[Answers will vary. Samples are given.]

1. _____[In my grandma's kitchen]_____ is my favorite place to eat.

2. _____[With plenty of cheese]_____ is the best kind of pizza.

3. _____[In my bedroom]_____ is the easiest place to nap.

4. _____[After dinner]_____ is a great time to relax.

5. _____[In my backpack]_____ is where I keep my homework.

102. Reviewing Prepositions

A. Underline each preposition. Circle its object(s).

1. Pecos Bill is a cowboy of (legend.)

2. Many elaborate stories about his cowboy (skills) have been made up.

3. As a tiny (baby,) Pecos Bill supposedly used a horseshoe as a teething (ring.)

4. The baby Bill fell from his parents' (wagon) and was lost in the (wilderness.)

5. He was raised by (coyotes.)

6. At a young (age,) he saw a cowboy and dreamt of a cowboy (life.)

7. He eventually joined a group of (cowboys) and soon distinguished himself through his (courage) and (cleverness.)

8. He is credited with the (invention) of the (lasso.)

9. Cowboys threw lassos around (cattle) to catch and control the animals.

B. Underline the correct word in parentheses.

10. Pecos Bill differed (from   with) other cowboys; he was faster and stronger than they were.

11. (Beside   Besides) his amazing strength, Bill also had intelligence and a daring spirit.

12. Bill lassoed and jumped on a rain cloud—which made the cloud angry (with   at) Bill.

13. The cloud bucked up and down (as if   like) it were a huge bucking bronco.

14. Bill got (off   off of) the rain cloud only after the cloud released its water onto the dry land.

C. On the line write **A** if the *italicized* word is used as an adverb or **P** if it is used as a preposition.

___[P]___ 15. Pecos Bill sat *on* the rain cloud.

___[A]___ 16. He was able to stay *on* for a long time.

___[P]___ 17. Bill rode the cloud clear *across* Texas.

___[A]___ 18. He bounced *up* and down.

___[A]___ 19. But the cloud couldn't throw him *off.*

Prepositions

CONTINUED

109

Name _____

D. On the line write **Adj** if the *italicized* prepositional phrase is used as an adjective, **Adv** if it is used as an adverb, or **N** if it is used as a noun.

[N] 20. *In a coyote den* was an early home of young Pecos Bill.

[Adv] 21. Later Bill left *for a nearby cowboy camp.*

[Adj] 22. On the way he caught sight *of a huge mountain lion.*

[Adv] 23. Bill was a bit frightened *by it.*

[Adv] 24. Suddenly the lion jumped *onto Bill's back.*

[Adj] 25. The lion wanted a fight *with Bill.*

[Adv] 26. A fierce fight continued *for hours and hours;* both Bill and the lion were too stubborn to give in.

[Adv] 27. Finally the exhausted lion surrendered *to Bill.*

[Adj] 28. Bill's request *for a ride* surprised the lion.

E. Underline each prepositional phrase. Above it write **Adj** if the phrase is used as an adjective, **Adv** if it is used as an adverb, or **N** if it is used as a noun.

29. The end [Adj] of the story was funny.

30. Bill rode [Adv] into the cowboy camp.

31. He wasn't seated [Adv] on a horse—he was riding a mountain lion.

32. [N] On a lion's back seemed a most unusual place for a cowboy.

33. Everyone immediately knew that Bill was a person [Adj] with extraordinary qualities.

34. He soon was accepted [Adv] as a cowboy.

35. Stories [Adj] about him can be found [Adv] in many books.

Try It Yourself
On a separate sheet of paper, write about a legend or a legendary person of interest.

Check Your Own Work
Choose a selection from your writing portfolio, a journal, a work in progress, an assignment from another class, or a letter. Revise it, applying the skills you have learned. This checklist will help you.

✔ Have you used prepositional phrases to add details to your sentences?

✔ Have you correctly used commonly confused prepositions, such as *beside, besides; between, among; differ with, differ on, differ from; angry at, angry with;* and *from* and *off?*

✔ Have you correctly used *like* as a preposition and *as if* as a conjunction?

Prepositions

Name _____

103. Declarative and Interrogative Sentences

A **declarative sentence** makes a statement. A declarative sentence ends with a period.

The Great Wall of China is one of the wonders of the world.

An **interrogative sentence** asks a question. An interrogative sentence ends with a question mark.

When was the Great Wall built?

Decide whether each sentence is declarative or interrogative.
Write your answer on the line. Add the correct end punctuation.

[interrogative] 1. When did construction of the Great Wall begin?

[declarative] 2. In the seventh century BC there were many warring states in China.

[declarative] 3. Each state built walls to keep out its enemies.

[declarative] 4. In 221 BC China was united under the emperor Shi Huangdi.

[declarative] 5. He restored the old walls and linked them with new construction.

[declarative] 6. The resulting wall was about 3,000 miles long.

[interrogative] 7. What was the wall made of?

[declarative] 8. Some parts of the Shi Huangdi wall are dry-laid stone.

[declarative] 9. Other parts are formed from layers of tightly packed earth.

[interrogative] 10. How long did this wall survive?

[declarative] 11. In 206 BC the Qin dynasty was overthrown.

[declarative] 12. The wall started to fall apart.

[interrogative] 13. Who rebuilt it?

[declarative] 14. In 206 BC the Han dynasty rose to power.

[declarative] 15. The emperor Han Wudi repaired the crumbling walls.

[declarative] 16. He extended the wall another 300 miles into the Gobi Desert.

[declarative] 17. Beacon towers were added to the walls.

[interrogative] 18. What were the towers for?

[declarative] 19. Columns of smoke from the towers warned of enemy attacks.

[declarative] 20. The beacons relayed messages faster than a man on horseback could.

104. Imperative and Exclamatory Sentences

> An **imperative sentence** gives a command or makes a request.
> An imperative sentence usually ends with a period.
>
> **Explain how the eye works.**
>
> An **exclamatory sentence** expresses a strong emotion.
> An exclamatory sentence ends with an exclamation mark.
>
> **That's impossible!**

A. Underline the sentences that are imperative.

1. <u>Place a glass of water on a table.</u>
2. <u>Stand a pencil behind the glass of water.</u>
3. <u>Look through the glass.</u>
4. You will see an image with two pencils.
5. <u>Close your left eye.</u>
6. The right-hand pencil will disappear.
7. What happens when you open your left eye and close your right eye?
8. The water acts as a cylindrical lens.
9. Each eye sees the image at a different angle.
10. <u>Try the experiment with containers of other shapes.</u>

B. Decide whether each sentence is imperative or exclamatory. Write your answer on the line. Add the correct end punctuation.

___[imperative]___ 1. Fill a shallow dish with water.

___[imperative]___ 2. Rest a flat mirror at an angle in the dish.

___[exclamatory]___ 3. Be careful!

___[imperative]___ 4. Position the dish so that sunlight hits the mirror.

___[imperative]___ 5. Hold a sheet of white paper in front of the mirror.

___[imperative]___ 6. Move the paper until you see a rainbow.

___[imperative]___ 7. Adjust the angle of the mirror if necessary.

___[exclamatory]___ 8. How amazing that is!

___[imperative]___ 9. Fasten the mirror in position with some modeling clay.

___[imperative]___ 10. Show your prism to your friends.

Sentences

Name _____

105. Simple Subjects and Simple Predicates

A sentence has a subject and a predicate. The **simple subject** is the noun or pronoun that names the person, place, or thing that the sentence is about. The **simple predicate** is the verb that tells what the subject does or is.

SIMPLE SUBJECT

Engineers

Chinese <u>engineers</u>

Chinese <u>engineers</u> of the Ming dynasty

SIMPLE PREDICATE

<u>build</u>.

<u>built</u> the Great Wall.

<u>built</u> many miles of the Great Wall.

A. Write the simple subject and the simple predicate of each sentence in the appropriate column.

	SIMPLE SUBJECT	SIMPLE PREDICATE
1. The Ming ruled China from 1368 to 1644.	[Ming]	[ruled]
2. Ming artists created beautiful porcelain.	[artists]	[created]
3. Chinese blue-and-white porcelain amazed Europeans.	[porcelain]	[amazed]
4. Ming trading ships sailed the seas.	[ships]	[sailed]
5. The ships carried tea, porcelain, silk, and spices.	[ships]	[carried]
6. The new drink became the rage in Europe.	[drink]	[became]
7. Ming engineers improved brick-making technology.	[engineers]	[improved]
8. Their bricks are as strong as modern masonry.	[bricks]	[are]
9. The Ming wall snakes across difficult terrain.	[wall]	[snakes]
10. The work of the Ming dwarfed earlier accomplishments.	[work]	[dwarfed]

B. Draw one line under the simple subject. Draw two lines under the simple predicate.

1. During the Tang dynasty (618–906) the <u>Chinese</u> <u>made</u> the first true porcelain.

2. A <u>potter</u> <u>shapes</u> pieces of porcelain on a potter's wheel.

3. Porcelain <u>workers</u> <u>decorate</u> the pieces in a variety of ways.

4. Surface <u>modification</u> <u>includes</u> carving, perforating, or embossing a piece.

5. Many <u>museums</u> <u>display</u> early Chinese porcelain.

Sentences

113

106. Complete Subjects and Complete Predicates

The **complete subject** of a sentence is the simple subject with all the words that describe it. The **complete predicate** of a sentence is the simple predicate with all the words that describe it.

COMPLETE SUBJECT
The 1900 Galveston hurricane

COMPLETE PREDICATE
destroyed almost the entire city.

SIMPLE SUBJECT
hurricane

SIMPLE PREDICATE
destroyed

Draw a vertical line between the complete subject and the complete predicate. Draw one line under the simple subject. Draw two lines under the simple predicate.

1. Forecasters during the early 1900s | had no radar or satellites.

2. They | lacked information about the forces of nature.

3. The city of Galveston | is on an island off the coast of Texas.

4. A report about a tropical storm | reached Galveston on September 4, 1900.

5. The forecasters in the weather bureau | thought the storm would hit Florida.

6. Showery weather | began in Galveston on the morning of September 8.

7. A high surf | pounded the shore.

8. Galveston residents | watched the waves.

9. Breezes from the sea | cooled the unseasonably hot air.

10. A hurricane | struck about eight o'clock that night.

11. An enormous surge of water | swept about 6,000 people to their deaths.

12. The low-lying, three-mile-wide island | offered no protection from the storm.

13. Residents trying to escape | found the roads impassable.

14. The winds at the height of the storm | reached 135 miles per hour.

15. The force of the hurricane | leveled thousands of buildings.

16. Terrified islanders | strapped themselves together with ropes.

17. People huddling in churches | died when the roofs collapsed.

18. Only three children in St. Mary's Orphanage | survived.

19. Almost a sixth of the island's population | perished in the storm.

20. The Galveston hurricane | was one of the deadliest natural disasters in U.S. history.

Name _____

107. Adjective Phrases and Adverb Phrases

A **phrase** is a group of words that does not have a subject and a verb. A phrase is used as a single part of speech, usually as an adjective or an adverb. A **prepositional phrase** consists of a preposition, its object, and any modifiers of the object.

The role _of insects_ is very important. (*Of insects* is an adjective phrase that describes the noun *role.*)

Many creatures eat insects _for food_. (*For food* is an adverb phrase that describes the verb *eats.*)

A. The prepositional phrase in each sentence is *italicized.* Circle the word it modifies. On the line write whether the phrase is used as an adjective or an adverb.

_____[adjective]_____ 1. The most abundant (creatures) *in the world* are insects.

_____[adjective]_____ 2. Scientists have named only a (third) *of them.*

_____[adverb]_____ 3. Insects (belong) *to the phylum Arthropoda.*

_____[adverb]_____ 4. The first insects probably (evolved) *from primitive sea worms.*

_____[adjective]_____ 5. The (body) *of the typical adult insect* has three parts: head, thorax, and abdomen.

_____[adverb]_____ 6. Most insects (feed) *on plants.*

_____[adjective]_____ 7. (Insects) *with chewing mouth parts* are the most destructive.

_____[adjective]_____ 8. Some can destroy large (areas) *of vegetation* quickly.

_____[adjective]_____ 9. Insects are an important food (source) *for many creatures.*

_____[adverb]_____ 10. Many plants (need) insects *for pollination.*

B. Find the prepositional phrase(s) in each sentence. Underline each phrase used as an adjective and circle each phrase used as an adverb.

1. Cockroaches are considered pests (by people.)

2. They invade food supplies <u>in homes</u>.

3. They can increase rapidly (in hospitable conditions.)

4. Most species <u>of cockroaches</u> live (in the tropics.)

5. Many cockroaches <u>in the tropics</u> have wings and can fly.

6. Most roaches are brown or black, but yellow and red appear (on some tropical species.)

7. Little bristles <u>on their legs</u> allow cockroaches to climb walls.

8. One type <u>of cockroach</u>, the Madagascar hissing cockroach, differs (in many ways) (from most cockroaches.)

9. It makes a sound <u>like a hiss</u>, lives (in rotten logs,) and feeds (on fallen fruit.)

10. Fossils <u>of some cockroaches</u> are more than 350 million years old.

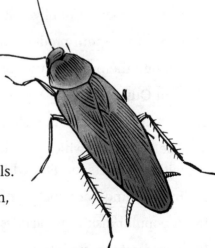

108. Adjective Clauses

A **clause** is a group of words that has a subject and a predicate. An **independent clause** expresses a complete thought and can stand on its own as a sentence. A **dependent clause** does not express a complete thought and cannot stand alone.

An **adjective clause** is a dependent clause used as an adjective. It usually begins with a relative pronoun *(who, whom, whose, which, that)* or a subordinate conjunction *(where, when, why)*.

Spain, which is on Mediterranean Sea, is part of the European Union.

Underline the adjective clause in each sentence. Circle the word it modifies.

1. Spain, which is in southwestern Europe, shares the Iberian peninsula with Portugal.

2. Famous Spanish cities that tourists visit include Madrid and Barcelona.

3. The main geographical feature of Spain is the central plateau, which lies an average of 2,000 feet above sea level.

4. Only a few miles separate Spain from Africa, whose culture has had a strong influence on that European country.

5. Spain is ruled by a constitutional monarch, who can propose candidates for prime minister.

6. The Cortes, which is Spain's legislature, consists of a chamber of deputies and a senate.

7. The members, who are elected every four years, have legislative power.

8. Spain, which was under Arab rule during the Middle Ages, has many lovely mosques.

9. The Alhambra, which is in Granada, was a palace of Moorish kings.

10. The Reconquista, which took more than seven centuries, was the retaking, or reconquest, of the Iberian peninsula by Christians.

11. Spain, which traditionally has been an agricultural country, is the world's largest producer of olive oil.

12. Crops that Spain produces include wheat, sugar beets, tomatoes, potatoes, and citrus fruit.

13. Among the products that Spain manufactures are textiles, steel, and chemicals.

14. Don Quixote, whom Miguel de Cervantes created, is a famous figure in Spanish literature.

15. Cervantes tells about a simple-minded knight who tries to right the world's wrongs.

16. The flamenco, which is a dance with fancy footwork and finger snapping with castanets, originated in southern Spain.

17. Bullfighting, for which Spain is well known, is considered an art, not a sport there.

18. A popular dish that includes rice, saffron, seafood, meat, and vegetables is known as paella.

19. Tapas, which are bite-sized snacks, are eaten between meals.

20. Gazpacho is a cold vegetable soup that is very popular in Spain.

Name _____

109. Restrictive and Nonrestrictive Clauses

> A **restrictive clause** is an adjective clause that helps identify a certain person, place, or thing and is a necessary part of the sentence.
>
> > The person <u>who founded the Round Table</u> was King Arthur.
> >
> > The sword <u>that Arthur found</u> was called Excalibur.
>
> A **nonrestrictive clause** merely adds information about the word it modifies and is not necessary to the sentence. It is separated from the rest of the sentence by commas.
>
> > King Arthur, <u>who founded the Round Table</u>, had many knights in his court.
> >
> > Excalibur, <u>which Arthur found</u>, was stuck in a stone.

Underline the adjective clause. Circle the word to which it refers.
On the line write **R** if it is restrictive or **N** if it is nonrestrictive.

[R] 1. The (stories) of the Round Table <u>that readers are most familiar with</u> feature several well-known characters.

[R] 2. The (knight) <u>who was the bravest of the knights</u> was Lancelot.

[N] 3. Lancelot fell in love with (Guinevere,) <u>who was King Arthur's wife.</u>

[R] 4. The (character) <u>who was an evil force</u> was Mordred.

[N] 5. (Merlin,) <u>who was a sorcerer and a prophet,</u> was King Arthur's advisor.

[N] 6. (Sir Galahad,) <u>who was one of King Arthur's knights and the son of Lancelot,</u> was perhaps the noblest of all the knights of the Round Table.

[R] 7. He occupied the (seat) <u>that was the most famous of all those at the Round Table.</u>

[R] 8. According to belief, any unworthy (person) <u>who sat in the seat</u> would be destroyed.

[N] 9. Miraculously, at Galahad's arrival at court, the seat's (label,) <u>which had read</u> "Seat Perilous," changed to "This is the seat of Galahad, the high prince."

[N] 10. That same year the knights saw a vision of the (Holy Grail,) <u>which was the holy cup, or chalice, from the Last Supper.</u>

[R] 11. All the (knights) <u>who were present</u> promised to search for the Holy Grail.

[R] 12. The (journeys) <u>that the knights undertook</u> were long and difficult.

[R] 13. The (one) <u>who found the Grail</u> would be the noblest and purest knight of all.

[R] 14. Eventually a (vision) <u>that appeared to Galahad</u> led him to a castle.

[N] 15. There he found the (Grail,) <u>which spiritual forces then carried up to the heavens along with the noble Galahad himself.</u>

Sentences

117

Name _____

110. More Adjective Clauses

Combine each pair of sentences into one sentence that includes
an adjective clause. [Suggested sentences are given.]

1. There are many different holidays. You may not know these holidays.

   [There are many different holidays that you may not know.]

2. Pulaski Day honors a Polish-American hero. It is a state holiday in Illinois.
   [Pulaski Day, which is a state holiday in Illinois, honors a Polish-American hero.]

3. Susan B. Anthony is honored on February 15. She was a leader in the
   women's movement.

   [Susan B. Anthony, who was a leader in the women's movement, is honored on February 15.]

4. March 3 in Japan is Dolls Festival. Dolls Festival is celebrated by displaying toys.

   [March 3 in Japan is Dolls Festival, which is celebrated by displaying toys.]

5. On National Gripers' Day in April, some people are happy. Those people like to
   complain.

   [On National Gripers' Day in April, people who like to complain are happy.]

6. National Nothing Day is a day not to commemorate anything! This day occurs on
   January 16.

   [National Nothing Day, which occurs on January 16, is a day not to commemorate anything!]

7. Cinco de Mayo celebrates a battle. In that battle the Mexicans defeated the French.

   [Cinco de Mayo celebrates a battle in which the Mexicans defeated the French.]

8. On National Fink Day people gather in Fink, Texas. These people
   have the last name Fink.

   [On National Fink Day people who have the last name Fink gather in Fink, Texas.]

9. National Left-Handers Day gives special attention to "lefties." The day is on August 13.

   [National Left-Handers Day, which is on August 13, gives special attention to "lefties."]

10. World Food Day occurs on October 16. The day's purpose is to make
    people aware of the fight against hunger.

    [World Food Day, whose purpose is to make people aware of the fight against hunger, occurs

    on October 16.]

Sentences

118

Name _____

111. Adverb Clauses

> An **adverb clause** is a dependent clause used as an adverb. It modifies a verb, an adjective, or an adverb. It is introduced by a subordinate conjunction such as *after, although, as, because, before, if, since, so that, unless, until, when, whenever, wherever, whether,* or *while.*
>
> **When humans first encountered wild horses**, they viewed them primarily as sources of food.

A. Underline the adverb clause in each sentence. Circle the word(s) it modifies.

1. When horses were first domesticated, they (were raised) for meat, milk, and hides.

2. If a group of ancient people moved, horses (were used) as pack animals.

3. Although wheeled carts appeared about 2,500 BC, oxen (were) usually (used) to pull them.

4. Horses (were) not generally (used) as draft animals until the light chariot was developed.

5. Horses then (became) draft animals, however, because they could travel faster than oxen.

6. While archeologists were excavating the tomb of King Tut, they (found) gold plaques showing the king hunting from a horse-drawn chariot.

7. Since the Romans were such fans of chariot racing, they (built) the Circus Maximus.

8. Roman engineers (constructed) roads wherever they went.

9. The roads (were built) to exacting specifications so that officials in chariots or on horseback could travel swiftly throughout the Empire.

10. After the Roman Empire declined, these roads (fell) into disrepair.

11. During the Middle Ages few people (traveled) unless the trip was absolutely necessary.

12. Although horses were still common, they (were used) mainly for farming, warfare, and hunting, but not for traveling.

13. Since chariots were no longer popular, most draft horses (pulled) farm wagons.

14. As vehicle design improved during the Renaissance, horses (were used) once more for transporting goods and people.

15. When Leonardo da Vinci made his famous drawings of horses, he (was reflecting) the interest of people in their beautiful animals.

B. Complete each sentence with an adverb clause. [Sample answers are given.]

1. _____ [After I finish high school] _____, I plan to attend college.

2. _____ [Because I want to get good grades] _____, I usually study hard.

3. I generally have a good time _____ [when I go out with my friends] _____.

4. I get up early in the morning _____ [unless I am on vacation] _____.

5. I often listen to music _____ [while I'm walking in the park] _____.

Sentences

119

Name _____

112. More Adverb Clauses

When an adverb clause begins a sentence, it is usually followed by
a comma. When an adverb clause is at the end of a sentence, it
usually is not separated from the rest of the sentence by a comma.

Combine each pair of sentences into one sentence that includes
an adverb clause. A subordinate conjunction is given for each.
[Sample answers are given.]

1. Bananas are a common food today in the United States.

    They used to be a rare commodity.

    although __[Although bananas are a common food today in the United States, they used to be a__

    __rare commodity.]__

2. Bananas have become common in the United States. Refrigerated transportation was invented.

    since __[Bananas have become common in the United States since refrigerated transportation was__

    __invented.]__

3. Bananas provide vitamin C, fiber, and potassium. They are a healthful food.

    because __[Because bananas provide vitamin C, fiber, and potassium, they are a healthful food.]__

4. Bananas probably originated in Malaysia. Many varieties of bananas are found there.

    because __[Bananas probably originated in Malaysia because many varieties of bananas are found__

    __there.]__

5. Alexander the Great conquered India. He supposedly saw bananas there.

    when __[When Alexander the Great conquered India, he supposedly saw bananas there.]__

6. Spanish explorers brought the banana to the Americas. It became a popular
    fruit in Central America.

    after __[After Spanish explorers brought the banana to the Americas, it became a popular fruit in__

    __Central America.]__

7. Much of Central America has a rich soil and a tropical climate. Bananas grow well there.

    as __[As much of Central America has a rich soil and a tropical climate, bananas grow well there.]__

8. Banana plants bear fruit only once. The plants are cut down to harvest the fruit.

    since __[Since banana plants bear fruit only once, the plants are cut down to harvest the fruit.]__

9. Bananas were introduced to the United States officially at an 1876 exhibition.

    They were wrapped in foil and sold for 10 cents each.

    when __[When bananas were introduced to the United States officially at an 1876 exhibition, they__

    __were wrapped in foil and sold for 10 cents each.]__

10. You want a good snack. Try a banana.

    if __[If you want a good snack, try a banana.]__

Sentences

113. Noun Clauses as Subjects

Dependent clauses can be used as nouns. These clauses are called **noun clauses**. A noun clause can function as a subject.

That many people admire Jackie Robinson is justified by his life story.

Underline the noun clause used as a subject in each sentence.

1. <u>That Jackie Robinson was a great baseball player</u> is indisputable.

2. <u>That he was a great role model</u> is also clear.

3. <u>What Jackie Robinson did</u> was to accept the difficult role as the first African American in major league baseball in modern times.

4. <u>Whoever was chosen for that role</u> faced a difficult road.

5. <u>That racial discrimination existed in the United States in the 1940s</u> is undisputable.

6. <u>That there were separate hotels, restaurants, and other facilities for African Americans</u> was an accepted part of life for most people in many areas of the country.

7. <u>That Jackie Robinson was an outstanding athlete</u> was clear even during his high school days.

8. <u>What the baseball executive Branch Rickey wanted</u> was to break the color barrier in baseball.

9. <u>Whether Robinson would be a good choice for that role</u> was unclear at first.

10. <u>That Robinson had once refused to go to the back of a bus</u> was on his record.

11. <u>That Robinson would have to face many insults because of his race</u> was a sad fact.

12. <u>How Robinson would react to the inevitable insults</u> was the issue.

13. <u>That he could never show anger in the face of insults</u> put a great burden on him.

14. <u>That he always acted in a dignified manner</u> was praised by many.

15. <u>That he played baseball extremely well</u> could not be questioned.

16. <u>That Robinson was an exciting base runner</u> made him fun to watch.

17. <u>Whoever saw him on the field</u> remembers his daring plays.

18. <u>That Robinson deserves his place in baseball's Hall of Fame</u> is an opinion that few would disagree with.

19. <u>What Robinson did</u> was to pave the way for minority athletes in all sports.

20. <u>That people will long remember Robinson for being a pioneer</u> seems clear.

Jackie Robinson faced a big challenge as a result of racial prejudice. Give an example of how you can treat people fairly.

114. Noun Clauses as Subject Complements

A noun clause can be used as a subject complement.
The question to answer is <u>why the Anasazi twice left their homes</u>.

Underline the noun clause used as a subject complement in each sentence.

1. The Four Corners of the Southwest is <u>where a group of Native Americans lived from about AD 200 to 1300</u>.

2. One of history's mysteries remains <u>what happened to the Anasazi people and their culture</u>.

3. The fact is <u>that by about AD 900 they had adopted agriculture as their way of life</u>.

4. Their greatest achievement, however, was <u>that they built sophisticated dwellings, stone pueblos of two or more stories that were aligned with the sun and the moon</u>.

5. A major part of the mystery surrounding their disappearance is <u>why they eventually abandoned the magnificent pueblos</u>.

6. The question is <u>whether they were driven from these homes or abandoned them willingly</u>.

7. One theory explaining their disappearance is <u>that a cult of warrior Mexicans from the south overcame them</u>.

8. Another suggestion has been <u>that the Anasazi at some pueblos brutalized subgroups of their own people</u>.

9. An item for speculation is <u>whether whatever drove them to abandon their homes also led them to build cliff dwellings capable of providing defense on all sides</u>.

10. A continuing mystery is <u>why the Anasazi also abandoned these cliff dwellings after a short period of time</u>.

11. One possible explanation for the final disintegration of Anasazi society is <u>that there was a serious drought</u>.

12. Another is <u>that the group depleted the resources of the area</u>.

13. The idea widely accepted is <u>that something terrible happened to the Anasazi</u>.

14. The accepted belief is <u>that the Anasazi were the ancestors of the current Hopi, Zuni, and Pueblo peoples of the Southwest</u>.

15. At the Anasazi Heritage Center at Four Corners, which houses more than three million artifacts, is <u>where visitors can become familiar with Anasazi history</u>.

115. Noun Clauses as Appositives

A noun clause can be used as an appositive. An appositive follows a noun or a pronoun and restates it.

> **The idea <u>that people had natural rights</u> was widespread in the 1800s.**
> (The noun clause *that people had natural rights* restates the subject; it can be substituted for the *The idea*.)

An adjective clause sometimes can be confused with a noun clause used as an appositive. An adjective clause describes a noun or a pronoun in the main clause.

> **The idea <u>that many people accepted</u> was that people had natural rights.**
> (The clause *that many people accepted* is an adjective clause describing the word *idea*; it cannot replace the word *idea*.)

A. Underline the noun clause used as an appositive in each sentence.

1. The idea <u>that "all men are created equal"</u> is part of the Declaration of Independence.

2. Also part of that document is the principle <u>that all people have the right to freedom</u>.

3. Despite their belief <u>that all men were equal</u>, many of the Founding Fathers owned slaves.

4. The fact <u>that both Thomas Jefferson and George Washington were slave owners</u> is well known.

5. The fact <u>that one Founding Father, Robert Carter, freed his slaves</u> is less known.

6. The understanding <u>that his religion would not support slave ownership</u> led to his action.

7. The U.S. Constitution included an acknowledgment <u>that there would be slavery in the new nation</u>.

8. Written into the Constitution was the statement <u>that slaves would be counted as three fifths of a person for representation purposes</u>.

9. The fact <u>that the nation did not yet live up to its principles of freedom and equality</u> was evident.

10. From an early period in U.S. history, however, many accepted the notion <u>that slavery had to be ended</u>.

B. On the line write **N** if the *italicized* clause is a noun clause or **A** if it is an adjective clause. Remember that an adjective clause describes a noun or a pronoun, while a noun clause used as an appositive can actually replace the word to which it refers.

___**[N]**___ 1. The Constitution is based on the view *that people should govern themselves.*

___**[A]**___ 2. The idea *that inspired the Constitution* went back to the ancient Greeks and Romans.

___**[N]**___ 3. The Constitution was based on the notion *that government gets its authority from the people.*

___**[A]**___ 4. The principle *that underlies monarchy* is that government gets its authority from one person—the monarch.

___**[N]**___ 5. The opinion *that the common person is capable of making important decisions* was held by the framers of the Constitution.

116. Noun Clauses as Direct Objects

A noun clause can act as a direct object.
**Since ancient times astronomers have studied
what they see in the skies.**

Underline the noun clause used as a direct object in each sentence.

1. Eratosthenes, an ancient astronomer, calculated <u>that Earth's circumference
   was 24,662 miles.</u>

2. Modern scientists have determined <u>that his conclusion was only
   50 miles off Earth's actual circumference.</u>

3. Ptolemy and other ancients believed <u>that the Sun
   revolved around Earth.</u>

4. Ptolemy thought <u>that Earth was the center of the universe.</u>

5. Copernicus, a 16th-century astronomer, did not
   believe <u>what previous scientists had stated.</u>

6. He theorized <u>that Earth orbits the Sun.</u>

7. Many people rejected <u>what Copernicus proposed.</u>

8. Johannes Kepler, a German astronomer of the early 1600s,
   showed <u>that orbits of the planets are shaped like ovals, not circles.</u>

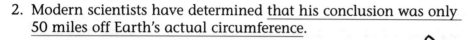

9. Galileo Galilei proved <u>that Copernicus was right.</u>

10. To support his ideas, Galilei used <u>what he saw through his telescope.</u>

11. He confirmed <u>that the Sun was the center of our solar system.</u>

12. He described <u>what the craters on the Moon were like.</u>

13. Isaac Newton discovered <u>what are known as the laws of motion.</u>

14. Newton's law of gravity explained <u>how planets orbit around the Sun.</u>

15. He theorized <u>that attraction exists between particles of matter.</u>

16. Edmund Halley showed <u>that comets have orbits.</u>

17. He believed <u>that comets return into view of Earth at predictable intervals.</u>

18. Some scientists believe <u>that the universe is expanding.</u>

19. Edwin Hubble explained <u>how this could be happening.</u>

20. Astronomers know <u>that the universe holds many unexplained mysteries.</u>

117. Noun Clauses as Objects of Prepositions

> A noun clause can be used as the object of a preposition.
> **Students are exploring ideas for <u>how they can celebrate International Peace Day</u>.**
>
> An adjective clause is sometimes confused with a noun clause used as an object of a preposition. An adjective clause describes a noun or pronoun in the main clause.
> **The students are looking for a way <u>in which they can promote humanitarian causes</u>.** (*In which they can promote humanitarian causes is an adjective clause that describes the noun way.*)

Underline each noun clause used as an object of a preposition.

1. The students were thinking about <u>what they could do as a project</u>.

2. They searched on the Web for <u>what other schools were doing as special projects</u>.

3. They learned about <u>how some schools were celebrating International Peace Day on September 21</u>.

4. The purpose of <u>what these schools were doing</u> was to make everyone aware of the importance of peace in a violent world.

5. The students learned about <u>how some schools were making pinwheels for peace</u>.

6. As part of the project, the students first reflect on <u>what peace means to them</u>.

7. The outcome of <u>what they think about peace</u> is then transferred as words and pictures onto pinwheels.

8. The students took a vote on <u>whether they wanted to participate in the pinwheel project</u>.

9. Their next discussion focused on <u>how they were going to implement their plan</u>.

10. The school principal would have to agree to <u>whatever they planned</u>.

11. The students found directions on the Web on <u>how simple pinwheels could be made</u>.

12. They found suggestions for <u>how students could decorate their peace pinwheels</u>.

13. The students decided that they would send invitations to <u>whoever wanted to participate in the project</u>.

14. They developed a plan for <u>how an after-school session on pinwheel making could be organized for interested participants</u>.

15. The decision on <u>whether a special ceremony should be held to place the pinwheels around the school</u> had to be made.

Name _____

118. Simple Sentences

> A **simple sentence** contains one subject and one predicate,
> either or both of which may be compound.
>
> SUBJECT   COMPOUND VERB
>
> **Murasaki Shikibu**   lived and wrote in Japan during the early 11th century.

Underline each simple subject once and each simple predicate twice.

1. Murasaki Shikibu lived about 1,000 years ago in Japan.

2. Many experts consider her book *The Tale of Genji* the first novel.

3. The book tells the story of Prince Genji, the "Shining One."

4. Murasaki's novel and diary are still read today.

5. She described and analyzed human emotions with great insight.

6. Murasaki was unusual for her time.

7. She had been well educated.

8. Unlike many women of her time, she read and wrote.

9. At the time in Japan, men and women used different writing systems and writing styles.

10. Women were allowed a freer, less formal style of writing.

11. Murasaki used lovely images from nature in her work.

12. Few facts are known about Murasaki's life, outside of her writings.

13. According to some sources, Murasaki married and had a daughter.

14. After her husband's death she went to live at the Japanese court.

15. Music, poetry, and gossip were common pastimes of the court.

16. Women lived in separate quarters and frequently hid behind screens.

17. Murasaki's writings give great insight into the life of the court.

18. Her long novel about Genji was written over a period of many years.

19. Prince Genji's life and loves are described in the book.

20. According to some, the end of the novel shows Murasaki's increasing belief in Buddhism and in the vanity of the world.

Murasaki lived in a world with many restrictions, yet she used her ability to create. Give an example of a special ability that you have.

Sentences

119. Compound Sentences

A compound sentence has two or more independent clauses. The clauses are connected by the coordinating conjunction *and, or, but, nor,* or *yet;* by a semicolon; or by a semicolon followed by an adverb such as *therefore* or *however.*

The Colosseum is an ancient Roman ruin, but it is the most famous of all.

The Colosseum is an ancient Roman ruin; it is the most famous of all.

The Colosseum is an ancient Roman ruin; nevertheless, it is the most famous of all.

Underline the independent clauses in each sentence and insert the proper punctuation.

1. The Colosseum was built more than 2,000 years ago, but it still stands in modern Rome.

2. The Colosseum is a famous ruin; thousands of tourists visit it every day.

3. The Colosseum was the largest amphitheater built by the ancient Romans; nevertheless, it was completed in less than 10 years.

4. The Colosseum was four stories high, and it had a seating capacity of more than 45,000.

5. The huge structure is about 600 feet long and some 500 feet wide; it rises 187 feet into the air.

6. The Colosseum had approximately 80 entrances; therefore, crowds could enter and leave quickly.

7. Under the floor of the Colosseum were passages; wild animals were kept there.

8. Entertainment was provided by the Roman emperors, and it was free to the public.

9. One of the main spectacles was combat between gladiators; another was hunting wild animals.

10. These events were for entertainment; however, the sports often ended in death.

11. Originally the victor determined the fate of the loser, but later the emperor gave the life-or-death signal—thumbs up or thumbs down.

12. The rewards for victors were considerable; they included precious gifts and gold coins.

13. The Colosseum has been damaged by earthquakes; moreover, people have stolen stones and marble seats from the structure.

14. In the past pieces of stone fell from the Colosseum, and the building had to be closed to tourists during repairs.

15. Today tourists can visit parts of the Colosseum; they can imagine it filled to capacity with spectators!

Sentences

127

120. More Compound Sentences

Combine each pair of simple sentences into a compound sentence. Use a coordinating conjunction, a conjunctive adverb, or just a semicolon. [Sample answers are given.]

1. Gold is a precious metal. People have valued it throughout history.
   [Gold is a precious metal, and people have valued it throughout history.]

2. Gold does not rust. Gold objects from ancient tombs often still shine.
   [Gold does not rust; therefore, gold objects from ancient tombs often still shine.]

3. Gold is a soft metal. It can be shaped into a variety of forms.
   [Gold is a soft metal; it can be shaped into a variety of forms.]

4. Gold conducts electricity well. Silver and copper are better conductors.
   [Gold conducts electricity well; however, silver and copper are better conductors.]

5. Jewelry has long been made from gold. Coins also have been made from gold.
   [Jewelry has long been made from gold, and coins also have been made from gold.]

6. The gold in jewelry is measured in karats. Pure gold is 24-karat gold.
   [The gold in jewelry is measured in karats; pure gold is 24-karat gold.]

7. About two thirds of all gold is made into jewelry. Gold is also used in electronic devices.
   [About two thirds of all gold is made into jewelry; gold is also used in electronic devices.]

8. Gold is found in many places on earth. It usually occurs with other metals.
   [Gold is found in many places on earth, and it usually occurs with other metals.]

9. There is gold in seawater. The cost of extracting it is expensive.
   [There is gold in seawater; however, the cost of extracting it is expensive.]

10. The largest gold field is in South Africa. Gold is mined in many places.
    [The largest gold field is in South Africa, but gold is mined in many places.]

11. A gold strike occurred in Nevada in the 1960s. An open pit mine still operates there.
    [A gold strike occurred in Nevada in the 1960s, and an open pit mine still operates there.]

12. During the Middle Ages people tried to turn other metals into gold. They were alchemists.
    [During the Middle Ages people tried to turn other metals into gold; they were alchemists.]

13. The Spanish sought gold in the Americas. They had heard of a land rich in gold.
    [The Spanish sought gold in the Americas; they had heard of a land rich in gold.]

14. There have been many gold rushes. Most people didn't strike it rich.
    [There have been many gold rushes, but most people didn't strike it rich.]

15. There was a gold rush to California in 1849. Alaska had a gold rush in the 1890s.
    [There was a gold rush to California in 1849, and Alaska had a gold rush in the 1890s.]

Name _____

121. Complex Sentences

> A **complex sentence** contains at least one independent clause and one or more dependent clauses.
>
> **The Inca civilization, <u>which was centered in Peru</u>, was conquered by the Spanish.**

A. Underline each independent clause once and each dependent clause twice.
Circle the relative pronoun or subordinate conjunction.

1. The Inca Empire, (which) controlled the Andes Mountains, survived fewer than 100 years.

2. The term *Inca* was the name of the group's ruler, (whom) the Incas worshipped as a god.

3. (Before) the Incas expanded in the 15th century, they were a small tribe near Cuzco in Peru.

4. (After) they were attacked by their neighbors, they began a series of conquests.

5. They started attacks (that) established Inca rule from Colombia to Chile.

6. The Inca rulers were worshipped (after) they died.

7. Their mummified bodies were carried into the main square every day (so that) people could worship them.

8. (Because) they didn't have written numbers, the Incas developed a clever counting system with knotted cords.

9. (Since) there was no writing, oral communication was important.

10. Messages were memorized and carried by runners, (who) could cover up to 150 miles a day.

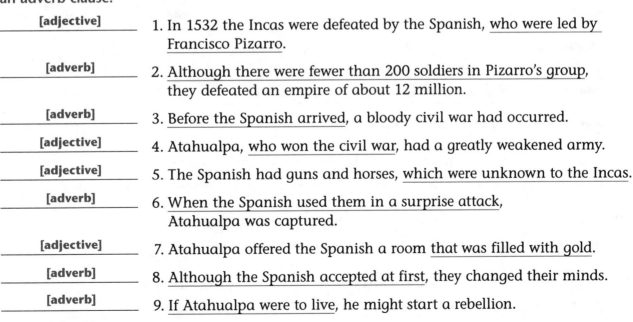

B. Underline each dependent clause. Identify each dependent clause as an adjective clause or an adverb clause.

_____[adjective]_____ 1. In 1532 the Incas were defeated by the Spanish, <u>who were led by Francisco Pizarro</u>.

_____[adverb]_____ 2. <u>Although there were fewer than 200 soldiers in Pizarro's group</u>, they defeated an empire of about 12 million.

_____[adverb]_____ 3. <u>Before the Spanish arrived</u>, a bloody civil war had occurred.

_____[adjective]_____ 4. Atahualpa, <u>who won the civil war</u>, had a greatly weakened army.

_____[adjective]_____ 5. The Spanish had guns and horses, <u>which were unknown to the Incas</u>.

_____[adverb]_____ 6. <u>When the Spanish used them in a surprise attack</u>, Atahualpa was captured.

_____[adjective]_____ 7. Atahualpa offered the Spanish a room <u>that was filled with gold</u>.

_____[adverb]_____ 8. <u>Although the Spanish accepted at first</u>, they changed their minds.

_____[adverb]_____ 9. <u>If Atahualpa were to live</u>, he might start a rebellion.

_____[adverb]_____ 10. The Inca empire ended <u>after Atahualpa was killed in 1533</u>.

Sentences

129

122. More Complex Sentences

Combine each pair of simple sentences into one complex sentence.

[Sample sentences are given.]

1. Coins and bills were invented. Previously people bartered goods.

   [Before coins and bills were invented, people bartered goods.]

2. The Chinese introduced paper money. It was first used in the eighth century AD.

   [The Chinese introduced paper money, which was first used in the eighth century AD.]

3. The Lydians began to use money in 700 BC. They invented coins.

   [The Lydians, who invented coins, began to use money in 700 BC.]

4. Much currency in history has been made of paper or metal. People have also used other items.

   [Although much currency in history has been made of paper or

   metal, people have also used other items.]

5. Seashell beads were used by European settlers in the Americas. They saw the beads used by Native Americans.

   [Seashell beads were used by European settlers in the Americas

   after they saw the beads used by Native Americans.]

6. Coins were usually stamped with a distinctive mark. This was often the image of a ruler.

   [Coins were usually stamped with a distinctive mark,

   which was often the image of a ruler.]

7. The first woman on a U.S. bill was Martha Washington. She appeared on a one-dollar bill in 1886.

   [The first woman on a U.S. bill was Martha Washington, who

   appeared on a one-dollar bill in 1886.]

8. A new copper penny was introduced in 1906. It was called the Lincoln penny.

   [A new copper penny that was called the Lincoln penny was introduced in 1906.]

9. Credit cards were introduced in 1950. They began to replace cash.

   [After credit cards were introduced in 1950, they began to replace cash.]

10. In 1999 the European Union created a new currency. It was called the euro.

    [In 1999 the European Union created a new currency, which was called the euro.]

Sentences

123. Reviewing Sentences

A. On the line write whether each *italicized* prepositional phrase is an adjective phrase or an adverb phrase.

___[adjective]___ 1. The age *of the Vikings* lasted for about 300 years.

___[adverb]___ 2. It began *in the eighth century AD*.

___[adverb]___ 3. The Vikings came *from the present-day Scandinavian countries*.

___[adverb]___ 4. They traveled *in longboats*.

___[adjective]___ 5. They conquered many areas *of Europe*.

B. Underline the simple subject once and the simple predicate twice.

6. Viking society had a number of classes.

7. Wealth and land ownership determined one's class.

8. A king ruled and had much power over his community.

9. Below him ranked rich noblemen and freemen.

10. At the bottom of the social ladder were slaves.

C. Underline each adjective clause and circle the word to which it refers.

11. The Vikings are most famous as fierce (warriors) who raided many parts of Europe.

12. The Vikings originally were (farmers) who produced their own goods.

13. Rapid population (growth,) which caused overcrowding, caused them to turn to the sea.

14. Some seagoing (vessels) that the Vikings built can be seen in museums today.

15. They built fast, maneuverable (ships,) which were known as longboats.

D. Underline each adverb clause and circle the word to which it refers.

16. After the Vikings developed wonderful boats, they (became) great sea traders.

17. The wood hull of a Viking ship (was painted) colorfully, while the craft's square sails were woven with strips of bright colors.

18. Because the Vikings had such advanced boats, they (could cross) the Atlantic.

19. Although they were the first Europeans in the Americas, they (did) not (establish) permanent settlements.

20. The Viking raids on Europe (ended) as feudal kingdoms there arose and gained strength.

CONTINUED

Name _____

E. Underline the independent clauses in the compound sentences.

21. <u>Aluminum is an abundant metal in the earth's crust</u>, but <u>it always occurs in compounds</u>.

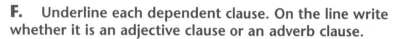

22. <u>The lead in a pencil is not actually lead</u>; <u>it is graphite</u>.

23. <u>Aquamarines and emeralds are gemstones from beryllium</u>.

24. <u>The ruby is the rarest of gems</u>, and <u>it can have a blood-red color</u>.

25. <u>The diamond is the hardest and most lustrous of all gems</u>.

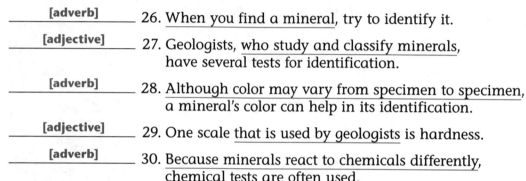

F. Underline each dependent clause. On the line write whether it is an adjective clause or an adverb clause.

_____[adverb]_____ 26. <u>When you find a mineral</u>, try to identify it.

_____[adjective]_____ 27. Geologists, <u>who study and classify minerals</u>, have several tests for identification.

_____[adverb]_____ 28. <u>Although color may vary from specimen to specimen</u>, a mineral's color can help in its identification.

_____[adjective]_____ 29. One scale <u>that is used by geologists</u> is hardness.

_____[adverb]_____ 30. <u>Because minerals react to chemicals differently</u>, chemical tests are often used.

G. Write on the line whether each sentence is simple, compound, or complex.

_____[complex]_____ 31. Magnetite, which contains iron and oxygen, is naturally magnetic.

_____[compound]_____ 32. Sulfur has a characteristic color, and jade has a bell-like ring.

_____[simple]_____ 33. Halite and borax have distinct tastes.

_____[complex]_____ 34. Minerals that contain calcite fizz in certain acids.

_____[simple]_____ 35. Minerals such as pyrite and arsenopyrite actually have distinctive odors.

Try It Yourself

On a separate sheet of paper, write a paragraph about a group of people in history. Be sure to use compound and complex sentences. Use the appropriate punctuation for those sentences.

Check Your Own Work

Choose a piece of writing from your portfolio, a journal, a work in progress, an assignment from another class, or a letter. Revise it, applying the skills you have reviewed. This checklist will help you.

✔ Have you used a variety of simple, compound, and complex sentences?

✔ Do all your sentences have subjects and predicates?

✔ Have you used appropriate punctuation in compound sentences and in complex sentences?

Sentences

Name _____

124. Coordinating Conjunctions

A **coordinating conjunction** joins words or groups of words that are similar, such as subjects or predicates. It also connects independent clauses to form compound sentences. The coordinating conjunctions are *and, but, or, nor, so,* and *yet.*

Sea otters are <u>furry</u> and <u>cute</u>. (words)
They open shellfish <u>with their claws</u> or <u>with tools</u>. (phrases)
<u>In 1911 several countries prohibited the hunting of otters</u>, so <u>the number of otters has increased</u>. (clauses)

Circle each coordinating conjunction. Underline the words or word groups that it joins. On the line write **W** if the conjunction joins words, **P** if it joins phrases, or **C** if it joins clauses.

[C] 1. <u>Sea otters are cute</u>, (yet) <u>they are also fascinating research subjects</u>.

[W] 2. Sea otters live in waters of the northern Pacific, along the coasts of <u>North America</u> (and) <u>Russia</u>.

[W] 3. <u>Otters</u> (and) <u>primates</u> are mammals that are known to use tools.

[W] 4. A sea otter may use a <u>rock</u> (or) another <u>object</u> to break open its prey.

[C] 5. <u>Otters eat marine animals</u>, (and) <u>they spend much of their day diving for food</u>.

[W] 6. Among the foods they eat are <u>mussels</u>, <u>crabs</u>, (and) <u>clams</u>.

[C] 7. <u>People valued otters' fur</u>, (so) <u>sea otters faced extinction</u>.

[C] 8. <u>The number of sea otters has been reduced to just a few thousand</u>, (so) <u>they are considered an endangered species by some governments</u>.

[P] 9. Otters are capable of surviving <u>in salt water</u> (and) <u>in cold temperatures</u>.

[P] 10. They are kept warm <u>by a thick layer of fine underfur</u> (and) <u>by an outer layer of coarse guard hairs</u>.

[C] 11. <u>An average human being has approximately 100,000 hairs on his or her head</u>, (but) <u>an otter has more than 600,000 hairs in each square inch of underfur</u>.

[W] 12. <u>Overfishing</u> (and) <u>oil spills</u> can destroy the environment of otters.

[W] 13. Otters' existence is also threatened by natural enemies such as <u>sharks</u> (and) <u>killer whales</u>.

[C] 14. <u>The sea otter has the thickest fur in the animal kingdom</u>, (but) <u>it doesn't have a layer of fat like that of other marine animals</u>.

[C] 15. <u>Otters have long, slim, streamlined bodies</u>, (and) <u>they are extraordinarily graceful and flexible</u>.

125. Correlative Conjunctions

> **Correlative conjunctions** are conjunctions that are used in pairs to connect words or groups of words that have equal importance in a sentence. The most commonly used correlative conjunctions are *both . . . and, either . . . or, neither . . . nor, not only . . . but also,* and *whether . . . or.*
>
> **Warm air <u>both</u> rises <u>and</u> expands.**

Underline the correlative conjunctions in each sentence. Circle the words or phrases connected by the conjunctions.

1. <u>Both</u> (water) <u>and</u> (ice) falling from a cloud are called precipitation.

2. The water may be in the form of <u>either</u> (rain) <u>or</u> (snow.)

3. <u>Both</u> (sleet) <u>and</u> (hail) are also forms of falling water.

4. <u>Not only</u> (snow) <u>but also</u> (sleet) can occur at low temperatures.

5. <u>Whether</u> (large) <u>or</u> (small,) hailstones can damage crops.

6. Hurricanes can bring <u>both</u> strong (winds) <u>and</u> heavy (rain.)

7. A hurricane may also be referred to as <u>either</u> a (typhoon) <u>or</u> a (cyclone,) depending on the part of the world in which it occurs.

8. Tornado Alley is an area of the United States that includes <u>not only</u> (Kansas) <u>but also</u> (Oklahoma.)

9. <u>Both</u> (hurricanes) <u>and</u> (tornadoes) can be called wild winds.

10. During a thunderstorm, <u>both</u> (lightning) <u>and</u> (thunder) occur.

11. Lightning usually strikes the highest point in an area, <u>whether</u> a (building) <u>or</u> a (tree.)

12. Lightning can appear <u>either</u> (as a streak) <u>or</u> (as a ball.)

13. Daytime air in a desert is usually <u>both</u> (hot) <u>and</u> (dry,)

14. The air in a rain forest is <u>not only</u> (hot) <u>but also</u> (humid.)

15. The trade winds blow <u>either</u> (from the northeast) <u>or</u> (from the southeast) toward the equator.

16. <u>Neither</u> the (North Pole) <u>nor</u> the (South Pole) receives as much sun as areas near the equator.

17. Some mountains are snow-covered in <u>both</u> (summer) <u>and</u> (winter.)

18. Most snowflakes are flat, but they may also be in the form of <u>either</u> (needles) <u>or</u> (columns.)

19. <u>Neither</u> the (cold) <u>nor</u> the (snow) prevents some animals, including penguins, from living in the Antarctic.

20. There are some very rainy areas in <u>both</u> (Hawaii) <u>and</u> (Colombia.)

126. Conjunctive Adverbs

A **conjunctive adverb** connects two independent clauses. A semicolon is used before the conjunctive adverb, and a comma is used after it. Some common conjunctive adverbs are *consequently, furthermore, however, moreover, nevertheless, still, therefore,* and *thus.*

> People have dreamed of labor-saving devices; **furthermore**, they have invented many.

A. Circle each conjunctive adverb. Insert semicolons and commas where needed.

1. Humanlike machines have long been envisioned; *nevertheless*, the word *robot* didn't come into use until 1920.

2. In that year a Czech writer named Karel Čapek first used the word in a play; *furthermore*, the play showed a world filled with robots.

3. In the play, robots did most of the work; *therefore*, the world at first seemed a paradise.

4. Humans had fewer jobs to do; *consequently*, there was soon unemployment and social unrest.

5. The robots in the play brought benefits; *nevertheless*, they also brought problems.

6. The science fiction writer Isaac Asimov coined the term *robotics* in 1941; *moreover*, he made up rules for robots, such as "They must obey human commands."

7. Robots had been built before this time; *however*, they didn't enter industry until the 1960s.

8. Most robots today are really computer-controlled arms and hands; *consequently*, they do not resemble the robots of early films.

9. Some early robots were used to mow lawns; *indeed*, similar robots that vacuum floors have been in use for a while.

10. Advances in technology are being made; *therefore*, more humanlike robots are likely to appear in the future.

B. Complete each sentence with a conjunctive adverb. **[Answers may vary.]**

1. People are interested in gadgets to do chores; __**[consequently]**__, many labor-saving devices are produced.

2. Many appliances do chores well; __**[nevertheless]**__, people want to improve them.

3. New houses are often equipped with such devices; __**[moreover]**__, some of them are "intelligent."

4. A leaking washing machine with a sensor may alert the resident to the problem; __**[therefore]**__, a plumber can be called immediately.

5. On the owner's command, a refrigerator may order groceries via the Internet; __**[moreover]**__, it can accept them when they are delivered.

127. Subordinate Conjunctions

A **subordinate conjunction** connects an independent clause and a dependent clause. A dependent clause does not express a complete thought and cannot stand alone. Some common subordinate conjunctions are *after, although, as, as if, because, before, if, in order that, since, so that, than, though, unless, until, when, whereas,* and *while.*

SUBORDINATE CONJUNCTION IN THE DEPENDENT CLAUSE
Because Arachne was proud,

INDEPENDENT CLAUSE
she was turned into a spider.

A. Circle the subordinate conjunction and underline the dependent clause in each sentence.

1. (Since) Arachne's weaving was so beautiful, she was famous throughout ancient Greece.

2. Tailors and weavers came from miles around (so that) they could see her at work.

3. Her hands moved over the loom smoothly, (as if) she were making music.

4. (Although) Arachne was skillful, she was also boastful.

5. (If) anyone challenged her to a spinning contest, Arachne was confident of winning.

6. (When) Arachne boasted of this one day, the goddess Athene appeared before her.

7. Arachne challenged the goddess to a contest, (although) this was disrespectful.

8. Two looms were set up (in order that) the rivals might compete.

9. (As) Athene and Arachne began to weave, a crowd gathered.

10. (Whereas) Athene's work honored the gods, Arachne's work made fun of them.

11. Arachne wove and wove more and more beautifully, (until) she was exhausted.

12. (When) Athene saw Arachne's work, she realized Arachne was the winner.

13. Athene, however, decided to punish Arachne, (because) she did not respect the gods.

14. (While) the crowd looked on, Athene turned Arachne into the first spider.

15. (As) Athene's command took effect, Arachne's body shrunk and turned black, her head grew smaller, and her fingers turned into legs.

B. Begin each sentence with a dependent clause introduced by a subordinate conjunction. **[Answers will vary. Sample answers are given.]**

1. _____**[Unless you start early]**_____, you will never make it up the mountain.

2. ____**[So that they maintain good health]**____, many people exercise regularly.

3. _____**[Though rain began to fall]**_____, he ran around and around the track.

4. __**[Because Molly wanted to improve her game]**__, she trained regularly.

5. ____**[When the girls finished swimming]**____, they were exhausted but proud.

Conjunctions and Interjections

136

128. Troublesome Words

Without is a preposition and introduces a prepositional phrase.
> **Without the right sunlight, a garden won't grow.**

Unless is a conjunction and introduces a dependent clause.
> **Unless you know the growing requirements for a plant, don't plant it.**

Like is a preposition and introduces a prepositional phrase.
> **This flower looks like a rose.**

As can be used as a preposition to introduce a prepositional phrase or as a conjunction to introduce a dependent clause. *As if* is a conjunction and introduces a clause.
> **As assistant landscaper, Harry helps water the plants.** (phrase)
> **He watches carefully as the other landscapers do their jobs.** (clause)
> **That plant looks as if it needs some water.** (clause)

A. Complete each sentence with *without* or *unless*.

1. _____[Without]_____ proper care a garden won't grow.

2. Don't start a garden _____[unless]_____ you're prepared to do some hard work.

3. _____[Unless]_____ a space with plenty of sunlight is available, planting a vegetable garden is not a good idea.

4. _____[Without]_____ adequate sun plants like tomatoes won't grow well.

5. _____[Without]_____ nutrients plants won't grow.

6. _____[Unless]_____ the soil is dark and spongy, you might want to add compost, mulch, or fertilizer.

7. Plants will die _____[without]_____ sufficient water.

8. Water them often _____[unless]_____ the soil is moist when you touch it.

9. No garden grows _____[without]_____ weeds, so you'll have to weed often.

10. Don't pull out anything, however, _____[unless]_____ you are sure that it is not one of your plants!

B. Circle the correct words in parentheses.

1. The garden looked (like (as if)) no one had tended it for a while.

2. The gigantic sunflower looked ((like) as) a scarecrow.

3. The old fence looked (like (as if)) it hadn't been painted in years.

4. Its wooden gate swung back and forth (like (as)) the wind blew.

5. The scent of the roses was ((like) as) that of a subtle perfume.

Name _____

129. Interjections

> An **interjection** is a word that expresses strong and sudden emotion. Some common emotions are annoyance, delight, disagreement, disappointment, disgust, joy, impatience, pain, surprise, relief, wonder, and warning. An interjection may be set off from a related sentence by an exclamation point, or it may be part of an exclamatory sentence.
>
> **What! The new science fiction movie is opening today?**

A. Underline each interjection, and write on the line the emotion it expresses. [Answers may vary.]

[joy]	1. Hooray! I can go to the movie!
[delight]	2. Good, we're here early!
[disappointment]	3. Ah! Look at the long line.
[impatience]	4. Hurry! Let's get our tickets.
[surprise]	5. Oops! I dropped my change.
[delight]	6. Great! Thanks for getting the popcorn.
[disgust]	7. Yuck! There's butter on my sleeve.
[surprise]	8. What, you can't find your stub!
[relief]	9. Whew! It was in your pocket!
[pain]	10. Ouch! I bumped my knee!
[disagreement]	11. Oh! Let's not sit here. Let's move closer to the screen.
[warning]	12. Shh! Don't talk during the movie.
[surprise]	13. Cool! That's a city on the moon.
[disgust]	14. Ugh! What an evil, slimy villain.
[delight]	15. Wow! That was a great chase scene!

B. Use interjections in sentences to express each emotion. [Sentences will vary. Sample sentences are provided.]

surprise   1. [Look! The tower is tilting.] _____

sorrow   2. [Gosh, I can't help you!] _____

disgust   3. [Oh my, that's revolting!] _____

pain   4. [No! Don't touch my elbow!] _____

impatience   5. [Indeed, we've waited long enough!] _____

Conjunctions and Interjections

138

Name _____

130. Reviewing Conjunctions and Interjections

A. On the line write **A** if the *italicized* word (or words) is a coordinating conjunction, **B** if it is a correlative conjunction, **C** if it is a subordinate conjunction, or **D** if it is a conjunctive adverb.

___[A]___ 1. Stonehenge is an ancient monument in southwestern England, *but* the meaning of this circle of stones remains a mystery.

___[A]___ 2. Scientists *and* archaeologists have long been puzzled by it.

___[C]___ 3. No one has a definitive answer about its purpose, *although* the monument has been studied for centuries.

___[B]___ 4. Many think that it served as *either* a religious center *or* an astronomical observatory.

___[D]___ 5. Over the centuries some stones fell or were moved; *however*, scientists have determined their original arrangement.

___[C]___ 6. *When* a person stands in the middle of the circle on the first day of summer or winter, the sun sets directly over a specific stone, the heel stone.

___[D]___ 7. Stonehenge clearly has a connection with the sun; *therefore*, scientists have developed various theories involving it.

___[B]___ 8. Some think that Stonehenge *not only* was connected to worship of the sun *but also* was used as a calendar.

B. Underline the coordinating conjunction, correlative conjunctions, subordinate conjunction, or conjunctive adverb. On the line identify each type of connector, using the letters from Exercise A.

___[A]___ 9. Stonehenge was built over centuries—between 2800 and 1500 BC.

___[C]___ 10. The British government has maintained Stonehenge since it began the monument's restoration in 1922.

___[B]___ 11. Both scientists and tourists are attracted to the mysterious structure.

___[B]___ 12. Some scientists believe that ancient people used it not only as a temple to the sun but also as a tool for understanding the heavens.

_[A, A]_ 13. Two or three scientists have done mathematical calculations that show a relationship between Stonehenge and celestial bodies.

___[D]___ 14. Their studies show that the positions of the stones relate to events in the heavens; therefore, they call Stonehenge a primitive astronomical computer.

___[A]___ 15. Some experts say that certain ideas about Stonehenge may seem strange, yet these ideas may have some merit.

___[D]___ 16. Many theories about Stonehenge persist; however, no one theory is accepted by the entire scientific community.

CONTINUED

C. Circle the coordinating conjunctions and the correlative conjunctions. Underline the words, phrases, or clauses connected by the conjunctions.

17. Some scientists think that the huge stones at the site were transported (both) over land (and) on the sea from Wales.

18. The British people of the time had no wheel, (but) somehow they managed to move the enormous stones needed to build Stonehenge.

19. Scientists cannot totally explain exactly how (or) why the monument was built.

20. Scientists continue to study Stonehenge, (yet) it remains an enigma.

21. Stonehenge is (not only) a monument for scientific study (but also) a major tourist attraction.

D. Circle the subordinate conjunction in each sentence. Underline the dependent clause.

22. The military uses codes during wartime (so that) secret information can be transmitted.

23. Battles can be lost (if) an enemy breaks an important code.

24. (While) World War II was raging, someone proposed an unusual idea for a code.

25. (Since) few people knew the Navajo language, it was used to send U.S. military messages.

26. (Because) specially trained Navajos used their Native American language to transmit information with this special code, they contributed to the Allied victory.

E. Circle the correct word or words in parentheses.

27. At the time of its discovery, the writing on the Rosetta Stone seemed (like (as if)) it could provide the key to understanding hieroglyphics.

28. The writing looked (like (as if)) it might repeat the same text in three languages.

29. Decipherers first searched for characters that looked ((like) as if) rulers' names.

30. The varied scratchings that had appeared ((like) as if) random images at last became decipherable.

Try It Yourself

On a separate sheet of paper, write about a mystery in history or in nature that interests you.

Check Your Own Work

Choose a selection from your writing portfolio, a journal, a work in progress, an assignment, or a letter. Revise it, applying the skills you have learned. This checklist will help you.

✔ Have you used conjunctions correctly?

✔ Do coordinating conjunctions and correlative conjunctions connect words or phrases that are parallel in form?

✔ Have you used *without, unless, like, as,* and *as if* correctly?

131. Periods

> A period is used at the end of a declarative sentence or an imperative sentence.
> **The new office building is a skyscraper.**
> **Look at the spires on top of that building.**
>
> Periods are used after most abbreviations and after initials in a name.
> **Mr. Jacob Meriwether, Jr.**   **H. G. Wells**

Insert periods where needed.

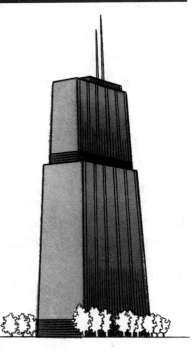

1. Have you been to the new H. M. Stellar Building yet?

2. Come with me and see what it is like.

3. Its address is 1300 E. Bristol Ave.

4. It is located next to a branch of the U.S. Department of the Interior at Third St. and Bristol.

5. I received an invitation to the grand opening.

6. It read "Inaugural Open House: Jan. 31 and Feb. 1."

7. "President's reception: Jan. 30 at 5:00 p.m."

8. "R.S.V.P. by Dec. 31."

9. It was signed "Gov. John S. Rill."

10. I telephoned Ms. Charlene Jones with my acceptance on Dec. 30.

11. My neighbor, Mrs. Clement, accompanied me to the reception.

12. There we met Mr. Roy Smith, Jr., another member of the Urban Renewal Committee.

13. A local news reporter, C. J. Hoff, was at the reception.

14. I saw a note that said "25 yd. red ribbon, 14 ft. blue felt, 9 in. gold tape."

15. There is a statue of J. P. Morgan, the banker, in the lobby.

16. My dentist, Dr. Hiromi Tanaka, will have her office on the 35th floor.

17. A line in the building directory read "Tanaka, Hiromi, D.D.S."

18. I saw a listing for our family lawyer, Morales, Michael, L.L.D.

19. A games company called TackyTime Corp. will be in the building too.

20. It was called The Games Co. until last year, when it moved from King Blvd. and Sixth Ave.

Punctuation and Capitalization

132. Commas—Part I

Commas are used
1. to separate items in a series: *volcanoes, earthquakes, and tornadoes*
2. to set off parts of dates, addresses, and place names: *in Naples, Italy, on May 11, 2006*
3. to separate words used in direct address: *Keith, do you have a question?*
4. after *yes* or *no* when it begins a sentence: *No, I don't.*

Insert commas where needed. Use the numbers above to describe how each comma is used.

[1] 1. Volcanoes are vents in the earth through which gases, lava, and ash escape.

[1] 2. Volcanoes are described as active, dormant, or extinct.

[2] 3. Lassen Peak Volcano in California was thought to be dormant until it exploded on May 19, 1915.

[3, 2] 4. Joe, you can get information about Lassen Peak Volcano by writing to Lassen Volcanic Park, P.O. Box 100, Mineral, CA 96063.

[2] 5. Mount Vesuvius, near Naples, Italy, erupted in the year 79.

[1] 6. The eruption buried the towns of Pompeii and Herculaneum under cinder, ashes, and mud.

[1] 7. The cities' temples, amphitheaters, and houses were "frozen in time."

[4] 8. Yes, much of the excavated towns can be visited by tourists today.

[4] 9. No, Vesuvius is not an extinct volcano.

[2] 10. On March 18, 1944, the volcano began its latest series of eruptions.

[1] 11. There are four types of volcanoes: cinder, shield, composite, and lava dome.

[1] 12. Kilauea, Hualalai, and Mauna Loa in Hawaii are three shield volcanoes that were formed from lava flows.

[1] 13. Composite volcanoes such as Mount Vesuvius, Mount Saint Helens, and Mount Fuji were formed from eruptions of lava and cinders.

[4, 3] 14. Yes, Henry, cinder volcanoes form when rocks shoot out of volcanoes and fall back to earth in small pieces.

[2] 15. The eruption of Mount Saint Helens on May 18, 1980, was the most significant eruption ever recorded in the lower 48 states.

Name _____

133. Commas—Part II

Commas are used
1. to set off a nonrestrictive appositive

   Joan of Arc, the French national hero, died in 1431.

2. to set off a parenthetical expression

   Joan is, I believe, a patron saint of France.

3. to set off a long introductory phrase or an introductory adverb clause

   When Joan told about her mission, many people followed her.

Insert commas where needed. Use the numbers above to describe how each comma is used.

___[1]___ 1. Joan of Arc, the Maid of Orleans, lived in the 15th century.

___[3]___ 2. Although she was a simple peasant girl, she helped lead the French to victory in a war.

___[2]___ 3. She is, as you may know, now a saint of the Catholic Church.

___[3]___ 4. When Joan was 13 years old, she claimed she heard voices.

___[3, 1]___ 5. According to accounts about Joan, these voices told her to assist the dauphin, the heir to the French throne.

___[1]___ 6. Joan wore armor and carried a banner with the fleur-de-lis, the French royal emblem.

___[1]___ 7. Orleans, a town near Paris, was important to the French cause.

___[1]___ 8. Joan helped the dauphin, later King Charles VII, defend Orleans against the English.

___[3]___ 9. When the dauphin was crowned king, Joan was given a place of honor near him.

___[3]___ 10. Later, fighting north of Paris, Joan was captured and sold to the English.

___[3]___ 11. Because there was no attempt to rescue her, Joan was turned over to a court that tried her for disagreeing with church teachings.

___[2]___ 12. The charges, many think, were made up by those who wanted to get rid of her.

___[3]___ 13. After Joan was burned at the stake, her dedication continued to provide inspiration.

___[2]___ 14. Many people, myself included, see Joan as someone truly committed to a cause.

___[3]___ 15. Although some of the details of Joan's story are unclear, she remains an important figure in French history.

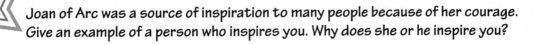

Joan of Arc was a source of inspiration to many people because of her courage.
Give an example of a person who inspires you. Why does she or he inspire you?

134. Commas—Part III

Commas are used

1. to separate the clauses of a compound sentence connected by *and, or, but, nor, so,* or *yet*
   Throughout history people have built tunnels, and they continue to build them.

2. to separate a nonrestrictive clause from the rest of the sentence
   The Mont Blanc tunnel, which goes through the Alps, connects France and Italy.

3. to set off a direct quotation or parts of a divided quotation
   "Did you know," Emmi asked, "that this tunnel is more than seven miles long?"

Insert commas where needed. Use the numbers above to describe how each comma is used.

__[2]__ 1. Tunnels, which are underground passageways, are built through mountains and under water.

__[1]__ 2. Tunnels have existed in many eras, and they have had different uses.

__[1]__ 3. Tunnels of the past were often built as burial places, but now tunnels are often built as roadways.

__[2]__ 4. The pyramids, which were used as tombs, had secret tunnels to burial chambers.

__[2]__ 5. Many tunnels were built by the ancient Romans, who used them to carry water to the city.

__[2]__ 6. The name for such a tunnel was aqueduct, which comes from the Latin words for *water* and *carry*.

__[1]__ 7. Medieval castles were designed to keep invaders out, yet some had secret tunnels for escapes during a siege.

__[2]__ 8. Tunnels today crisscross below large cities, where they are used for transportation and other basic services.

__[2]__ 9. Today's most famous tunnel is the Channel Tunnel, which connects England and France.

__[2]__ 10. The tunnel, which is considered a wonder of the modern world, consists of three tubes.

__[1]__ 11. Two of the tubes are used for high-speed trains, and the third is used for services and security.

__[1]__ 12. Passengers can ride on the train, or they can stay in their own vehicles on special rail cars.

__[3]__ 13. "The tunnel is 31 miles long," Quinn explained, "and is commonly called the Chunnel."

__[2]__ 14. The Galera Tunnel, which is in the Andes Mountains of Peru, is the highest tunnel.

__[1]__ 15. It is about three miles above sea level, and its trains are equipped with oxygen to assist passengers' breathing.

135. Reviewing Commas

A. Insert commas where needed.

1. Gary Soto, the writer and poet, was born on April 12, 1952.

2. He grew up in a Spanish-speaking neighborhood in Fresno, California.

3. Since Soto's grandparents had come from Mexico, he considered himself Mexican American.

4. When Soto was still quite young, his father was killed in a factory accident.

5. His mother had to rear her three children on her own, but she did have the help of the children's grandparents.

6. When he was growing up, Soto became fascinated by poetry.

7. Soto eventually went to college, and he earned a degree in literature.

8. After Soto finished college, he became a professor at a university in Berkeley, California.

9. He began to publish poetry, and soon his works gained recognition.

10. Soto has written award-winning poetry, novels, short stories, and essays for both young people and adults.

11. He often writes about the ordinary events in the lives of children and teens: playing sports, running through a lawn sprinkler, or having a first date.

12. *The Pool Party*, one of Soto's novels, is about a teen who brings a huge inner tube to a pool party.

13. Because Soto describes his experiences while growing up so well, he brings to others the sights and sounds of the barrio.

14. Have you read any works by Gary Soto, Michael?

15. Yes, I've read *Living up the Street*, *Buried Onions*, and *Neighborhood Odes*.

B. There is one comma error in each sentence. Cross out unnecessary commas or add commas where needed.

16. *Taking Sides*, one of Gary Soto's novels, has Lincoln Mendoza as its main character.

17. Lincoln's family, which is Mexican American, moves from the barrio of San Francisco to Sycamore, California.

18. Lincoln, who is in a new school, has to decide whether to show, or hide his heritage.

19. Because he is uncertain of his place in the new surroundings, he has conflicts with his basketball coach and teammates.

20. *Pacific Crossing*, which is another of Soto's novels, continues Lincoln's story.

136. Exclamation Points and Question Marks

> An exclamation point is used after an interjection and at the end of an exclamatory sentence.
>
> **Amazing! I didn't know that there were so many things to see at the natural history museum.**
>
> **What a big diamond that is!**
>
> A question mark is used at the end of an interrogative sentence.
>
> **Do you know the name of the natural history museum in your area?**

Add an exclamation point or a question mark where needed. Also add periods as end marks where needed. **[Answers may vary.]**

1. What can you see in a natural history museum?

2. Have you ever visited one?

3. Many natural history museums have a wide variety of objects.

4. My goodness, that's a huge dinosaur skeleton!

5. What was the average height of a *Tyrannosaurus rex*?

6. Cool! We can create a Jurassic scene in the dinosaur education center.

7. What exhibits about Native Americans are at the museum?

8. How interesting the Pawnee earth lodge is!

9. What does it look like?

10. It's constructed of cottonwood and willow and covered with earth.

11. Awesome! Seeing the museum exhibit, I felt as if I were visiting the Great Plains some 200 years ago.

12. Did you know you could also visit a Saharan market at the museum?

13. Great! Let's go see it!

14. What's that strange item?

15. It's a saddle for a camel, and those are amulets that supposedly had magical powers.

16. Did you know that there is a butterfly conservatory?

17. What is a butterfly conservatory?

18. It is a place that provides the perfect environment for butterflies, with a variety of tropical plants that supply nectar.

19. Wow! That butterfly is emerging from its chrysalis.

20. What a fun place this museum is!

Name _____

137. Semicolons and Colons

A semicolon is used
- to separate the clauses of a compound sentence when they are not joined by a conjunction or when they are joined by a conjunctive adverb such as *however, therefore, moreover, nevertheless*
- before *as* and *namely* when they are used to introduce examples

A colon is used
- before a list
- after the salutation of a business letter

Insert semicolons and colons where needed.

1. Dear Mr. President:

2. President Theodore Roosevelt enjoyed several sports:wrestling, judo, and polo.

3. President Ulysses S. Grant was given a ticket for speeding in a carriage;consequently, he had to pay a twenty-dollar fine.

4. What presidents' pictures are on these coins:the nickel, the dime, and the quarter?

5. The tallest president was Abraham Lincoln;the shortest president was James Madison.

6. President Andrew Jackson loved horses;indeed, he kept a stable of thoroughbreds on the White House grounds.

7. Two men were bachelors when they were elected president;namely, James Buchanan and Grover Cleveland.

8. The oldest person elected president was Ronald Reagan;the youngest person was John F. Kennedy.

9. Two sets of father and son have been elected president;namely, John Adams and John Quincy Adams, and George H. W. Bush and George W. Bush.

10. The Twenty-Second Amendment limits presidents to two terms in office;therefore, Franklin D. Roosevelt is likely to remain the president with the longest term in office.

11. James Earl Carter, Jr., was his full name;however, he was always called Jimmy.

12. William Henry Harrison died of pneumonia after only a month in office;he was the first president to die in office.

13. I have looked for information on past and present presidents in these sources:a history book, an encyclopedia, the Internet, and the newspaper file at the library.

14. I learned that in 1971 a single holiday, Presidents Day, was created to honor all past presidents;previously two presidents, Abraham Lincoln and George Washington, had been honored on separate days in February.

15. Libraries honoring 12 past presidents have been established by the federal government; they contain records and other information about each president's term in office.

138. Quotation Marks and Underlining

Quotation marks are used before and after direct quotations and around every part of divided quotations. For quotations within a quotation, use single quotation marks.

"I am looking for information on the constellations," Rob told the librarian.

Quotation marks set off the titles of stories, poems, songs, magazine and newspaper articles, individual episodes within television series, and radio programs.

The librarian replied, "The magazine article 'Seeing Stars' is a good resource."

Titles of books, magazines, newspapers, movies, and works of art are usually printed in italics. When these titles are handwritten, they are underlined.

My Dad reads the <u>New York Times</u> on his way to work.

Insert quotation marks, punctuation marks, and underlining where needed.

1. Josh said,"I need to find information on mummies for my report."

2. "I have some research to do on astronomy,"replied Rob,"and I want to get some information on snowboarding."

3. "So let's go to the library together,"Josh suggested.

4. Josh found a book on mummies called <u>Mummies in Ancient Egypt</u>.

5. Rob found an article on snowboarding in the magazine <u>Sports Illustrated for Kids</u>.

6. He also found"Extreme Sports"in <u>Sports Today</u>.

7. Josh noticed that there was a TV show titled <u>Ancient Mummies</u> available on video.

8. "May I take out videos?"Josh asked the librarian.

9. "Yes, you may,"the librarian answered,"but some of them have a dollar fee."

10. Josh noticed a novel called <u>The Egypt Game</u>.

11. "The novel is about two children who get involved in an exciting game,"said a librarian.

12. "Where can I check out books?"asked Rob.

13. Rob selected the book of short stories that contained"Baseball in April"by Gary Soto.

14. "Let's watch the baseball game on TV,"suggested Rob.

15. Josh answered,"I have to finish my report on Alfred Noyes's poem'The Highwayman'for English."

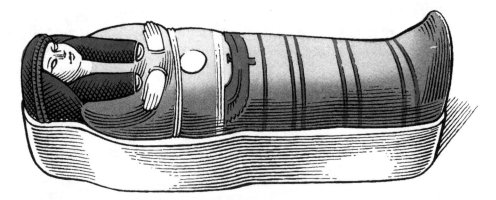

Name _____

139. Apostrophes, Hyphens, and Dashes

> An apostrophe is used
> * to show possession or a relationship: *my mother's story*
> * to show the omission of a letter(s) or numbers: *I'm not in the class of '03.*
> * with an *s* to form the plural of a small letter or of a capital letter that might be mistaken for a word: *There are two s's in my name. The A's on the poster should be blue.*
>
> A hyphen is used
> * in compound numbers from twenty-one to ninety-nine
> * to separate the parts of some compound words: *sister-in-law, forget-me-not*
> * to divide a word at the end of a line when you are writing
>
> A dash is used to indicate a change in thought.
>
>   **Blizzards—thank goodness they don't happen often—can cause many problems.**

Insert apostrophes, hyphens, and dashes where needed.

1. Do you remember the blizzard of '79?

2. I don't remember it.

3. That's not surprising since you weren't born yet.

4. My parents met at least they tell me this at a dance in 1984.

5. I sometimes hear my parents' recollections of that blizzard.

6. Apparently twenty-six inches of snow fell in less than twenty-four hours.

7. After the storm almost everyone's electricity was off.

8. It was really cold cold enough to see your breath inside before the heat returned.

9. My mother's story about the blizzard was in a journal in her mother's attic.

10. My grandmother looked for the journal, because Dad, who of course is her son-in-law, wanted to read Mom's story.

11. The dust-covered folder with the story had Mom's maiden name on it.

12. There were twenty-nine handwritten pages!

13. It's going to be boring, I thought.

14. I couldn't put the story down; however, the problems imagine no electricity for two days were quite serious.

15. "Mom, it's a great story," I said.

16. Well, last week's blizzard was bad.

17. My parents' suggestion was that I write about it so that I don't forget.

18. It's an idea that seems OK to me.

19. I'll be able to use it for my personal writing assignment in Mr. Wright's class.

20. How many *z's* are in *blizzard*?

149

Name _____

140. Capital Letters

Use a capital letter for
1. the first word in a sentence, a direct quotation, and most lines of poetry
2. proper nouns and adjectives and the pronoun *I*
3. a title when it precedes a person's name
4. *North, South, East,* and *West* when they refer to sections of the country
5. names of deities and sacred books
6. the principal words in titles but not articles, prepositions, and coordinate conjunctions unless they are the first or last words
7. initials in a name and abbreviations of words that would normally be capitalized

A. Use the proofreading symbol (=) to show which letters should be capitalized.

1. in social studies class we're studying the american west.

2. hoping to find gold, many easterners settled in the west.

3. during the gold rush to california in 1849, people arrived from europe, china, and mexico.

4. a railroad across north america was completed in 1869.

5. on may 10, 1869, the union pacific railway and the central pacific railroad linked up in utah.

6. there was a big rush to alaska in the 1890s.

7. gold was found by george w. carmack near the klondike river.

8. the find was near the border between alaska and canada.

9. this event is described in donna walsh shepherd's book *the klondike gold rush.*

10. the author writes, "people from over fifty countries came with dreams of gold but with little knowledge about the difficulties."

B. Rewrite each phrase, using capital letters where necessary.

1. the grand canyon   [the Grand Canyon]

2. jack london's <u>the call of the wild</u>   [Jack London's <u>The Call of the Wild</u>]

3. the battles of gen. ulysses s. grant   [the battles of Gen. Ulysses S. Grant]

4. robert service's <u>spell of the yukon</u>   [Robert Service's <u>Spell of the Yukon</u>]

5. the short story "to build a fire"   [the short story "To Build a Fire"]

Name _____

141. Reviewing Punctuation and Capitalization

A. Insert commas and periods where needed.

1. We traveled through three states: Pennsylvania, Delaware, and Maryland.

2. After we went through those states, we visited Washington, D.C.

3. We stopped at Gettysburg, Pennsylvania.

4. Gettysburg, which is in the southern part of the state, was the site of a great Civil War battle.

5. Gen. George Meade, I believe, defeated Gen. Robert E. Lee in that battle.

6. Abraham Lincoln, the president during the Civil War, delivered a speech there.

7. Yes, it is called the Gettysburg Address, one of his greatest speeches.

8. Lincoln talked about the meaning of the war, and he praised the soldiers who fought and died there.

9. Pres. Abraham Lincoln said, "The world will little note, nor long remember what we say here, but it will never forget what they did here."

10. Although Lincoln said this years ago, we still remember his words today.

B. Insert colons, semicolons, and quotation marks where needed.

11. In Washington we went inside three sites: the Capitol Building, the White House, and the Lincoln Memorial.

12. "It's gigantic," I said, when I saw Lincoln's statue.

13. We also visited the Smithsonian Institution; it consists of a number of different museums.

14. In the National History Museum we saw many things: dinosaurs, diamonds, insects' nests, and a copper mine.

15. In the Air and Space Museum I asked, "What's that odd-looking thing?"

16. "It's an early rocket ship," a guide answered.

17. On the trip I took photos with a digital camera; Dad used his video camera.

18. Lori Perkins, in her guidebook to Washington, D.C., discusses these attractions: monuments, museums, hotels, and restaurants.

19. One of the most moving sites was the Vietnam Memorial; it is a polished black granite wall with the names of dead soldiers engraved on it.

20. I said, "Let's come back again next year."

CONTINUED

Name _____

C. **Insert apostrophes, hyphens, and dashes where needed.**

21. There were fifty-five people at the reunion of my Dad's family.

22. Some of them can you imagine? hadn't seen one another in years.

23. The last reunion was in '99.

24. My Dad's sister-in-law was one of the few people who couldn't make it.

25. We spell our name Welles, with two e's.

D. **Circle the correct example of capitalization in each row.**

26. (the Guggenheim Museum)	Fifth avenue	St. Patrick's cathedral
27. House Of Representatives	(the *Washington Post*)	the Potomac river
28. (the Civil War)	general Sherman	Appomattox courthouse
29. (*To Kill a Mockingbird*)	Elizabeth g. Speare	the american colonies
30. the vatican	pope Leo X	(St. Peter's Square)
31. king Richard	the middle ages	(*The Tales of Robin Hood*)
32. (Microsoft Corporation)	Redmond, washington	the pacific northwest
33. thursday	french club	(Lincoln High School)
34. Labor day	Summer	(Silver Lake)
35. *Sports illustrated*	(the World Series)	Fenway park

Try It Yourself
On a separate piece of paper, write a paragraph about a trip you have taken.
Be sure to use punctuation and capitalization correctly.

Check Your Own Work
Choose a piece of writing from your portfolio, a journal, a work in progress, an assignment from another class, or a letter. Revise it, applying the skills you have reviewed. This checklist will help you.

✔ Do your sentences end with the correct punctuation marks?

✔ Have you inserted commas where needed and not used them where they aren't needed?

✔ Have you used quotation marks around direct quotations?

✔ Have you used commas and semicolons correctly in compound sentences?

✔ Have you used apostrophes where needed?

✔ Have you capitalized all proper nouns and adjectives?

✔ Have you used correct capitalization and punctuation (quotation marks or underlining) for titles of works?

142. Simple Sentences

A **diagram** is a visual outline of a sentence. It shows the relationship between the words in a sentence.

- The subject, the verb, the direct object, the subject complement, and the object complement go on the main horizontal line.

- A vertical line that cuts through the main line separates the subject from the verb, and a vertical line that does not cut through the main line separates the direct object from the verb.

- A line that slants left separates a subject complement from the verb, and a line that slants right separates an object complement from the direct object.

- Indirect objects, adjectives, and adverbs are placed under the words to which they relate. Prepositional phrases, which usually act as adjectives or adverbs, go under the words they describe.

SENTENCE: **Luke plays drums.**

| Luke | plays | drums |

SENTENCE: **Luke is a drummer.**

| Luke | is \ drummer
                    \ a

SENTENCE: **They named the baby Serena.**

| They | named | baby / Serena
                 \ the

SENTENCE: **I told Michael the joke.**

| I | told | joke
      \ Michael   \ the

SENTENCE: **The big ship with many decks moved slowly into the harbor.**

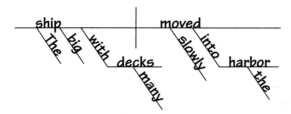

Diagram each sentence.

1. Maureen quickly set the table.

2. The peso is the currency of Mexico.

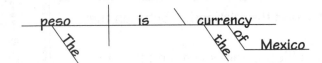

3. My parents have promised me new gym shoes.

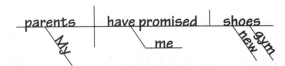

4. The children named the white rabbit Snowball.

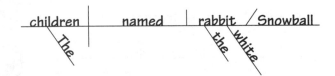

5. The cuteness of pandas makes them a popular attraction in zoos.

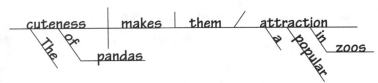

6. The left part of the brain controls the right side of the body.

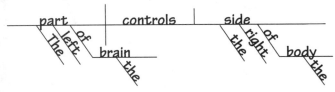

7. We showed Cecile pictures of our trip to Rome.

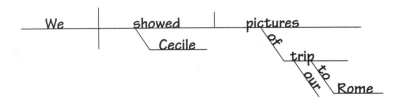

143. Appositives

- An appositive is placed in parentheses to the right of the word it identifies.
- Words that describe the appositive go under it.

SENTENCE: **Our class studied Langston Hughes, a famous American poet.**

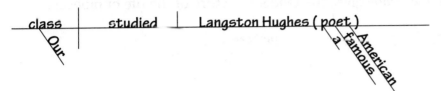

Diagram each sentence.

1. My dog, Max, can do many tricks.

2. The word *volcano* comes from Vulcan, the Roman god of fire.

3. Arthur Conan Doyle created the character of Sherlock Holmes, an early detective in literature.

4. A surname, a person's last name, is a family name.

CONTINUED

Name _____

Diagramming

5. My brother is visiting Seoul, the capital of South Korea.

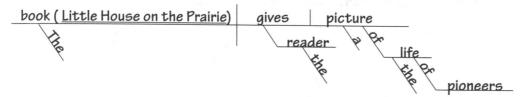

6. The book *Little House on the Prairie* gives the reader a picture of the life of pioneers.

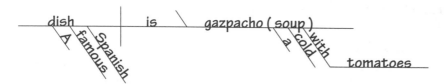

7. A famous Spanish dish is gazpacho, a cold soup with tomatoes.

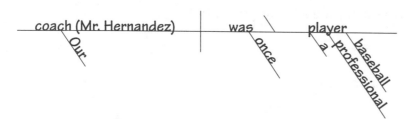

8. Our coach, Mr. Hernandez, was once a professional baseball player.

9. An early design for a parachute was made by Leonardo da Vinci, a famous artist of the Italian Renaissance.

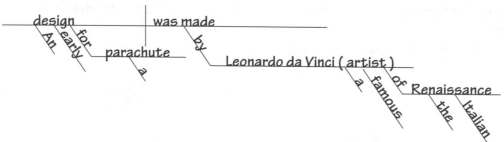

10. A kayak—a long, narrow boat—was used by Native Americans.

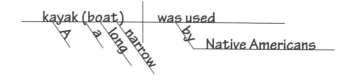

156

Name _____

144. Compound Sentences

- Each independent clause of a compound sentence has its own horizontal line, with its subject, verb, objects, and complements in their usual positions.
- The coordinating conjunction or conjunctive adverb that connects the clauses is placed on a vertical dashed line that touches the left edges of the main horizontal lines.

SENTENCE: **I worked for five hours, yet I did not finish my report.**

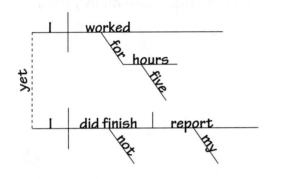

SENTENCE: **Poodles are cute dogs; consequently, they are popular pets.**

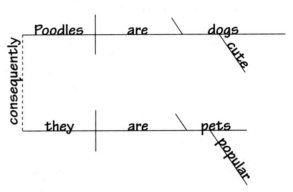

Diagram each sentence.

1. Wolves are the largest wild dogs, and they hunt together in packs.

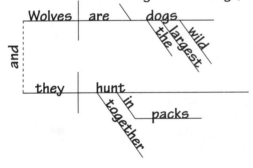

2. We were late for the movie, so we went for pizza.

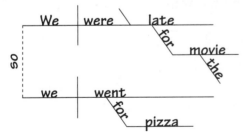

3. Venezuela grows many crops, but oil provides the most income.

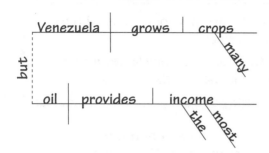

4. Bicycles are an efficient form of transportation; however, their riders face danger from other vehicles on city streets.

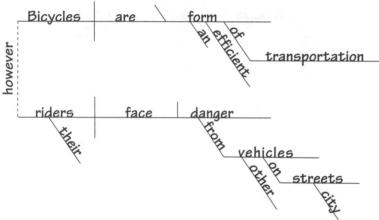

5. Hamburgers originated in Germany; however, people now consider them an American food.

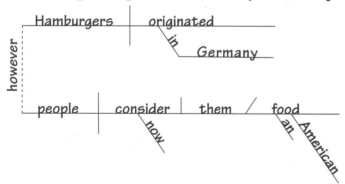

6. I wanted some juice, but someone had taken the last bottle from the refrigerator.

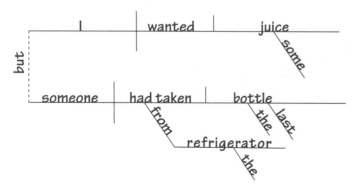

145. Compound Sentence Elements

- Compound subjects and compound predicates are placed on two separate horizontal lines that are joined to the main horizontal line.
- The conjunction connecting the compound parts is placed on a vertical line between them.
- Each subject may have its own modifiers, and each verb may have its own objects, complements, and modifiers.
- Words other than subjects and verbs may also be compound. They are diagrammed in a similar way.

SENTENCE: **I completed and signed the application form.**

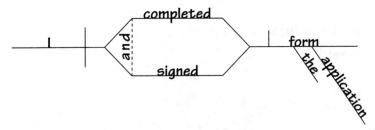

SENTENCE: **Dad and I were late and missed part of the movie.**

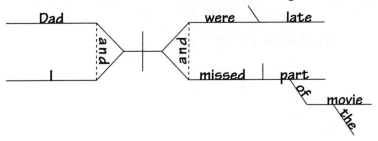

Diagram each sentence.

1. Another name for a swamp is bog or fen.

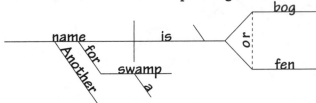

2. The soup in the pot bubbled and boiled.

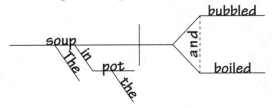

3. We met Kevin and Petra at the mall.

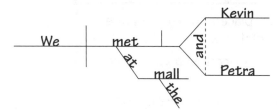

4. The mayor described and praised the plans for a new ice rink.

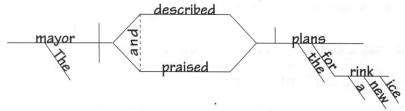

5. The eye's retina registers pictures and sends images to the brain.

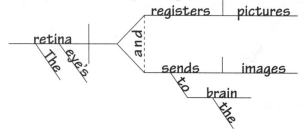

6. In pantomime, gestures and facial expressions tell the story.

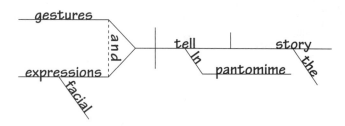

7. Her arguments are always logical and clear.

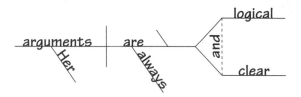

8. Abraham Lincoln had little formal education but taught himself.

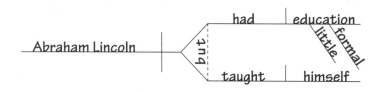

146. Participles

- The participle in a participial phrase starts on a slanted line under the noun or pronoun it describes and extends onto a horizontal line.
- Any direct object or complement is placed on the horizontal line after the participle.
- Modifiers of the participle, of its object, or of its complement go on slanted lines under the word being described.
- A participle that precedes the noun it describes is positioned as other adjectives are.

SENTENCE: **Watching the film closely, I noticed small figures in the background.**

SENTENCE: **An unopened book lay on the floor.**

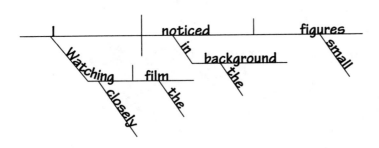
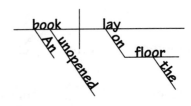

Diagram each sentence.

1. Seeing me at the gate, my dog barked.

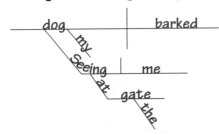

2. Having climbed the mountain, we had a magnificent view of the distant hills.

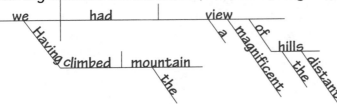

3. The American Red Cross, founded by Clara Barton, helps people in times of disaster.

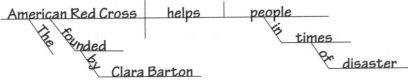

4. The heart is a pump made mostly of muscle.

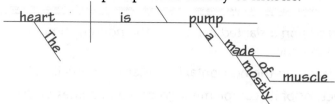

5. Rising explosively from the ground, a geyser's water is an impressive sight.

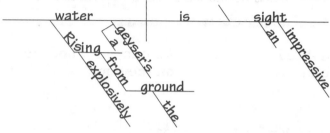

6. A biome is a community of living things adapted for survival.

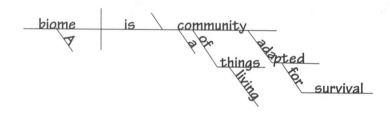

7. Lava flowing from a volcano can cause great destruction.

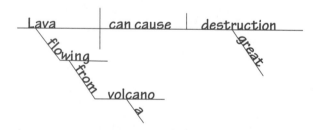

8. Excited by the team's victory, the girl jumped and clapped.

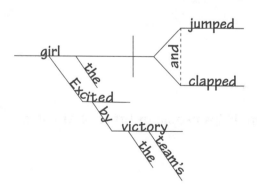

147. Gerunds

- A gerund is placed according to its function in a sentence—as a subject, a subject complement, an object of a verb, an object of a preposition, or an appositive.
- The gerund is placed on a stepped line that extends onto a horizontal line.
- A direct object or a complement is placed after the gerund. Modifiers are placed as usual.
- When used as the object of a preposition, a gerund goes on a stepped line but is not raised.

SENTENCE: **Writing adventure stories is my hobby.**

SENTENCE: **Jake is good at giving oral presentations.**

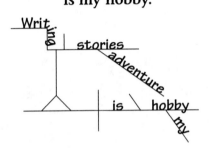

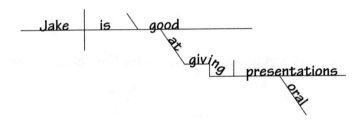

Diagram each sentence.

1. Setting goals is important.

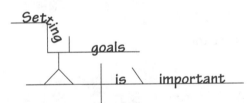

2. My chore is feeding the cat.

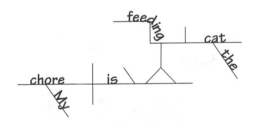

3. Mozart began writing music at the age of five.

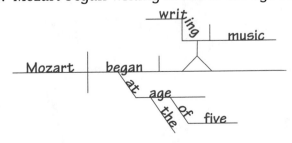

CONTINUED

163

4. The class discussed reasons for learning a foreign language.

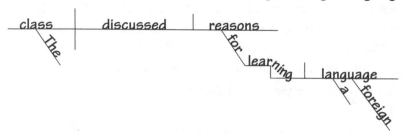

5. Being fit can protect you from illness.

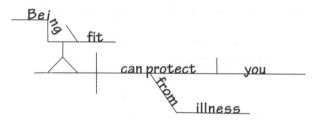

6. Ricardo got an A by studying for the entire weekend.

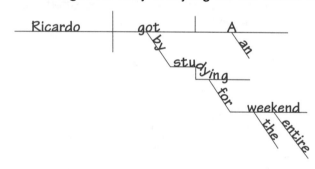

7. Our French teacher recommended getting an e-pal in France.

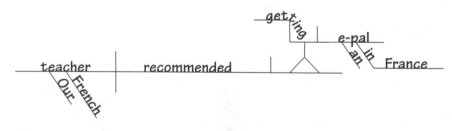

8. Bees signal the location of flowers by dancing a special dance.

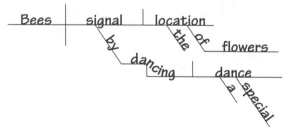

148. Infinitives

- An infinitive is placed according to its function in a sentence—as a noun, an adjective, or an adverb. When used as a subject, a direct object, a subject complement, or an appositive, an infinitive is placed in the appropriate position over a stem above the main line.
- As in a prepositional phrase, the word *to* is placed on a slanted line; the verb is on a horizontal line.
- A direct object or a complement of the infinitive follows the verb on the horizontal line. Modifiers are placed in their usual positions.
- When used as an adjective or an adverb, an infinitive is placed under the word it describes.

SENTENCE: **We plan to meet at the mall.**

SENTENCE: **We need some salt to be healthy.**

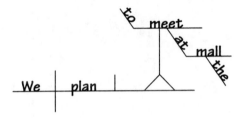

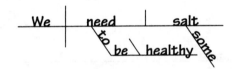

Diagram each sentence.

1. Alex forgot to put his homework in his backpack.

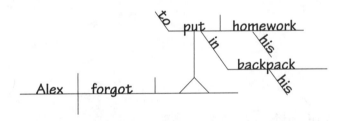

2. The last student to finish the test was Jackie.

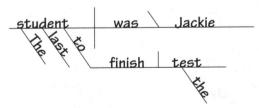

3. To become a citizen requires a series of steps.

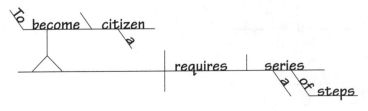

CONTINUED

Diagramming

4. The bulky package was hard to carry.

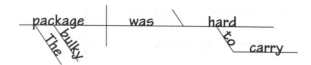

5. Martina decided to take guitar lessons.

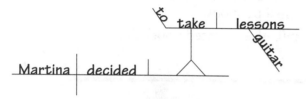

6. My plan is to join the photography club.

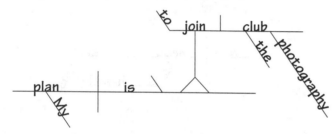

7. Cacti are structured to survive in the desert.

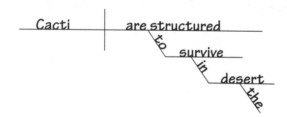

8. My hope, to become a vet, requires years of study.

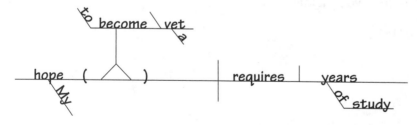

9. To move the various parts of the body, the brain sends signals through the nerves.

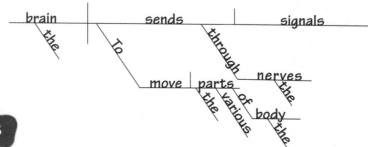

Name _____

149. Adjective Clauses

- An adjective clause is placed on a horizontal line parallel to and under the horizontal line of the independent clause.
- A dashed line connects the relative pronoun or the subordinate conjunction in the adjective clause to the word in the independent clause that the clause describes. *Whose*, like other possessives, goes under the noun it is associated with.
- A relative pronoun is placed according to its function within the adjective clause.

SENTENCE: **I have some friends who live in Los Angeles.**

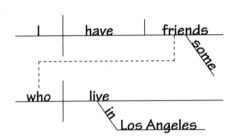

SENTENCE: **The artist whose paintings I really like is Vincent Van Gogh.**

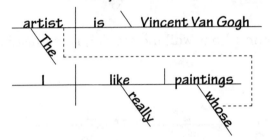

Diagram each sentence.

1. Evelyn was wearing a necklace that had belonged to her grandmother.

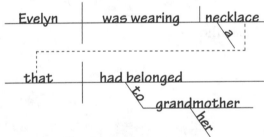

2. The alphabet that we now use is based on the Roman alphabet.

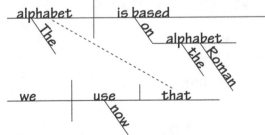

3. Fusion food, which blends the cuisines of Europe and Asia, is gaining popularity.

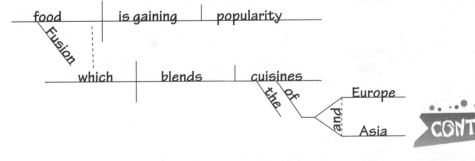

CONTINUED

4. Queen Victoria, whose reign lasted for 63 years, ruled during the great expansion of the British Empire.

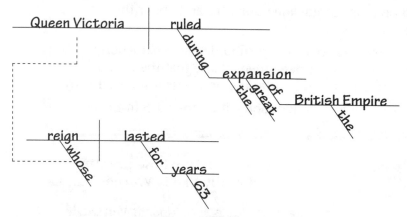

5. The man who is walking the dog is my neighbor.

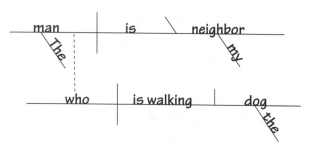

6. The woman whom I met on the train was from Australia.

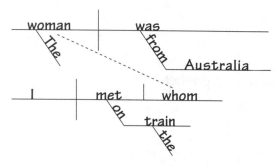

7. Crystals are solids that have a regular arrangement of atoms.

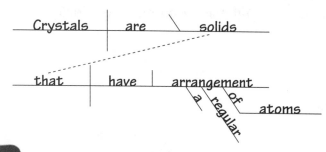

150. Adverb Clauses

- An adverb clause goes on a horizontal line under the independent clause.
- The subordinate conjunction is placed on a slanting dashed line that connects the verb in the adverb clause with the word in the independent clause described by the adverb clause. The word described by an adverb clause is usually the verb.

SENTENCE: **Before you answer, you should read each test item carefully.**

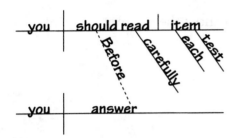

Diagram each sentence.

1. I did not understand the problems with fractions until my sister explained them to me.

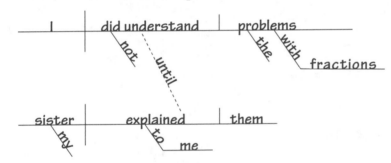

2. Because Mom forgot to water the plant, it died.

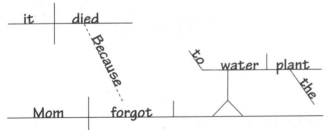

3. A rainbow can be seen when the sun is behind you.

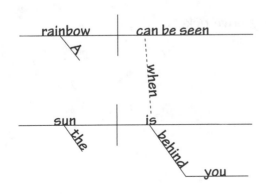

4. As people watched a silent movie, an organist played appropriate music.

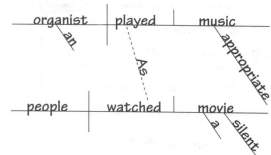

5. The stories of Robin Hood became popular because they show the triumph of good.

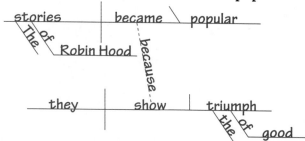

6. After the Nineteenth Amendment was ratified in 1920, women in the United States had the right to vote.

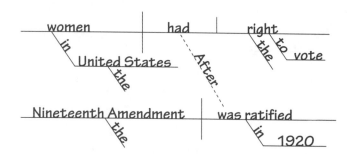

7. While Richard was riding the Ferris wheel, the lights of the carnival blinked below him.

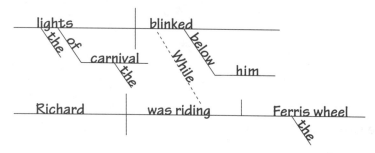

8. You will not get into the concert unless you already have tickets.

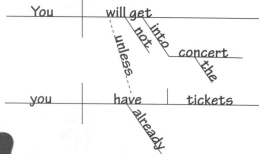

Name _____

151. Noun Clauses

- A noun clause is placed according to its function in the sentence. It has its own horizontal line that rests on a stem connecting it to the horizontal line of the independent clause.
- Noun clauses, with the exception of those used as objects of prepositions, are placed above the main clause.
- If the word introducing the noun clause has a specific function in the noun clause, it is placed according to that function. If it has no specific function, it is placed on the vertical line that connects the noun clause to the independent clause.

SENTENCE: **I have decided that I will go to summer camp.**

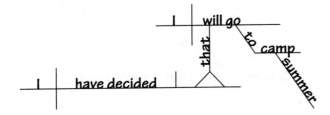

SENTENCE: **The owners will give a reward to whoever finds the lost dog.**

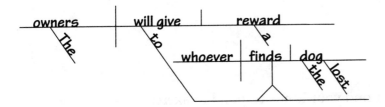

Diagram each sentence.

1. Many scientists believe that the first beaches appeared during the Ice Age.

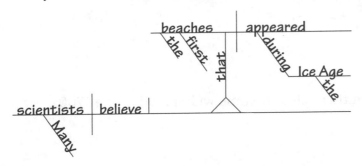

2. Everyone wondered what made the strange noise.

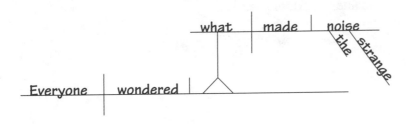

171

3. We talked about what we would do for Mom's birthday.

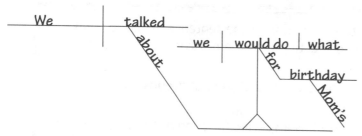

4. That the fruit is ripe seems obvious.

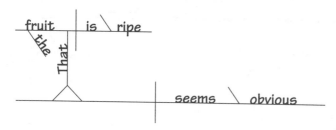

5. Paul Revere warned the colonists that the British troops were coming from Boston.

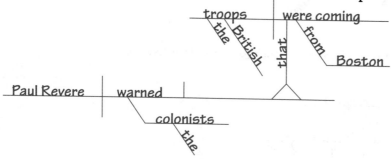

6. A sign of fitness is how your heart and your lungs respond to exercise.

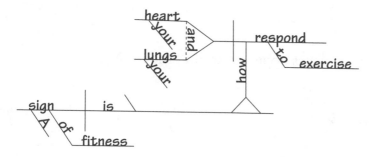

7. The idea that people should govern themselves became widespread in the 1700s.

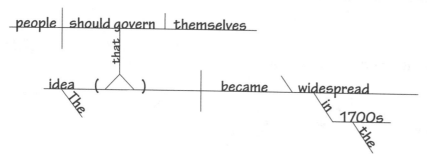

152. Diagramming Review

- Subjects, verbs, direct objects, and complements go on the main horizontal line. Adjectives, adverbs, prepositional phrases, and participles go under the words they describe.
- Gerunds and infinitives may go above or below the main line depending on how they are used in a sentence.
- Compound sentences and sentences with adjective clauses, adverb clauses, and noun clauses have two horizontal lines, one for each clause. An adjective clause or an adverb clause is placed under the line for the main clause. The line for a noun clause rests on a stem.

Diagramming

SENTENCE: **After planning the big dinner, I decided to go to the supermarket for groceries.**

SENTENCE: **To be fit depends on exercising regularly.**

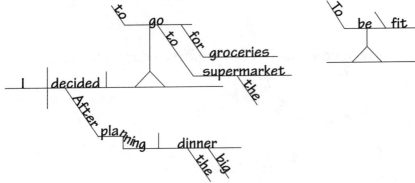
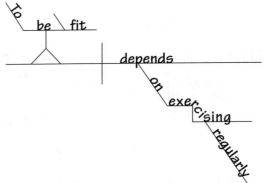

SENTENCE: **Susan can make beautiful signs because she knows a graphics program.**

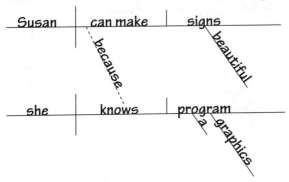

Diagram each sentence.

1. Rain falls after clouds fill with large drops of water and ice.

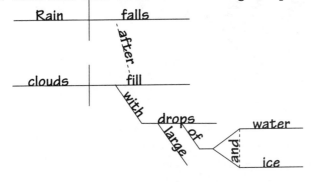

173

Name _____

2. To solve the problem, we need to get some creative ideas.

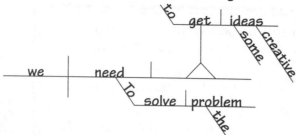

3. Touring the city on a bus, we enjoyed seeing the major sites.

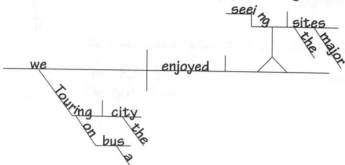

4. The two witnesses contradicted each other about what happened during the accident.

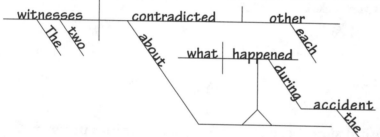

5. The dump contained many abandoned cars that were arranged in piles.

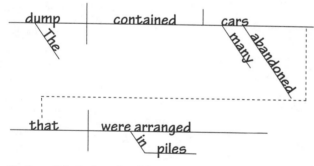

6. Before I left for the library, I checked that I had my library card in my wallet.

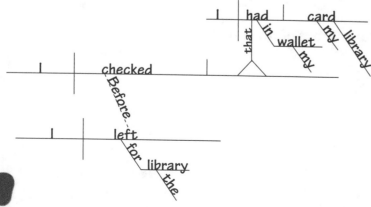

Handbook of Terms

ADJECTIVES

An **adjective** points out or describes a noun.

An **article** points out a noun. *A, an,* and *the* are articles: *a* game, *an* apple, *the* rules.

A **demonstrative adjective** points out a specific person, place, or thing. *This, that, these,* and *those* are demonstrative adjectives: *this* book, *those* pencils.

A **descriptive adjective** tells about age, size, shape, color, origin, or another quality of a noun. A descriptive adjective usually comes before the noun it describes, but it may follow the noun. It may also follow a linking verb: It was a *sunny* morning. The popcorn, *crunchy* and *salty,* tasted *great.*

An **indefinite adjective** refers to any or all members of a group. Indefinite adjectives include *all, another, any, both, each, either, few, many, more, most, much, neither, other, several,* and *some: both* boys, *either* girl.

An **interrogative adjective** is used in questions. *What, which,* and *whose* are interrogative adjectives: *Whose* book is this?

A **possessive adjective** shows possession or ownership. The possessive adjectives are *my, your, his, her, its, our, your,* and *their: my* car, *your* motorcycle.

A **proper adjective** is formed from a proper noun. A proper adjective begins with a capital letter: *American* history.

See also **antecedents, clauses, comparisons, participles, prepositions, sentences, subject-verb agreement.**

ADVERBS

An **adverb** modifies a verb, an adjective, or another adverb.

- An **adverb of affirmation** tells that something is positive or gives consent or approval: The music is *certainly* beautiful.
- An **adverb of degree** answers the question *how much* or *how little:* The boy is *very* tall.
- An **adverb of manner** answers the question *how,* or *in what manner:* Jason draws *well.*
- An **adverb of negation** expresses a negative condition or refusal: The door is *not* locked.
- An **adverb of place** answers the question *where:* Sit *here* by the gate.
- An **adverb of time** answers the question *when* or *how often:* It rained *yesterday.*

An **adverbial noun** is a noun that functions as an adverb. An adverbial noun expresses time, measure, value, or direction: Every *Sunday* we attend church. He ran six *miles*.

A **conjunctive adverb** is used to connect two independent clauses. The principal conjunctive adverbs are *consequently, however, moreover, nevertheless, therefore,* and *thus:* Jill had studied journalism; *therefore,* the newspaper editor hired her.

An **interrogative adverb** is used in asking questions. *Why, where, when,* and *how* are interrogative adverbs: *When* did you do that?

See also **clauses, comparisons, prepositions.**

ANTECEDENTS

The noun to which a pronoun or a possessive adjective refers is its **antecedent.** A pronoun or a possessive adjective must agree with its antecedent in person and number. A third person singular pronoun or possessive adjective must also agree in gender.

See also **adjectives, pronouns.**

CAPITALIZATION

Capital letters are used for many purposes, including the following:

- The first word of a sentence: The bell rang.
- Proper nouns and proper adjectives: Betsy Ross, American flag
- An abbreviation if the word it stands for begins with a capital letter: Rev. for Reverend
- The first word and the name of a person addressed in the salutation of a letter and the first word in the complimentary close of a letter: Dear Marie, Yours truly,
- The principal words in the titles of books, plays, works of art, and poems: *A Tale of Two Cities, Romeo and Juliet, Mona Lisa,* "Fire and Ice"
- The first word of a direct quotation: Mother said, "It's time for my favorite television program."
- Titles when used in direct address as substitutes for the names of persons: Thank you, Professor.
- North, East, South, West when they refer to sections of the country or the world. They are not capitalized when they refer to directions: the old West. He drove west on Main Street.
- The pronoun *I*
- Names referring to the deity or to sacred books: God, the Bible
- Two-letter state postal abbreviations: MA, NY, CA

CLAUSES

A **clause** is a group of related words that contains a subject and predicate.

A **dependent clause** does not express a complete thought and cannot stand alone. A dependent clause, together with an independent clause, forms a complex sentence.

- An **adjective clause** is a dependent clause used as an adjective. An adjective clause is usually introduced by a relative pronoun, such as *who, whom, which, whose,* or *that:* The roses *that he bought* were yellow.

- An **adverb clause** is a dependent clause used as an adverb. An adverb clause is usually introduced by a subordinate conjunction such as *after, although, as, because, before, for, since, that, though, unless, until, when, where,* or *while: After we had canoed down the river,* we went to a clambake on the beach.

- A **noun clause** is a dependent clause used as a noun. Most noun clauses begin with an introductory word such as *that, who, whom, whoever, whomever, how, why, when, whether, what, where,* or *whatever: That he was late* disappointed me.

An **independent clause** expresses a complete thought. An independent clause can stand alone as a sentence.

A **nonrestrictive clause** is a dependent clause that adds information about a person, place, or thing, but it is not necessary to the meaning of the sentence. A nonrestrictive clause is separated from the rest of the sentence by commas: New York City, *which is located on the eastern seaboard,* contains many skyscrapers.

A **restrictive clause** is a dependent clause that points out or identifies a certain person, place, or thing. A restrictive clause cannot be omitted without changing the meaning of a sentence: The girl *who runs fastest* will win the prize.

See also **sentences.**

COMPARISONS

Many adjectives and adverbs can be used to compare two or more persons, places, things, or actions.

- The **positive degree** describes one or more persons, places, things, or actions: The *tall* boy ran *fast.*

- The **comparative degree** compares two persons, places, things, or actions. Form comparatives by adding *-er* to the positive degree or by putting *more* or *less* before the positive degree: The *younger* child cried *more sadly.*

- The **superlative degree** compares three or more persons, places, things, or actions. Form superlatives by adding *-est* to the positive degree or by putting *most* or *least* before the positive degree: The *tallest* boy ran *most quickly.*

Few, fewer, and *fewest* are used to compare count nouns. *Little, less,* and *least* are used to compare noncount nouns: *few* dimes, *little* money.

Farther and *further* are used both as adverbs and as adjectives. *Farther* refers to distance; *further* denotes an addition: She went *farther* into the forest. *Further* research is necessary.

Comparisons with *as . . . as* may be made in positive or negative sentences. Comparisons with *so . . . as* may be made only in negative sentences. *As* is never used with *equally* in a comparison: Bill is *as* tall *as* Kelly. John cannot run *so* fast *as* Mike.

The conjunctions *than* and *as* are used to join clauses to make comparisons. Often part of the second clause is omitted. The omitted part must be added mentally to determine whether the pronoun needed is a subject pronoun or an object pronoun: Gary was *as* surprised *as she* (was surprised). Laura gave Tom more candy *than* (she gave) *me*.

CONJUNCTIONS

A conjunction is used to connect words, phrases, or clauses in a sentence.

A **coordinating conjunction** connects words, phrases, or clauses of the same rank and function. *And, or, but, so, nor,* or *yet* are coordinating conjunctions: Todd *or* Cindy will come early to help us.

Correlative conjunctions are conjunctions used in pairs: *Neither* Tom *nor* Laurie came to the party.

A **conjunctive adverb** connects two independent clauses. It is preceded by a semicolon and followed by a comma: The meal was expensive; *however,* I wasn't surprised.

A **subordinate conjunction** introduces a dependent clause and connects it to an independent clause: He missed gym class *because* he was sick.

See also **adverbs, clauses, sentences.**

GERUNDS

A **gerund** is a verb form ending in *-ing* that is used as a noun. A **gerund phrase** is a gerund along with any direct object, complement, and/or modifiers. A gerund or a gerund phrase can be used as a subject, a subject complement, a direct object, an object of a preposition, or an appositive: *Swimming* is good exercise. She enjoys *cooking elaborate meals.*

A gerund may be preceded by a possessive noun or a possessive adjective. The possessive describes the doer of the action of the gerund: *My* arriving early was a surprise.

INFINITIVES

An **infinitive** is a verb form, usually preceded by *to*, that can be used as a noun, an adjective, or an adverb. An **infinitive phrase** is an infinitive and its direct object, complement, and/or modifiers. An infinitive or an infinitive phrase used as a noun can be a subject, a subject complement, a direct object, an object of a preposition, or an appositive: *To win* was our goal. He wanted *to earn some money.*

A **hidden infinitive,** one in which the word *to* is not used, appears after verbs such as *hear, see, know, feel, let, make,* and *help* and with the prepositions *but* and *except* and the conjunction *than*: I helped her *construct* the framework.

A **split infinitive** results when an adverb is placed between *to* and the verb. Split infinitives generally should be avoided.

INTERJECTIONS

An **interjection** expresses a strong or sudden emotion, such as delight, disgust, pain, agreement, impatience, surprise, sorrow, or wonder. An interjection is grammatically distinct from the rest of the sentence: *Oh! Shh! Ouch! Wow!*

MOOD

Mood shows the manner in which the action or state of being of a verb is expressed.

- The **imperative mood** is used to give commands: Please *call* me.

- The **indicative mood** is used to state a fact or ask a question: Where *are* you?

- The **subjunctive mood** is used to express a wish or a desire or a condition that is contrary to fact. The subjunctive is also used to express a demand or a recommendation after *that:* She wishes she *were coming* with us. If she *had* more money, she would come. Her mother recommended that she *get* a job.

NOUNS

A **noun** is the name of a person, place, or thing.

An **abstract noun** names a quality, a condition, or a state of mind. An abstract noun names something that cannot be seen or touched: *anger, idea, spirit.*

A **collective noun** names a group of persons, places, or things considered as a unit. A collective noun usually takes a verb that agrees with a singular noun: The *crew* is tired. The *herd* is resting.

A **common noun** names any one member of a group of persons, places, or things: *queen, city, church.*

A **concrete noun** names a thing that can be seen or touched: *brother, river, tree.*

A **count noun** names something that can be counted: *nickels, bags, emotions.*

A **noncount noun** names something that cannot be counted: *money, luggage, fear.*

A **plural noun** names more than one person, place, or thing: *boys, berries, geese.*

A **possessive noun** expresses possession or ownership.

- To form the possessive of a singular noun, add -'s to the singular form: *architect's.*

- To form the possessive of a plural noun that ends in *s*, add an apostrophe to the plural form: *farmers'.*

- To form the possessive of a plural noun that does not end in *s*, add -'s to the plural form: *children's.*

- To show separate possession, add -'s to each noun: *Meg's* and *Mike's* dogs.

- To show joint possession, add -'s to the last noun only: *Jack* and *Jill's* pail.

A **proper noun** names a particular person, place, or thing. A proper noun is capitalized: *Queen Elizabeth, London, Westminster Abbey.*

A **singular noun** names one person, place, or thing: *boy, river, berry.*

See also **clauses, gerunds, infinitives, prepositions, sentences, subject-verb agreement.**

PARTICIPLES

A **participle** is a verb form that can be used as an adjective. Present participles end in *-ing,* and past participles often end in *-ed.* A participle used as an adjective can come before or after the noun it modifies or after a linking verb: The *broiled* chicken tasted great. The cake *baking* in the oven smelled delicious. The lemonade was *refreshing.*

A participial adjective that does not modify any noun or pronoun in a sentence is called a **dangling participle.** Sentences with dangling participles must be rewritten.

PREPOSITIONS

A **preposition** is a word that shows the relationship between a noun or a pronoun and some other word in the sentence. The **object of a preposition** is the noun or pronoun that follows the preposition: The huge mountain lion leaped *through* (preposition) the tall *grass* (object of the preposition).

A **prepositional phrase** is a phrase that is introduced by a preposition.

- An **adjective phrase** is used as an adjective and modifies a noun or a pronoun: The cabin *in the woods* burned down.

- An **adverb phrase** is used as an adverb and usually modifies a verb: The river flows *into the sea.*

- A **noun phrase** is used as a noun. It can be used as a subject or a subject complement: *Before dinner* is a good time to do your homework.

PRONOUNS

A **pronoun** is a word that takes the place of a noun or nouns.

A **demonstrative pronoun** points out a definite person, place, or thing. *This, that, these,* and *those* are demonstrative pronouns: *This* is mine. *Those* are yours.

An **indefinite pronoun** refers to any or all of a group of persons, places, or things. Among the indefinite pronouns are *all, another, both, each, either, few, many, neither, nothing, several, some,* and pronouns beginning with *any* or *every: Each* wants to be on the team. *Both* must pass physicals.

An **intensive pronoun** is used to show emphasis. The intensive pronouns are *myself, yourself, himself, herself, itself, ourselves, yourselves,* and *themselves:* I *myself* cooked the entire dinner.

An **interrogative pronoun** is used to ask a question. The interrogative pronouns are *who, whom, which, what,* and *whose:* To *whom* does this belong?

An **object pronoun** is used as the direct or indirect object of a verb or as the object of a preposition. The object pronouns are *me, you, him, her, it, us,* and *them.*

Personal pronouns have different forms.

- A personal pronoun shows **person:** the speaker **(first person)**, the person spoken to **(second person),** or the person, place, or thing spoken about **(third person).** The first person pronouns are *I, me, mine, we, us,* and *ours.* The second person pronouns are *you* and *yours.* The third person pronouns are *he, him, his, she, her, hers, it, its, they, them,* and *theirs.*

- A personal pronoun shows **number.** It is **singular** when it refers to one person, place, or thing. The singular pronouns are *I, me, mine, you, yours, he, him, his, she, her, hers, it,* and *its.* A personal pronoun is **plural** when it refers to more than one person, place, or thing. The plural pronouns are *we, us, ours, you, yours, they, their,* and *theirs.*

- The third person singular pronoun shows **gender.** It can be **masculine** *(he, him, his),* **feminine** *(she, her, hers),* or **neuter** *(it, its).*

A **possessive pronoun** shows possession or ownership. The possessive pronouns are *mine, yours, his, hers, its, ours,* and *theirs.* A possessive pronoun takes the place of a noun and its possessive adjective. Although possessive pronouns show ownership, they do not contain apostrophes: The new skates are *hers.*

A **reflexive pronoun** can be used as a direct or an indirect object or as the object of a preposition. The reflexive pronouns are *myself, yourself, himself, herself, itself, ourselves, yourselves,* and *themselves:* She made *herself* a sandwich.

A **relative pronoun** connects a noun clause to the person, place, or thing it modifies. The relative pronouns are *who, whom, whose, which,* and *that:* Hal, *who* grew up in Indonesia, now lives in Boston.

A **subject pronoun** is used as a subject or a subject complement. The subject pronouns are *I, you, he, she, it, we,* and *they:* We played soccer. The goalie was *he.*

See also **antecedents, clauses, comparisons, gerunds, sentences, subject-verb agreement.**

PUNCTUATION

An **apostrophe** (') is used as follows:

- To show ownership: the *cook's* hat, the *girls'* horses

- To replace letters or numbers that are omitted: *wasn't, '76*

- With *s* to show the plural of small letters but not capital letters unless the plural could be mistaken for a word: *p's* and *q's, Rs* and *A's*

A **colon** (:) is used as follows:

- After the salutation in a business letter: Dear Sir:

- Before a list when terms such as *follows* or *the following* are used: We bought the following: eggs, limes, bread.

A **comma** (,) is used to make reading clearer. Among the comma's uses are the following:

- To separate words or groups of words in a series and adjectives of equal importance before nouns: On a hot, sunny day we saw elephants, giraffes, hyenas, and monkeys.

- To set off parts of dates, addresses, or geographical names: January 1, 2003; 321 Spring Road, Atlanta, Georgia

- To set off a word in direct address: Josie, I'm so pleased that you called me this morning.

- After the word *yes* or *no* when it introduces a sentence: Yes, I agree with you completely.

- To set off a direct quotation, unless a question mark or exclamation point is required: "We have only vanilla and chocolate today," he said in an apologetic tone.

- Before a coordinating conjunction or after a conjunctive adverb in a compound sentence: She called his name, but he didn't answer her. She became angry; however, she soon got over it.

- After the salutation of a friendly letter and after the closing of a letter: Dear Ben, Sincerely yours,

- To set off a parenthetical expression—a word or a group of words that is inserted into a sentence as a comment or explanatory remark but is not necessary to the thought of the sentence: The time, I think, is up.

- After a long introductory phrase or after an introductory clause: As the band marched down the street, the class cheered and applauded.

- To separate nonrestrictive phrases and clauses from the rest of the sentence: Chicago, which is the largest city in Illinois, is not the state capital.

A **dash** (—) is used to indicate a sudden change of thought: The boy jumped—indeed soared—over the hurdle.

An **exclamation point** (!) is used after an interjection and after an exclamatory sentence: Wow! What a celebration that was!

A **hyphen** (-) is used as follows:

- To divide a word at the end of a line whenever one or more syllables are carried to the next line.

- In the words for numbers from twenty-one to ninety-nine and between the parts of some compound words: *soldier-statesman, half-baked* plan.

A **period** (.) is used at the end of a declarative or an imperative sentence and after initials and some abbreviations: Pres. J. F. Kennedy was from Massachusetts.

A **question mark** (?) is used at the end of an interrogative sentence: What time is it?

Quotation marks (". . .") are used as follows:

- Before and after every direct quotation and every part of a divided quotation: "Let's go shopping," said Michiko. "I can go with you," Father said, "after I have eaten lunch."

- To enclose titles of short stories, poems, and magazine articles. Titles of books, magazines, newspapers, movies, TV shows, and works of art are usually printed in *italics* or are underlined: I read "The Lost City" in *Newsweek*.

A **semicolon** (;) is used as follows:

- To separate the clauses of a compound sentence when they are not separated by a conjunction: I can't ride my bike; the wheel is damaged.

- To separate the clauses of a compound sentence that are connected by a conjunctive adverb: Helga plays the violin; however, she can barely read music.

- To separate phrases or clauses that have internal punctuation: We went to Paris, France; Rome, Italy; and London, England.

- Before expressions such as *for example* or *namely* when they are used to introduce examples: He achieved his goals; namely, acceptance into college and a scholarship.

SENTENCES

A sentence is a group of words that expresses a complete thought. A sentence must have a subject and a predicate and may contain other elements.

- An **appositive** is a word or group of words that follows a noun or a pronoun in a sentence and renames it: Kanisha Taylor, the *president* of our class, will make the first speech.

- A **direct object** is the receiver of the action of a verb. A noun or an object pronoun can be used as a direct object: Nat helped *him* with his homework.

- An **indirect object** is a noun or an object pronoun that tells *to whom, to what, for whom,* or *for what* the action in a sentence is done: I gave *him* a present.

- A **predicate** tells something about the subject. The **simple predicate** is a verb or verb phrase: Teresa *waved.* The **complete predicate** is the verb with all its modifiers, objects, and complements: Teresa *waved to the child from the window.*

- An **object complement** follows a direct object and completes the thought expressed by the verb. An object complement can be a noun or an adjective: They elected Jim *president.* He found the job *difficult.*

- A **subject** names the person, place, or thing a sentence is about. The **simple subject** is a noun or a pronoun: The *man* is riding his bike. The **complete subject** is the simple subject with all its modifiers: *The tall, athletic, young man* is riding his bike.

- A **subject complement** is a word that completes the meaning of a sentence that has a linking verb. A subject complement may be a noun, a pronoun, or an adjective: Broccoli is a green *vegetable.* The winner was *she.* The sea will be *cold.*

A **complex sentence** contains one independent clause and one or more dependent clauses: *If you want to win, you must jump higher.*

- A **dependent clause** does not express a complete thought and cannot stand alone: *If you want to win*

- An **independent clause** expresses a complete thought: *You must jump higher.*

A **compound sentence** contains two or more independent clauses.

- The clauses in a compound sentence are usually connected by a conjunction or by a conjunctive adverb: Usually Jane drives to work, *but* today she took the train. She left early; *nevertheless,* she was late for work.

- A semicolon may be used to separate the clauses in a compound sentence: She left on time; the train was late.

A **declarative sentence** makes a statement. A declarative sentence is followed by a period: The sun is shining.

An **exclamatory sentence** expresses strong or sudden emotion. An exclamatory sentence is followed by an exclamation point: What a loud noise that was!

An **imperative sentence** gives a command or makes a request. An imperative sentence is followed by a period: Go to the store. Please pick up the papers.

An **interrogative sentence** asks a question. An interrogative sentence is followed by a question mark: Where is my pen?

A **simple sentence** contains one subject and one predicate. Either or both may be compound. Any objects and/or complements may also be compound: *Ivan* and *John* argued with the grocer. The baby *walks* and *talks* well. Wear your *hat, scarf,* and *gloves.*

See also **clauses, subject-verb agreement.**

SUBJECT-VERB AGREEMENT

A subject and a verb must always agree.

- A phrase or a parenthetical expression between the subject and the verb does not affect the verb: A *crate* of bananas *was* hoisted off the boat.

- Indefinite pronouns such as *anyone, anything, everybody, no one, nobody, nothing, one, somebody,* and *something* and indefinite adjectives such as *another, each, either, neither,* and *other* always require the verb that agrees with the third person singular. Possessive adjectives and pronouns that refer to these words must be singular: *Everyone* in this class *works* hard for *his* or *her* grades. *Neither* girl *was doing her* homework on the bus.

- Indefinite pronouns and indefinite adjectives such as *both, few,* and *many* and indefinite pronouns and indefinite adjectives such as *all, any, most,* and *some* generally require the verb that agrees with the third person plural. Possessive adjectives and pronouns that refer to these words must be plural: *Few look* to *their* left before turning. *Most* puppies *enjoy their* treats.

- A collective noun is singular if the idea expressed by the subject is thought of as a unit: The orchestra *plays* tomorrow. A collective noun is plural if the idea expressed by the subject is thought of as individuals: The family *are* living in Georgia, Virginia, and the Carolinas.

- In sentences beginning with *there,* use *there is* or *there was* when the subject that follows is singular. Use *there are* or *there were* when the subject is plural: *There is* no cause for alarm. *There were* many passengers on the bus.

- Compound subjects connected by *and* are generally plural. If, however, the subjects connected by *and* refer to the same person, place, or thing or express a single idea, the subject is considered singular: Bob and Ted *are* making breakfast. Ham and eggs *is* their favorite meal.

- When compound subjects are connected by *or* or *nor,* the verb agrees with the subject closer to it: *Neither* Ken *nor* the twins *are* here. *Neither* the twins *nor* Ken *is* here.

- When two or more subjects connected by *and* are preceded by *each, every, many a,* or *no,* the subject is considered singular: *Every* teacher and student *has heard* the news.

TENSES

The tense of a verb shows the time of its action.

- The **simple present tense** tells about something that is true or about an action that happens again and again: I *play* the piano every afternoon.

- The **simple past tense** tells about an action that happened in the past: I *played* the piano yesterday afternoon.

- The **future tense** tells about an action that will happen in the future. The future is formed with the present and the auxiliary verb *will* or the verb phrase *be going to:* The piano recital *will be* on Sunday. I *am going to play* two songs.

- The **present progressive tense** tells what is happening now. The present progressive tense is formed with the present participle and a form of the verb *be:* He *is eating* his lunch now.

- The **past progressive tense** tells what was happening in the past. The past progressive tense is formed with the present participle and a past form of the verb *be:* He *was eating* his lunch when I saw him.

- The **present perfect tense** tells about a past action that is relevant to the present. The present perfect tense is formed with *have* or *has* and the past participle: I *have lived* here for six years now.

- The **past perfect tense** tells about a past action that happened before another past action. The past perfect tense is formed with *had* and the past participle: I *had lived* in Memphis for a year before I moved here.

- The **future perfect tense** tells about an action that will be completed by a specific time in the future. The future perfect tense is formed with *will have* and the past participle: I *will have finished* dinner by the time you get here.

VERBALS

A **verbal** is a verb form used as a noun, an adjective, or an adverb. *See* **gerunds, infinitives, participles.**

VERBS

A **verb** is a word that expresses action or state of being.

An **intransitive verb** has no receiver of the action. It does not have a direct object: The sun *shone* on the lake.

A **linking verb** links a subject with a subject complement (a noun, a pronoun, or an adjective).

- The verb *be* in its many forms *(is, are, was, will be, have been,* etc.) is the most common linking verb: He *is* happy. They *are* students.

- The verbs *appear, become, continue, feel, grow, look, remain, seem, smell, sound,* and *taste* are also considered linking verbs: This *tastes* good. She *became* president.

Modal auxiliary verbs such as *may, might, can, could, must, should,* and *would* are used to express permission, possibility, ability, necessity, and obligation: You *should* hurry. We *might be* late.

A verb has four **principal parts:** the present, the present participle, the past, and the past participle.

- The present participle is formed by adding *-ing* to the present: *walking, running.*

- The simple past and the past participle of **regular verbs** are formed by adding *-d or -ed* to the present: *skate, skated; walked, walked.*

- The simple past and the past participle of **irregular verbs** are not formed by adding *-ed* to the present: *ran, run.*

A **transitive verb** expresses an action that passes from a doer to a receiver. The receiver is the direct object of the verb: The dog *chewed* the bone.

A **verb phrase** is a group of words that does the work of a single verb. A verb phrase contains one or more **auxiliary verbs** *(is, are, has, have, will, can, could, do, would, should,* and so forth) and a **main verb:** She *had forgotten* her hat.

VOICE

In the **active voice** the subject is the doer of the action: Betty *wrote* a poem.

In the **passive voice** the subject is the receiver of the action. Only transitive verbs can be used in the passive voice: The poem *was written* by Betty.